Religious Science Fiction
in *Battlestar Galactica*
and *Caprica*

Religious Science Fiction in *Battlestar Galactica* and *Caprica*

Women as Mediators of the Sacred and Profane

JUTTA WIMMLER

McFarland & Company, Inc., Publishers
Jefferson, North Carolina

ISBN 978-1-4766-6253-4 (softcover : acid free paper) ∞
ISBN 978-1-4766-2265-1 (ebook)

LIBRARY OF CONGRESS CATALOGUING DATA ARE AVAILABLE

BRITISH LIBRARY CATALOGUING DATA ARE AVAILABLE

© 2015 Jutta Wimmler. All rights reserved

No part of this book may be reproduced or transmitted in any form or by any means, electronic or mechanical, including photocopying or recording, or by any information storage and retrieval system, without permission in writing from the publisher.

Front cover: (left to right) Tricia Helfer, James Callis and Lily Duong-Walton from Season 3 of *Battlestar Galactica* (Sci-Fi/Photofest)

Printed in the United States of America

McFarland & Company, Inc., Publishers
Box 611, Jefferson, North Carolina 28640
www.mcfarlandpub.com

Für meinen Vater Karl Wimmler,
der mich zu einer kritischen Feministin und
reflektierten Agnostikerin erzogen hat

Table of Contents

Acknowledgments ix
Introduction 1

1. Religious Science Fiction 9
2. Saviors: Women Bring Salvation 34
3. With God's Voice: Angels and Prophets 56
4. The Religious Machine 78
5. "Fallen" Women: Razors and Delusions 101
6. Men Without God(s) 123
7. Violence and Crisis: Religious Men 145
8. The Ambiguity of Dr. Baltar 167

Conclusion 185
Episode Guide 191
Chapter Notes 195
Bibliography 199
Index 211

Acknowledgments

I would first like to thank my teacher and supervisor Theresia Heimerl for encouraging me to engage with popular culture texts. I am deeply indebted to her and the rest of the staff at the Institut für Religionswissenschaft at the University of Graz for my education in the study of religions. A special thanks to Alexander Darius Ornella for introducing me to the issues of posthumanism and encouraging my interest in the academic study of *Battlestar Galactica*.

Lisa Kienzl has been my most important academic "sounding board" the last couple of years and many of the thoughts expressed in this book profited from our conversations about the relationship between religion, gender and popular culture. In this crazy world of academia, she has become a valued friend who always understands the difficulties and frustrations that go along with it, and we have shared quite a few breakfasts and coffee breaks complaining and laughing about it. I'm grateful!

Despite the fact that I'm actually employed to research the social and economic history of Europe, European University Viadrina has supported my "extra-curricular" academic activities from the very beginning. Thanks to the head of my department, Klaus Weber, and the entire staff, especially our student aide Robert Simon for his help in the

Acknowledgments

final stages of preparing the manuscript. I consider myself lucky to be working with all of you.

Finally, I always had the unconditional support of my family, especially my father Karl—without him, I would not be where I am today. I also thank my mother Edith, my siblings Ruth, Jakob and Manuela, my niece Magdalena, my grandparents Sibylle and Karl and my aunt Irmgard for years of support and encouragement.

Introduction

"Delusional machines! What's the universe gonna come up with next?" When Cavil, a member of the robotic Cylon species, rhetorically poses this question in the third season of *Battlestar Galactica* (*BSG*; Sci-Fi 2003–2009), he refers to the curious fact that the machines of his world are highly religious—and thus, according to him, delusional. Seeing religion as a delusion, as something outside of reason and close to mental illness, is nothing new in the world of science fiction. After all, this is the genre of science and rationality. Not entirely by coincidence, it is also a traditionally male genre. Curiously, not only are *BSG*'s machines religious, but they are also predominantly female. Cavil is right: something strange is happening.

Science fiction has indeed long been seen as one of the most "masculine" genres, especially when it comes to mainstream sci-fi. While the genre is certainly difficult to define (Johnson-Smith 2005, 15–17; Gözen 2012, 20), science and technology are vital components, a fact that largely discouraged feminine reinterpretations. Like the genre of science fiction itself, the connection between science, rationality and masculinity dates back to the 19th century. By the same logic, women were associated with nature and emotion, and thus disconnected from reason (Newmark 2010, 43, 50; Reckwitz 2010, 66). The emerging genre of science fiction adopted these associations and thus "naturally" excluded women from participating prominently—and subversively—in its narratives (Merrick 2003, 241; Hollinger 2003, 126). Sci-fi texts presented women as the "other," portrayed them as irrational or emotional, and commented on gender through androgynous aliens, or alien societies governed by women. Yet ultimately, most science fiction portrayed female power and femininity as potentially dangerous to the established ("good") social order (Merrick 2003, 243–244).

As woman was othered in science fiction, so was religion. Perceived as equally "other" since it was outside of reason and science, the genre portrayed religion as "backwards" from the 1960s onwards, a primitive and potentially dangerous state of mind that needed to be overcome by rational science (Mendelsohn 2003, 264–265, 269). Within this pattern, religion was and is frequently present in sci-fi texts, a trend that is also visible in televised sci-fi. On *Stargate SG-1* (Showtime and Sci-Fi Channel 1997–2007), a group of human military officers and academics battles evil aliens who declare themselves gods on less technologically developed planets. *Babylon 5* (PTEN and TNT 1993–1998) lets the viewer (and the characters) believe that angels and demons are real, before completely smashing this idea in the fourth season, when the "angels" and "demons" are revealed as an evolutionary species of the mind. Sci-fi often plays with the idea of immaterial beings, or of human evolution towards such a state, but this kind of "spirituality" is always closely connected to scientific reason.[1] We can summarize that sci-fi is fascinated by religion, but in the end, science must be the ultimate explanation. Or, to follow Matthias Hurst, the irrational flares up only to be contained and explained by reason and logic (Hurst 2000, 58–59).

This attitude towards religion has become increasingly unsustainable—maybe this is the reason for the genre's recent "crisis" as proclaimed by some scholars (Broderick 2009, 12). Popular culture scholars have begun to acknowledge that religious narratives, symbols, and topics have increased on the small screen in the last 10 to 15 years, in particular following 9/11 (Winston 2009a, 1; McAvan 2012). A lack of such motives suddenly seems antiquated. Scholars have noted this shift and have started to analyze the implications. However, the field of television studies is not exactly populated by academics trained in the study of religions. While several books have been published on religion and film (e.g., Rebiger 2007; Ernst 2007; Baynes 2012; Neusner 1990) or religion and popular culture in general (Lynch 2007; Lynch

2008; Forbes, Mahan 2005; Hannah 2007), only one essay collection concerned explicitly with religion and television has been published so far (Winston 2009b). Monographs on the subject are even scarcer.

I believe that the field of popular culture studies can benefit considerably from the expertise of scholars of religion—we can add to a discourse that has so far mostly been shaped by colleagues trained in English and American studies. The field has also been dominated by Anglo-American scholarship, with little to no input coming from continental Europe. Part of the reason for this is of course that popular culture is hardly recognized as a viable research field in academia, especially in Central Europe. Non-English-speaking Europeans can offer both an outside perspective (on U.S.-American culture) and a different kind of insider perspective (on Western culture from a European point of view). We also have better access to non-English scholarship (in my case notably in the German language) and can bring this body of work to the discussion more easily. Most importantly, U.S.-American television series are highly popular in Central Europe as well, which makes a trans-national approach all the more vital.

The television series *Battlestar Galactica* (*BSG*) was certainly amongst those U.S.-American exports to Central Europe. This science fiction show, broadcast in the U.S. throughout the Bush era from 2003 until 2009, curiously exemplified the return of religion more than any other series. Scholars were quick to point out what makes *BSG* such a quality show. Several edited collections and articles analyzed the discussion of 9/11 and the war on terror, the portrayal of gender equality and gender relations, issues of identity and philosophy, and the role of posthumanist thought in the series.[2] Some papers have pointed to the relevance of religion and faith in *BSG* (Wetmore 2012; Butler, Winston 2009; "In the Name of God(s)" 2008; Eberl 2008b; Kukkonen 2008), or to the association between women and technology (Kirkland 2008; George 2008; Jowett 2010). However, the complicated yet revealing relationship between gender, religion, and technology has so far escaped serious investigation. While watching the series, it had already occurred to me that it feminized both religion and technology, which seemed odd when compared to more conventional science fiction stories. Recently, Emily McAvan noted that the connection between religion as irrational and mechanical as rational in *BSG* was curious, but she did not elaborate on the issue (McAvan 2012, 140). In addition, scholarly discussions about *BSG*'s short-lived prequel series *Caprica* (SyFy 2009–2011) are only just beginning (Wimmler 2014; Anders 2013; Wetmore 2012). Concerning the relationship between gender, religion and technology, this series, too, has much to offer.

The purpose of this book is to bridge this gap in scholarship, asking how contemporary discourses of gender, religion, and science are reflected and interpreted in these products of popular culture. By analyzing how religion and technology are "gendered" and who and what the series codes as "good" or "bad," I will argue that *BSG* and *Caprica* both employ and rearrange stereotypes about the irrationality of woman and religion. I contextualize these stereotypes both historically and regarding current trends and discourse on the role of science in society and assess the series' interpretation of Judeo-Christian concepts and narratives, illustrating how conventions of the science fiction genre (e.g., humanism) are both employed and re-interpreted. Methodically, I largely rely on content and discourse analysis. Though this approach is rather traditional and positioned along the lines of Anglo-American scholarship on popular culture, the novelty of my approach is my academic training in history and religion that I hope will provide some fresh insights.

Since religion is such an important aspect in the two series, it is not surprising that the (to my knowledge) only monograph so far published on *BSG* and *Caprica* investigates its religious dimension (Wetmore 2012). Kevin J. Wetmore's *The Theology of Battlestar Galactica: American Christianity in the 2004–2009 Television Series* nevertheless takes a different perspective than this study, which is already indicated by the use of the term "theology" in the title.[3] A theological approach differs from a religious studies approach in several ways. Wetmore starts from the assumption that *BSG* can be read "as a theological text that makes explicit and implicit statements about the nature of faith and reality" (Wetmore 2012, 3). Consequently, as Wetmore further explains, the book is interested in finding normative answers about the world in this text of popular culture, or at least to analyze the way in which the series engages with such theologically relevant questions as the meaning of salvation or the nature of good and evil. Wetmore reads *BSG*'s theologies against "real world" theologies, suggesting that we can gain more insights about Christian theological matters by doing so.

In contrast, this book is not interested in finding real religious meaning in a popular culture text that can then be "transferred" to everyday life. It does not imply that the series is theologically significant or can be used to convey Christian theological contents to viewers. Rather, the book is interested in the way religion is used in the series and what cultural traditions are being followed in doing so. Religion is understood as part of a culture's interpretative framework, a set of references that can be used to convey meaning. The same can be said for gender and science, where a certain cultural pool of stereotypes, narrative conventions and subversive interpretations can be referred to in a popular culture text to tell a story. The book is interested in how these series tap into this pool of cultural references and to what end they do so. I suggest that they mix and mingle stereotypes form the three "cultural meaning pools" of religion, science and gender to create a complex new image of all three areas that still remains somewhat contradictory. To put it bluntly, I am not interested in whether we can learn something about the true nature of God or redemption from the series—this would be a theological question. I am, however, interested in how the two series construct God in relation to gender and science, and what traditions and discourses they engage by doing so.

I will suggest that both religion and technology are coded feminine in the series and will analyze how this connection is constructed and how it re-interprets gender roles and stereotypes. I will also provide the reader with background information on religious codes and concepts, and the possibilities and limits of reinterpreting these elements in a popular culture text. This will also illustrate the extent to which Western culture is based on "Judeo-Christian" ideas. I suggest throughout this book that the series are not simply placed in a Judeo-Christian context (to a certain extent, every story produced in the West is), but explicitly so: *BSG* and *Caprica* try to reconcile religion and science— to bring science fiction into a 21st century world that has learned that religion is nowhere near dead. It makes sense that they would bring religion into the genre through the likewise excluded "irrational" woman.

The book is divided into eight chapters. Chapters two to five analyze the relationship between women and religion and technology, while chapters six to eight deal with the connection between men and religion and technology. I will ease into the subject with a more general chapter that illustrates how *BSG* and *Caprica* construct a religious narrative. This will include an introduction to the stories themselves that is especially relevant for those readers who are unfamiliar with the series, but are interested in the subject matter itself. I will then put the narrative in a larger context by discussing the role of *Star Trek: Deep Space Nine* as a precursor for *BSG*, which will illustrate that *BSG*, though certainly revolutionary in many respects, did not happen entirely outside of mainstream sci-fi. We will follow this up with a more thorough discussion of the two most important ideological strands employed in the series, namely the use of posthumanist and Judeo-Christian concepts. The first chapter will consequently set the stage for the rest of the book, which will provide an in-depth analysis of specific subject matters.

In the second and third chapters, I will discuss how religious concepts such as savior, angel, prophet, and the use of scripture are gendered in the series. It will offer a bridge between the origin and development of these concepts and their current use in American popular culture, and especially look towards the confluence of posthuman and Judeo-Christian ideas. This connection will be further investigated in the fourth chapter that is devoted entirely to the "religious machine," namely the female Cyborg. This chapter will rely heavily on the rather extensive corpus of Cyborg scholarship. The reader will be presented with a more detailed examination of posthumanism, building on the background from the first chapter. I will discuss how the creation of technology is turned into a female affair in the series, and why this marks a shift away from the traditional image of the Cyborg. I suggest that the female Cyborg is the embodiment of the series' re-interpretation of classic science fiction stereotypes, as she unites femininity and a religious worldview (the "irrational") with technology (the "rational"). Finally, the fifth chapter will analyze female "evil," or rather the concept of "fallen" women in both series. By the end of chapter five, you should have a good idea of how the shows deal with women and their relationship to technology and religion.

Chapter six will open our investigation into the men of the series,

Introduction

starting with the majority of male "unbelievers." We will analyze how and if unreligious characters are able to act morally and how normative masculinity is reinforced and undermined in the series. In the following chapter, we will look at religious men and compare them to our female believers. This chapter will test my theory that religion and technology are feminine spaces, as I will consider how religious men deal with technology. I will argue that these men are in fact not associated with technology in the same way as women. Finally, I will end my investigation with an in-depth analysis of Gaius Baltar, who many would identify as the biggest challenger for my argument. By the end of chapter eight, you will either be convinced of my theory that women are the main mediators of both religion and technology in these TV series, or be inspired to write a book or article to refute it. Either way, I hope you enjoy it.

1

Religious Science Fiction

Battlestar Galactica and *Caprica* differ from other mainstream sci-fi texts when it comes to the use of religion. Specifically, the construction of a religious narrative sets the series apart. But what is a religious narrative, anyhow? Some would argue that *Superman* qualifies, since the main character is established as a Jesus-like figure, and his story is told as a modernized Christian messiah narrative (Kozlovic 2002). The same is true for *The Matrix*, where the character Neo fills this role (Stucky 2005). Others might suggest that a religious narrative is a story based on the Bible either in content or in structure. When I speak of a religious narrative, I use a more strict definition: I propose that a story's narrative can be called "religious," if the characters act in an explicitly religious environment—a world in which God or gods are not just elements of faith but exist in the story's "reality." To clarify: There's a difference between a world where vampires are real and a world in which some people believe vampires to be real (and some people pose as vampires). In the same manner, a story where God or gods are real differs from a world where some life forms act like gods and others believe in them.

Of course the boundaries are not always clear-cut. Emily McAvan has quite correctly pointed out that the last two seasons of *Stargate SG-1* shifted attention to ascended beings that actually possessed "mystical powers" (McAvan 2012, 131). However, not once does the series suggest that these beings might actually be gods who control the contemporary and historical development of the entire universe. Rather, they are "evil" aliens who use their superior powers (that are presented as scientifically explainable) in order to convince technologically "backwards" beings to worship them. Effectively, they are not much different from the Goa'uld who had previously been the series' villains. Thus neither *Superman* nor *Stargate SG-1* qualify as religious narratives, as they do not include actual gods, but only aliens acting like gods or having God-like powers that are nevertheless accessible through rational science.

Following my stricter definition, a religious narrative can only exist if the story accepts the existence of supreme beings or a supreme being that can actively influence events in "reality" at will and describes these beings as "divine." The nature of these beings (as well as their actions) must elude scientific or rational explanations. In this chapter, we will explore how *BSG* and *Caprica* built a religious sci-fi narrative, describing the influence of the televised sci-fi tradition, Judeo-Christian ideas, and posthumanist thought as constitutive elements. I will also offer a short introduction to the *Battlestarverse* (the fictional "universe" of *Battlestar Galactica* and *Caprica*) to introduce the story to those unfamiliar with the narrative or, more likely if you're reading this book, to refresh your memory. This chapter thus serves as a first introduction into the nature of religious narrative in a science fiction context.

Sci-Fi and Posthumanism

Science fiction has always been a thoroughly humanist genre—the human being with its claim to absolute truths stands at the center of the story. Of course the term "humanism" is a highly controversial one in scholarship. Its meaning has changed over time and was adapted to various contexts. We especially need to distinguish between what is often called "Renaissance humanism," centered on the general study of Roman and Greek literature and culture (Mann 1996), and the more specific and contemporary interpretation of the term that refers to a universalist ideology (Holderegger 2011). This humanist ideology presumes the existence of a fundamental and unchangeable human nature with likewise unchangeable (and of course universal) morals and values.

1. Religious Science Fiction

Although the intellectual origins of humanism can be traced to antiquity (and are also a central element of "Renaissance humanism") (Cancik and Cancik-Lindemaier 2011, 83–92; Augustijn 2003, 53–54), the ideology only asserted itself as part of Western mainstream culture in the course of 18th century enlightenment thought. The most prominent example of humanist thought is the declaration of human rights that proclaims universal morality: humans have an exceptional position in nature and are thus privileged as a species, which ensures fundamental rights for every human being (Holderegger et al., 2011, 14). This fundamentally unchanging nature of humanity is also the topic of traditional science fiction—and the alien, monster, or comparable "other" reinforces its existence.

The central question of traditional science fiction is about the nature of the human being—a thoroughly humanist issue. Mary Shelley's *Frankenstein, or the modern Prometheus* (1817), considered one of the foundational texts of modern science fiction, laid the groundwork for this central topic. Dr. Frankenstein uses science to create another creature that is then used to explore the human condition. The humanist world view assures that humanity's wish to create is bound by stable morals: if we dare to create life without thoroughly considering the moral implications, it is usually doomed to failure. Our technological creations get out of hand and turn against us. If they do not, it is because we have taught them to be human and thus moral. In traditional sci-fi, technology needs to be controlled and checked by humanism's universal moral code.

Humanism also enters the world of sci-fi on another level. Within traditional sci-fi's construction of the world, the nature and inviolability of the human being is a central concern. Technology that changes the nature of humanity (in particular invasive technologies) is usually portrayed as dangerous and doomed to failure (Gözen 2012, 113–114). *Star Trek*'s Cyborg species (the Borg) are "evil" (or at least dangerous for our treasured individuality) because technology has completely invaded their humanity. So when the Borg Seven of Nine on *Star Trek: Voyager* (UPN 1995–2001) has to learn to become human again, this transformation is accompanied visually by the removal of her technological implants.[1] In traditional sci-fi, technology advances humanoid societies, but only as a tool to be used by heroic, often scientifically trained characters. Technology does not, however, change human nature. As Jiré Emine Gözen has observed, this position is in fact a rather technophobe one: it allows us to use technology, but refuses to let it come too close to our bodies and minds (Gözen 2012, 102). The boundaries between us and our technology need to remain insurmountable in order to preserve our humanist existence.

Humanism belongs to the kind of grand narratives that came under attack with the notion of postmodernity.[2] The postmodern questions the validity of universal truths and embraces complexity and self-reflexivity. It exposes the humanist position as white, male, heterosexual and rational and highlights the subjective realities of the "other," namely women, non-white males and non-heterosexuals (Bertens 1995, 8). For this reason, Hans Bertens proposed that the postmodern originates in a "crisis of representation" (Bertens 1995, 11) because the humanist position fails to adequately represent this conceived "other." The term reflects a general dissatisfaction with modernity, which is increasingly seen as unsustainable and elitist. Yet it also rejects the notion of going back, of becoming "traditional" again. Instead, the term suggests that we need to move beyond modernity, to leave it behind and become "postmodern" (Griffin 1989, iv–x).

A critique of humanism is also inherent in the term "posthumanism," an intellectual ideology that has both a theoretical and a practical dimension. Theoretically, scholars such as Donna Haraway have used the image of the Cyborg—a human-machine hybrid—as a metaphor for the posthuman that consists of multiple identities, being post-gender, post-race, post-class, and so on. In "A Cyborg Manifesto," Haraway explains that the inclusion of minorities such as women, ethnic minorities, people with HIV or AIDS, or homosexuals can only be accomplished by eroding our humanist perception of the world. Humanism is sentimental, according to Haraway, because it proposes a normative view of humanity that is highly exclusive (Haraway 2004; Halberstam and Livingston 1995). On the theoretical end, posthumanism is a change of perspective: from the idea of a universalist human nature towards the notion of plurality.

On the more practical side of things, posthumanism is also a concrete ideology that proposes both mankind's gradual evolution through technology and the possibility of artificial sentience—and thus the creation of a new non-human species. In this case, the Cyborg is not a metaphor but a reality—a human-machine hybrid that will, eventually, guarantee eternal or at least extended life.[3] Again, this ideology is strongly anti-humanist. Neither the human nor his or her body is sacred, humanity does not have a privileged position, nor is human nature unchanging. Posthumanists argue that we have to give up on those ideas in order to survive the eventual demise of our sun and live beyond our planet and, possibly, our bodies (Herbrechter 2009, 8). Obviously the theoretical and the practical side are strongly interconnected, especially in their anti-humanist view of the world: their subject is the dethroned human being with its claim to superiority.

The humanist worldview was also attacked by sci-fi writers known as "cyberpunk" authors, among them William Gibson (*Neuromancer*, 1984), Bruce Sterling (*Shismatrix*, 1985), and John Shirly (*Eclipse*, 1985). Cyberpunks remove what they perceive to be the humanist barrier from their vision of future human development, and portray a future without moral boundaries to technological evolution. They define the "Frankenstein barrier" as the antiquated notion that technological and scientific development is bound by universal morals and reason. According to cyberpunks, no such boundaries exist—they consequently build worlds where highly evasive technologies are part of everyday life and have changed human nature completely. In cyberpunk worlds, humans do not build "monsters"—they become them (Gözen 2012, 115–117). These stories lack a recognizable moral message and often center on morally ambivalent or unlikeable characters, again as a critique of sci-fi's traditional humanist heroes.

Cyberpunk authors consciously understand their fiction as posthumanist, and many academics understand their work as *the* expression of postmodernity (Gözen 2012, 110, 125, 279). Yet cyberpunk is also a rather elitist strand of literature that has never become mainstream and effectively began and ended in the 1980s. Considering their lack of moral codes and unlikeable protagonists, this is hardly surprising. The movement nevertheless had a strong impact on the genre, and most contemporary sci-fi texts are infused with its topics and imagery. It would be hard to imagine contemporary sci-fi steering clear of digital culture, eroding boundaries between (wo)man and machine, near futures, and antiheroes. Yet cyberpunk's general critique that a humanist world view is no longer sustainable has only been acknowledged reluctantly in televised sci-fi (and film for that matter). While the classical 90s space opera no longer populates the small screen, it is unclear at the moment which direction the genre will take in this medium. It seems to be stuck somewhere between humanism and posthumanism, as was certainly the case for *BSG* and *Caprica*.

As a critique of humanism, both postmodernity and posthumanism also allow for the re-emergence of religion that had been discarded during enlightenment. Classical enlightenment thinkers had assumed that religion would disappear with the advancement of reason and science—a notion appropriated by science fiction. While posthumanists consider themselves to be highly scientific and unreligious, the posthuman debate does not lack for religious motifs. They search for a transformed self or world or even attempt to achieve "godhood" (Walker 2011). Recently, Robert M. Geraci has referred to posthumanist thinking as "Apocalyptic AI," suggesting that posthumanist visions of the future advocate eternal life in a perfect heavenly sphere (cyberspace) in a very similar manner as do Christian apocalyptic traditions (Geraci 2010; Robins 1995, 135–136). Posthumanists emphasize a strict mind-body dualism envisaging the separation of the mind or self from the physical body, or (in posthuman terms) of software from hardware. When this becomes possible, we can live eternally in a computer or comparable hardware.[4]

This idea of a mind-body dualism is reminiscent of religious concepts frequently associated with Gnostic thought. The controversial term "Gnosticism" refers to unorthodox Christian religious thought in Antiquity that was deemed "heretical" by the emerging Church (King 2003, 2–8). One particularly "heretic" concept (that nevertheless crept up regularly in the history of Christianity and other religions) was mind-body dualism: the body was, just like the world itself, a material creation—and thus "evil." Everything material was understood as a creation of an evil being—a creator God (or Demiurge) who was sometimes identified as Satan himself (Rudolph 1990, 68–69). Only the mind or "self" was (potentially) divine—the mind thus needed to be separated from the evil body. Although posthumanists would never use the concepts of good and evil, their affinity towards the mind and rejection of the human body as "inferior"—something that holds us back from evolution—clearly evokes this kind of thinking. This link to Judeo-Christian tradition is a major indicator for this ideology's postmodern nature.

After all, the conflict between science and religion is largely a modernist, a humanist one. The reconciliation between these two seemingly opposing concepts is made possible through the challenge of postmodernity and posthumanism. While the humanist position is inherently anti-religious (Cancik and Cancik-Lindemaier 2011, 35), posthumanism (and postmodernity) allow for the return of religious belief. As discussed by David Ray Griffin, modernity was incompatible with God, while postmodernity is not (Griffin 1989, 51). We could argue that a perspective that is both posthumanist and postmodern is a precondition for a religious sci-fi narrative. However, such a perspective does not necessarily guarantee a religious narrative, let alone a Judeo-Christian one as found in *BSG* and *Caprica*. This was illustrated by Emily McAvan who introduced the term of the "postmodern sacred" to discuss the introduction of postmodern religion in contemporary fictional genres (McAvan 2012). Yet most of the stories she discusses would not qualify as religious narratives as I defined them in the introduction to this chapter. A religious interpretation can nevertheless only work once humanism is dispersed as the foundational principle of the established worldview—postmodernity is the first pillar of a religious sci-fi narrative.

We should keep in mind that a story should also discuss scientific or technological issues in order to remain a sci-fi narrative—this is where posthumanism comes in. Theories of sci-fi usually mention the two interconnected elements of estrangement and cognition when defining the genre (and distinguishing it from other genres such as fantasy) (discussed by Freedman 1987). What theorists mean is that sci-fi takes place in a world that is removed from our own to such an extent that we cannot with certainty identify it as "our" world, but close enough so that we could imagine it to be our world at some point (estrangement). Additionally—and in opposition to other genres—sci-fi is fond of explanations and reasoning, specifically of the scientific and technological kind (cognition). Without dwelling too much on the complex issue of defining a genre, most sci-fi theorists would agree that examinations of science and technology are inherent components of any sci-fi text. Like postmodernity, posthumanism erodes the humanist world view and shares its critical disruptive potential. Yet it also has an inherent interest in technology and science, and thus a built-in bridge between science and religion. We will see that both our series frequently tackle issues connected to this posthumanist ideology. In order to understand how this is achieved, we first need to know what these stories are about.

The Stories of BSG *and* Caprica

Battlestar Galactica is based on an earlier series by the same name created by the Mormon Glenn A. Larson in the 1970s, while the new series was created by *Star Trek* veteran Ronald D. Moore. Known as "re-imagined," the series premiered in 2003 with a two-part television movie (commonly referred to as *Miniseries*) that because of these films' success followed up with a first season in 2004. The series was concluded in 2009 after four seasons. The major plot involves the conflict between humans and Cylons, Cyborg machines that were created by humans to serve them. The series takes place 40 years after the Cylon war, which ended with an armistice and the Cylons' disappearance from the 12 colonies (planets) of mankind. *Miniseries* opens with the Cylons' return and the destruction of the 12 colonies through nuclear bombs. The humans, who have stopped distrusting technological "enhancements," are wiped out almost completely by this enemy who is able to hack into their computers and hamper their defenses. The only surviving Battleship is the Galactica, an antiquated ship that was just about to be sent into retirement and had already served in the Cylon war. Because its commander, William Adama, participated in this war, he does not allow technological advancements on his ship—a decision that now saves his crew.

Meanwhile, secretary of education Laura Roslin, who participated in Galactica's decommissioning ceremony, finds herself the only surviving member of the government and is sworn in as president of the 12 colonies. She begins to collect survivors, and is able to lead about 50.000 remaining humans and their ships to Galactica, whose most pressing duty is the protection of the survivors. Since they cannot return to their planets that are now under Cylon control, they turn to the Holy Scriptures and decide to search for the mythical planet Earth, to which a 13th tribe of humanity supposedly emigrated when their forefathers left Kobol, the original planet. The Cylons are intent on wiping out all of humanity and consequently follow them through space. The story is complicated by the fact that the Cylons are overtly religious and see the genocide as a will of God, who has turned away from his sinful children and "ensouled" the Cylons, his new creation. They also see the humans as blasphemers, as they follow a polytheistic faith and do not accept the existence of a single, all-powerful God.

The physical appearance of the Cylons is a major plot twist that also sharply distinguishes the re-imagined series from the original. While we do encounter mechanical versions that can clearly be identified as machines (called Centurions), the Cylons have now "evolved" to look like humans. There are 12 humanoid Cylon "models" that are almost impossible to distinguish from actual humans and exist in many copies. This plot device turns Cylons into an intimate enemy, as anyone can be revealed as a Cylon. Throughout the series, we are left wondering which humans may be Cylons and whether they are even aware of their identity. Because some Cylons are completely unaware and understand themselves as humans and most Cylons strive to be more human, issues of identity are prevalent in the show. It is clear that in such a narrative, the Cylons cannot be completely "evil." Their actions are initially fuelled by revenge and belief. Likewise, humans are not univocally "good," as they frequently refuse to accept Cylons as sentient beings and refer to them as "things," and consequently also mistreat them. The series continuously reflects upon issues of the Bush era, especially the legitimacy of the War on Terror, by making both points of view accessible for the audience. The final goal of the series is the reconciliation of the two "species," and the discovery of a new home where a future can be built. This is, however, a long and bumpy road.

By the end of season two, the Cylons have changed their policies towards the humans. They no longer intend to eradicate humanity, but instead try to reconcile with them by living together on a planet they call New Caprica. This experiment has little success because power is not distributed evenly: the Cylons are occupiers, while humans are suppressed. Because the Cylons still feel superior and the humans are not yet ready to acknowledge the Cylons as sentient beings, reconciliation does not work. The humans revolt against Cylon occupation and finally manage to escape once again. In season three, some Cylons decide to let go of their superiority complex to live in peace with humans, while others move further away from them. At the same time, some humans refuse to compromise with the Cylons whom they still regard as soulless machines. Both human and Cylon purists need to be defeated in order to find a compromise—and in order for the more conciliatory fractions to live together in peace. At the end of season four, this alliance decides to settle on a new planet they call Earth. They had previously found the "original" Earth (Earth I) that had turned out to be a complete wasteland. After this paradigm-altering revelation, they move on to find "our" Earth where they settle on the African continent. This entire process of reconciliation and finding a new home is placed firmly within the show's religious narrative: God speaks to both sides through angels and uses chosen mediators and guides to implement his plan. The ending establishes that God was indeed actively present throughout this journey.

After the conclusion of *BSG* in 2009, a prequel series called *Caprica* was launched in the same year. The series was created by Remi Aubuchon and Ronald D. Moore, began with a straight-to-DVD movie in April 2009 (an extended version of the first episode) and premiered on SyFy in January 2010. The series was cancelled in 2011 after one season. *Caprica* took place roughly 60 years before the events of *BSG* and explored the creation of the Cylons and the events leading up to the first Cylon war. In the pilot episode of *Caprica*, teenager Zoe Graystone is killed in a terrorist attack conducted in the name of the monotheist extremist group Soldiers of the One (STO), of which Zoe is also a member. The girl is a computer genius who had infused a virtual version of herself ("The Zoe Graystone Avatar") with consciousness. Her best friend Lacy reveals the Avatar to Zoe's father by accident. Millionaire Daniel Graystone, CEO of Graystone Industries and inventor of the popular virtual-reality holoband, attempts to access this virtual version of his dead daughter, transferring her consciousness into a mindless robot body and thus creating the first Cylon.

Daniel bonds with Joseph Adama, who has also lost his daughter (as well as his wife) in the same terrorist attack and creates a virtual

1. Religious Science Fiction

version of Tamara Adama using his daughter's technology. In the second half of the series, the two avatars are trapped in v-world, the cyberspace accessible form the real world through the holoband. V-world is presented as a place of unrestrained urges, in particular the "hacked worlds" within it. Eventually, the avatars decide to cleanse the virtual world from what they perceive as sin and to recreate this world according to their own imagination. The series thus presents the creation of Cylons as an accident and places it in the context of intense family drama. *Caprica* continues and intensifies the issues of identity and the recognition of Artificial Intelligence as sentient beings that were already laid out in *BSG*. It also explores the origins of Cylon monotheism, which—as we previously learned in *BSG*—did not originate with the humanoid Cylon models, but with the Centurions (who are now clearly coded female). A strong focus on the monotheist religion and the fundamentalist STO explores ideology in the context of violence, but also of technology.

The *Battlestarverse* was expanded to the internet through Webisodes that were broadcast between the individual seasons of *BSG*. *The Resistance* explored humanity's struggle with the Cylon occupation of New Caprica, while *The Face of the Enemy* analyzed the journey of one particular character from idealism to racial purism. *Razor Flashbacks* was eventually incorporated into the movie *Razor* that focused on the Battlestar Pegasus that had entered the scene in season two. Another movie, *The Plan* tried to tie up loose ends after the series' finale in 2009. In 2012–2013, the pilot for a new series *Battlestar Galactica: Blood and Chrome* was released on the web and then broadcast on SyFy, although it was already clear that this new series would not go into production. *Blood & Chrome* was set in between the events of *Caprica* and *BSG* and focused on a young Bill Adama's role in the first Cylon war. With the decision not to produce this spin-off, the franchise can (for now) be seen as a complete whole that can be analyzed as such.

The two series—in particular through their connections to each other—can clearly be described as sci-fi narratives with a strongly religious tone, connecting the two spheres through notions of the posthuman that are also reminiscent of cyberpunk science fiction. *BSG* and *Caprica* incorporate cyberpunk elements in several ways. They are set in worlds that seem only marginally futuristic. *Caprica* in particular is rather close to our own world in its stage of technological development, though the series takes place on a different planet with a different history. *BSG* was known for its "realist" settings, approaching cyberpunk's focus on public spaces, ordinary daily life, and worn out technologies (Gözen 2012, 90–95, 125–134). Both series broach the issue of eroding boundaries between human and machine without automatically suggesting that this erosion is immoral. The Cylons seem to be in keeping with sci-fi's fear of out-of-control machinery or creations, but eventually turn into likeable and sentient creatures that are accorded a place in evolutionary human development.

Yet as a product of popular culture, the series cannot stray completely from the humanist perception of the world, and thus exist in an area of conflict. They cannot present a completely immoral world or unlikeable characters and have to adhere to several traditional elements of narrative construction as well as the conventions and rules of television itself. Although the series are morally complex, they generally subscribe to a common Western moral code. Since *BSG* is based on a space opera from the 1970s and 1980s, it cannot completely escape this sub-genre's traditions. Overall, *BSG* and *Caprica* can both be subsumed under the general category of the "postmodern space opera" (Westfahl 2003, 206) as they merge traditional sci-fi conventions based on ships in space with postmodern cyberpunk elements and posthumanism.

BSG and *Caprica* are well-rounded religious narratives, as their religious dimension is not retro-fitted into the story at a later point but already introduced in the very beginning, through *Miniseries*. The fact that the writers opted against a final scientific explanations was not well received by either critics or fans,[5] who obviously expected something very different from a show they understood as science fiction. This illustrates that religious sci-fi narratives are understood as unconventional. The genre is still expected to be more humanist, a genre of rational science in opposition to irrational belief—despite the postmodern infusions as described by McAvan. The ending of another sci-fi series was likewise contested—*BSG*'s major precursor *Star Trek: Deep Space Nine*. Maybe unsurprisingly, this series also included religion rather prominently, and chose not to discredit it completely, as we shall now explore.

The Legacy of Star Trek: Deep Space Nine

BSG-creator Ronald D. Moore has repeatedly stated that his most pressing wish was to create something very much different from the *Star Trek* franchise (Rogers 2008). Having been a writer and producer on both *Star Trek: The Next Generation* (1987–1994) and *Star Trek: Deep Space Nine* (*DS9*), Moore was dissatisfied with many of the genre's conventions. You could not imagine anyone actually living aboard the Enterprise, he stated, and the focus on high-tech gadgets as solutions to every problem was as uninventive as the camera work.[6] Consequently, everything was difficult on the Galactica. It was exhausting to open doors, people shared bathrooms, you had to get everywhere by foot (no beaming!), people frequently looked dirty and tired, and the camera seemed to be a distinctive character on board the ship. While Moore certainly succeeded in creating an original visual environment and viewer experience (Pank and Caro 2009), he was clearly influenced by the *Star Trek* franchise concerning the content of his story—which, to my knowledge, scholars have not noted so far. Either consciously or unconsciously, Moore and his writing staff (some of whom were likewise *DS9* veterans!) borrowed some major plot elements from *DS9*—including the idea of a religious narrative. I'm not convinced that this was a conscious move. However it happened, *DS9* can certainly be seen as a precursor to *BSG*, which also illustrates that, though *BSG* was certainly innovative, its novelty did not come out of nowhere.

DS9 was highly controversial because it flew in the face of some of the franchise's major statements, especially the superiority of science to religion. The *Star Trek* franchise as a whole was deeply committed to a scientific explanation of the world and did not leave much room for the supernatural or religious, as repeatedly stated by the franchise's founder Gene Rodenberry. In keeping with the traditional sci-fi paradigm, the usual pattern in both *Star Trek* (NBC 1966–1969) and *Star Trek: The Next Generation* (*TNG*) was to understand religion as a part of culture, not an objective reality. As such, it tended to be seen as a negative influence on societies, whose free will was portrayed as impaired by the power of religion (Rorie 2011). If evidence for the objective existence of religion appears, it is eventually explained by science—for example when a "re-born" Khales, mythical figure of the Klingons, turns out to be a clone (*TNG* 06.23 "Rightful Heir"). The power of religion is acknowledged in the episode, as many Klingons continue to believe in the returned Khales despite evidence that he is a clone because the Klingons need a strong moral leader. Yet the major Klingon character Worf's faith is severely shaken (see Kraemer et al., 2001, 168). On *Star Trek*, Religion is a powerful delusion, but a delusion nonetheless.

As a product of Western culture—which is in itself highly infused with religious elements—religious symbols and statements sometimes entered the scene, for example occasional quotes from the Bible or the Christmas celebration in the 1994 film *Star Trek: Generations* whose screenplay, by the way, was written by Ronald D. Moore and Brannon Braga (for religion in *Star Trek* see Kraemer et al., 2001). Probably the most significant appearance of Western religious heritage is the use of religious concepts such as the savior or the idea of a soul. Although produced after the controversial *DS9*, *Star Trek: Voyager* (UPN 1995–2001) returned to these roots, though the series showed a little more appreciation for the dimension of belief than either *TOS* or *TNG*, including a (postmodern) willingness to accept ambivalences and contradictions. Yet overall, the franchise usually rejected religion as a scientifically unexplainable reality—with the exception of *DS9*.

DS9 was the first *Star Trek* Series to air after Rodenberry's death. It tells the story of a space station that suddenly finds itself in a vital strategic part of the universe, when the first and only stable wormhole is discovered—a wormhole that reduces a journey of decades to a few seconds. The space station, Deep Space 9, belongs to the Bajorans, inhabitants of the nearby planet Bajor. After decades of oppressive occupation by the Cardassians, who had their military basis on the space station formerly called Terok Nor, the Bajorans ask the Federation and their scientific and military wing, Starfleet, for support in rebuilding their planet. After the wormhole's discovery, Bajor becomes a major economic and political player, and the station is suddenly highly contested. The highly religious Bajorans believe that the wormhole is really the "Celestial Temple" that is inhabited by their gods, the so-called Prophets. Life forms are indeed found in the wormhole, but they are called "wormhole aliens" by Starfleet officers. The main religious conflict presented on *DS9* is between the traditional Bajorans and the "advanced" Federation.

1. Religious Science Fiction

The series consciously moved away from much of the "comfort" typical for the *Star Trek* universe. It presented a broken world filled with broken characters (Steinrötter 2004, 53). This "brokenness" was also put into place on a visual level: the space station was not built by the Federation, but by Bajor's former oppressors, who had different ideas about necessities on a space station. They also employed different technologies, which often caused problems when they needed to be coupled with Starfleet technology. Especially in the beginning of the series, the station required a "hands-on" approach in much the same way as the Galactica on *BSG*: the space station Deep Space 9 was left to the Bajorans in bad shape and needed to be brought back to life. Since the station was technically Bajoran, not Federation, the legal situation was likewise different than on a typical Starfleet spaceship: Bajoran law applied. Thus the station's promenade was filled with shops and a gambling establishment, both of which require money, which is untypical in the utopian *Star Trek* universe. As stated by the producers, the tone of the series was to be conflict (Steinrötter 2004, 49) and, as a consequence, a large dose of discomfort. Conflict and discomfort were certainly at the heart of *BSG* as well, which included conflict and discomfort concerning religious world views.

BSG also constructed an enemy that is reminiscent of *DS9*. While the wormhole initially promised valuable scientific and economic benefits, Bajor and the Federation were soon faced with an unexpected threat, the Dominion, which was headed by a species of "changelings," who could change their shape to look like anything or anyone. *BSG* borrows this concept of an invisible enemy from *DS9*. The Federation was almost helpless against the changelings, who infiltrated many planets by posing as influential government officials or military leaders. They also had their own military force, the callous Jem-Hadar, who were genetically bred for the purposes of war and were unable to refuse orders. In *BSG*, the humanoid Cylons perform a very similar function to that of the Changelings. Since they are indistinguishable from humans physically, they can infiltrate the human fleet. This leads to immense suspicion amongst the humans—the same is true for *DS9*. The Cylons also have their Centurions, who can be compared to the Jem-Hadar. It is their purpose to be soldiers, and they are also unable to refuse orders. Thus the enemy constructed in *BSG* resembles that of *DS9*.

Religious Science Fiction in *Battlestar Galactica* and *Caprica*

The idea of a religious sci-fi narrative can also be traced to *DS9*, which was always understood as a "darker" *Star Trek* series. Its creators, Rick Berman and Michael Piller, had a similar goal as Moore (who joined the *DS9* writing staff in season three): to create a more realistic setting, where coherent stories could develop and characters could grow (Gregory 2000, 68–69). Significantly, the idea of a "more realistic" sci-fi show included a religious dimension. The Bajorans were overtly religious, and through the (female!) character of Kira Nerys (*DS9*'s Bajoran second in command), the viewer was offered intimate knowledge of their belief system. It is not a coincidence that religion would creep up in the "darker" *DS9*, if we consider the close connection between science fiction and utopia: religion is often lacking because a utopian world has no need for God (Linford 1999, 83–84). *DS9*, however, is not at all utopian. While other Star Trek series (and most science fiction) discredited religion as unscientific, *DS9* opened up an opposition between the rational Starfleet officers and the irrational and seemingly "backwards" Bajorans, but for the most part refused to take sides in the battle between science and religion. The series leaves it up to the viewer to decide. The prominent use of religion (which, curiously, was frequently overlooked by critics and investors) was an artistic choice that found support neither with the producing studio, nor with fans (Steinrötter 2004, 105). Religion did not equal high ratings—and yet the authors remained committed to this choice.

While *DS9* was never as explicit about its religious interpretation of the world as *BSG*, its ending does suggest the possibility that the "wormhole aliens" are indeed gods. Or at least, the series proposes that there is no real difference between "actual" gods and beings that are able to act God-like and to influence human (or Bajoran) events. As Chris Gregory noted, a big contribution of the series was that religious experiences or events were not easily "explained away" by science as had been customary in the *Star Trek* franchise (and, I would add, mainstream sci-fi as a whole) (Gregory 2000, 87). Jennifer Porter and Darcee McLaren even suggested that the franchise had previously proposed to substitute faith with "rational scientific humanism" (Porter and McLaren 1999, 3). On *DS9*, this became increasingly difficult, as illustrated through its reluctant messiah, Starfleet officer Benjamin Sisko, who eventually came to believe not only in the prophet-gods, but also in his own role as an "emissary" of the prophets. The narrative even turns him into a "son of God" by revealing that his mother had been a prophet. In the final episode, Sisko joins the prophets in their celestial temple, effectively becoming a god himself (or returning to his people). This religious aspect did not enter the series at a later stage, but was already introduced in the very first episode that, significantly, was entitled "Emissary." The series also ended on this note, making the religious narrative a thorough and well-rounded one.

The *Star Trek* franchise had of course always employed religious and mythical themes as well as spirituality as such. Messianic characters, stories of sacrifice and redemption, or eternal life where regularly present. Yet the basic humanist interpretation of the world was always kept intact. Other sci-fi narratives also toyed with the idea of religion, but none came as close to constructing a religious sci-fi world as *DS9* (Porter, McLaren 1999, 3).[7] Some would argue that religious explanations offer an "easy way out" of a complicated narrative (*Lost* comes to mind). While this may sometimes be the case, it is also an unexpected way of telling a science fiction story. Kolja Steinrötter has called *DS9* a "postmodern vision of the future": the story thrives on ambivalence and the merging of concepts that seem to be mutually exclusive (Steinrötter 2004, 51–52). The prime example for this is the construction of religious sci-fi, which merges a religious with a scientific world view. *DS9* tipped its toe into the "holy water" of religious narratives if you will, and illustrated that it could work for sci-fi. *BSG* would build on that later.

BSG thus did not invent the idea of a religious sci-fi narrative. However, it contributed to the idea significantly, especially through its Judeo-Christian dimension. *DS9* may possess some Christian concepts such as the messiah or the opposition between good and evil, but they are only superficially connected to the Judeo-Christian tradition, in a similar way as *Superman* can be said to be a "Christian" story. Some elements of *DS9*'s religious narrative actually make it difficult to speak of religious narrative as I have described it. First, the series leaves the viewer with a considerable amount of uncertainty concerning the nature of the prophets and the transformation of Sisko. While it leans towards a "divine" interpretation, it is still possible to see the prophets as "wormhole aliens," as simply another life form. In addition, as Linford has noted, the prophets are not universal gods —they are very much local (Linford 1999, 96–

99). They have a special connection to Bajor and its inhabitants. Their involvement in "human" affairs is limited—they rarely take conscious action to influence events, unless their emissary is somehow involved (they are actively engaged in the conception of Benjamin Sisko and intervene on behalf of Bajor if he asks them to do so). The divinity introduced in *BSG*, on the other hand, is very much universal and has a very specific plan for its creation(s) which it actively promotes.

DS9 was a precursor to *BSG*—it can be located somewhere in between the humanism of traditional sci-fi and the posthuman sci-fi of *BSG* and *Caprica*. It was certainly a more postmodern series because it embraced contradictions and questioned the superiority of the human being, the idea of progress, and the existence of universal morals. Yet the connection between religion and science seemed uneasy on the individual level: traditional (religious) characters like Major Kira were usually skeptical about technologies, while scientists remained skeptical about religion. When it comes to religion, *DS9* was unconventional, but remained committed to the traditional sci-fi tradition of focusing either on vague Judeo-Christian concepts or altogether on other spiritual traditions. Of course parallels to the Judeo-Christian tradition can be found, especially when it comes to narrative structures: the trials of a chosen one who finally sacrifices himself for the common good, the struggle between good and evil, the appearance of prophecy and miracles; but the specifics are not that similar: the messiah is called an emissary and has to teach the gods about human existence rather than tell humans about God, while the divinity is not a single all-powerful entity, but a collective that actually resides in a certain location (the wormhole or celestial temple). Overall, *DS9* does not strike us as "biblical." *BSG* and *Caprica*, on the other hand, could almost be read as a missing book from the Bible—or an alternative version of it. This brings us to the last pillar of the *Battlestarverse*'s construction of religious narrative: its Judeo-Christian heritage.

Judeo-Christian Sci-Fi

In her recent publication about the religious in science fiction and fantasy, Emily McAvan has stated that the "postmodern sacred" as she calls it derives most of its component from New Age spirituality, interspersed with Christian elements (McAvan 2012, 6–8). Yet some TV series have recently stood out in their use of overtly Judeo-Christian concepts (interspersed with some New Age elements), namely the fantasy-horror series *Supernatural* (The CW since 2005) and the sci-fi series *BSG* and *Caprica* that are the subject of this book. These series focused strongly on scriptures, Judeo-Christian concepts of God, angels, and (in the case of *Supernatural*) demons, including the concept of "chosenness" within this framework. They discussed the ideas of heaven or hell as well as the question of free will in a universe infused with divinity. God was a real constant in these stories, he actually existed—even if we never saw him in *BSG* and he seemed to have "left the building" in *Supernatural*. Lisa Kienzl has recently explored the specifics and consequences of such overtly Judeo-Christian elements in *Supernatural* (and its fan fiction) with regard to gender (Kienzl 2014), but these issues remain largely unexamined for *BSG* and its precursor *Caprica*.

In the case of *BSG*, this Judeo-Christian context has a back-story. The first series of this name was created in the 1970s by the Mormon Glenn A. Larson. Because Larson was explicitly interested in communicating Mormon ideas, the franchise always had a peculiar relationship to religion, in particular Christianity. When Ron Moore created the "re-imagined" series, he left some of the Mormon structures in place: the planet Kobol (an anagram of the star Kolob mentioned in Mormon scripture), the Quorum of 12 as the political cabinet (reminiscent of the Mormon ruling council by the same name), the focus on the exodus story (which is of course not restricted to Mormon faith). However, as Ivan Wolfe has pointed out, Mormon contents are largely missing in the new series. Freedom of choice, humanity's journey towards Godhood, the creation of the Cylons by "Count Iblis" (a clear reference to Satan, called Iblis in Islam)—all of these elements were central to Larson's original version, but absent from Moore's "reimagined" Galactica (Wolfe 2008). After all, Ronald Moore is not a Mormon.

According to Moore, he came up with the idea of equipping both Cylons and humans with religion, because he felt that this would be more realistic (Rogers 2008). He stated that "the religious aspects of the show developed naturally out of my intention to reflect every aspect of the human experience" (Vallant 2008, 18). Once again, he wanted to be different than *Star Trek* where religion was largely irrelevant—though we have seen that *DS9* needs to be mentioned as a precursor. Ironically, Moore also felt that science fiction was a rather safe genre for treating religion since the stories are far enough removed from our own reality to create comparatively little controversy. There is certainly truth to that—yet treating religion as a subject and creating a religious world are still two different things.

Moore deserves credit for not sticking with the sci-fi stereotype of borrowing religious concepts from eastern or Nordic religions while largely ignoring the Judeo-Christian religions that have shaped Western Culture. He decided to make humans polytheists and the Cylons monotheists, based on the idea that polytheistic religions were historically driven out by monotheist religions (Rogers 2008). The polytheism displayed in the series is based on the Greco-Roman pantheon, which certainly arose from the original series' use of character names such as Apollo and Athena. The monotheism displayed is vague enough to be interpreted as any of the three Abrahamic faiths (Judaism, Christianity, or Islam), though I will argue in this book that it leans especially strongly towards Judaism when it comes to religious content.

Of course Moore and the other writers never espoused a specific religious tradition, and it would be wrong to propose that the narrative follows a particular doctrine as had been the case with Larson's original. Rather, popular culture texts tend to conflate various aspects of Western heritage, including (but not limited to) several Jewish and Christian structures and ideas. The presence of a disproportional number of Catholic directors in Hollywood, for example, has led to a strong presence of Catholic concepts in U.S. popular culture, where reformed Christianity (Calvinists, Lutherans, and their off-shoots) is otherwise dominant. Judaism had already influenced Western culture in medieval and early modern Europe, although it did so mainly through its intellectually dominant Sephardic branch—the "Spanish" Jews who were expelled from the Iberian Peninsula in 1492. These were also the first Jewish settlers of America. By the 19th century, Ashkenazi ("German") Jews had become dominant in the United States, and in the 20th century they would influence the entertainment industry and thus popular culture significantly.[8]

1. Religious Science Fiction

Religious systems are not static, but dynamic. It cannot be the goal of any study concerned with religion in popular culture to suggest such static systems by assigning particular stories, story lines, or concepts to a specific religious system. The term "Judeo-Christian" points to the close connection between the religious worlds of Judaism and Christianity, the two religions that have most strongly shaped Western culture. Since they are strongly intertwined and share many of the same religious concepts, scholars of religion speak of the three "Abrahamic" religions Judaism, Christianity, and Islam as an entity. Some elements discussed could consequently also be interpreted as Islamic—however, if religious concepts from the Abrahamic religions entered Western culture, they usually did so via Judaism or Christianity, and not via Islam.

We are all aware that there are several currents in both belief systems that evolved historically, often in debate and conflict with one another. We distinguish between Reformed, Catholic, and Orthodox Christianity and sub-groups within them, as we do Reformed, Conservative, and Orthodox Judaism and their sub-groups. Both historically and in contemporary thought these sub-groups are often at odds when it comes to controversial topics such as life after death, free will, or eschatology—let alone gender issues or "correct" forms of worship. These conflicts have also manifested themselves in a variety of ways historically. So when I suggest that a concept is "Jewish" or an idea "Lutheran-Calvinist," these are generalized remarks that describe a tendency rather than a stable, historically static reality. In fact, the appeal of popular culture's use of religion is that it reveals how intermingled all of these religious ideas and debates are in Western thought. A concept can be both Jewish and Calvinist, with some Catholic elements, and still be recognizable to the viewer as part of their religious heritage.

The series introduces religion as a factor right from the beginning, in *Miniseries*. The Cylon Caprica Six appears as a God-fearing femme fatal, while her lover Gaius Baltar cannot understand why a smart woman would be so "superstitious." Through Bill Adama's encounter with the Cylon Leoben, we also learn that the Cylons understand themselves to be "ensouled" by God, and believe the genocide of humanity to be God's will. We are also introduced to human polytheism when we find Kara "Starbuck" Thrace praying to the gods while holding a wooden statue, and listen to the priest Elosha's reading of the Holy Scriptures as well as Bill Adama's insistence that he knows the location of the mythical 13th planet of humanity. In the *Battlestarverse*, religion is present from the very beginning, and it mixes and juxtaposes Judeo-Christian and Greco-Roman elements.

The Judeo-Christian world of *BSG* and *Caprica* is presented through the use of concepts and ideas associated with that tradition. God sends messengers (also called angels) to a chosen few to guide them to their destiny. A few messiahs, referred to also as prophets, "anointed leaders," or "saviors," must guide their people to "salvation" or "paradise." References to the story unfolding on the Galactica can be found in their Holy Scriptures. And on *Caprica*, the Christian idea of "heaven" is frequently employed. The series embrace Judeo-Christian religious concepts overtly, going so far as to use the "correct" terms. The next chapters will elaborate on the use of the concepts "messiah" (chapter three), "angels," "prophets" (chapter two) and "heaven" (chapter five). Before we do this, however, it is necessary to assess how the two series understand the concepts of God and salvation.

BSG and *Caprica* propose the actual existence of a divine being that is identified as male. Although the writers tried to diminish the issue of gender in the last episode by having one of the angels refer to the orchestrating being as an "it," the male pronoun is used constantly throughout the series. The finale also constructs a small amount of uncertainty about its "God-ness" by proposing that "it" does not appreciate being called "God." However, the entire narrative structure is directed at some all-powerful being who orchestrates the unfolding events in order to accomplish a certain goal. This goal is reconciliation and entry into the Promised Land. *BSG*'s divinity cannot be explained by reason and science, which is why the narrative can be called religious. As such, the series put much emphasis on the idea of salvation.

The concept of salvation seems straightforward but is in fact rather difficult to define. In its broadest sense, it evokes an existence that is free from the pain and restraints associated with present existence (Freedman 1987, 33). How exactly salvation is to be attained—and what constitutes these "pains and restraints" differs according to ideology, as does the imagined result of salvation. Judaism and Christianity share some basic ideas concerning salvation: resurrection, life in a netherworld, and the idea of messianic guidance. However, Judaism is altogether more concerned with this world than the next, and most stories of salvation are consequently connected to earthly existence rather than an idea of "heaven." Judaism also understands salvation in more collective terms than Christianity, which is focused on the individual (Steinrötter 2004, 1–3). The ways of achieving salvation likewise differ, as Judaism connects salvation more strongly to strict obedience to God's law. This connection between salvation and the total submission to God's will in Judaism (expressed though the observance of the law as laid down in the Torah) was a historical development dating back to the first centuries CE (Neusner 1990, 33–37).

The series are guided by an idea of salvation that is understood in rather Judeo-Christian terms. On *BSG*, salvation is associated with collective safety for the humans (also noted by Wetmore 2012, 76–77)—a return to a paradisiacal home where they will be safe from further Cylon assaults. This return will be guided by a mythical leader, making this story reminiscent of the Bible's exodus story, where the Jews tried to escape prosecution in Egypt, led by their religious leader Moses. Associating salvation with the plights of a minority group that needs to be saved is rather typical for Judaism (Kraemer et al., 2001, 299, 313). For the Cylons, the birth of the hybrid child Hera (half human, half Cylon) is associated with salvation, as it rescues the Cylons from their inability to reproduce naturally. This failure is seen as a barrier between them and God, and the child bridges that gap. This is at least partially reminiscent of the Christian tradition, where the birth of a child was likewise seen as the precondition for salvation. God heals Cylons and humans through Hera, just as God healed Israel through Jesus (Pomykala 1995, 7). Jesus signaled that salvation was possible through God, and Hera does the same for the Cylons (Freedman 1987, 39). On *Caprica*, on the other hand, the concept of salvation is more frequently employed by negative characters or "villains," who connect (individual) salvation to virtual space in a rather posthuman way (to be free of the constraints of a human body and thus find eternal life). We have already seen that this posthuman idea has Judeo-Christian roots. So does the idea that the righteous will eventually be rewarded. Not only is the series' entire concept of salvations influenced by the Judeo-

Christian tradition, but the series also understand this idea in religious terms.

Besides the simple fact that *BSG* and *Caprica* propose the existence of a Supreme Being and use religious concepts such as salvation, messiahs, and angels, other elements support my assertion that we are dealing with "religious narratives." God interferes with human affairs. If we accept that Cylons are people, then we must conclude that God has actively given them a soul because, as Bill Adama said, "we didn't include a soul in the programming" (*BSG Miniseries*). The events of *Caprica* support this assertion, as we witness how avatar prototypes are infused with a "soul" through religious intervention—God gives Zoe Graystone "the gift to create," transmitted through an angel. God actively decides to provide souls for the Cylons. God also decides that he wants his two creations to co-exist (as Baltar states in the finale, "our two destinies are entwined in its force")—so he sends angels to both of them to guide them to paradise. Strictly speaking, this God is physically absent. Unlike the Ori of *Stargate SG-1*, he does not need a large amount of humans or Cylons to believe in him and pray to him in order to survive—he has always and will always exist. He does not have a superiority complex either. This is a typical monotheistic (specifically Christian) God without much of a personality. As we have seen, he is a universal, not a local God as the prophets had been on *DS9*. This God is a reality, a universal constant.

Both narratives talk about religion excessively, but they do more than that: they create a world with an active divine power that influences events and sends messengers to chosen people in order to guarantee a certain outcome. As already stated, I propose that this is a precondition for speaking of a "religious narrative"—a precondition that not many science fiction narratives meet. After all, science fiction per definition does not create religious narratives, it creates scientific ones. We have seen that this apparent contradiction is gapped through their postmodern-posthuman interpretation of the world and of humanity that strongly questions humanism and erodes the boundaries between religion and science. The second particularity which especially distinguishes *BSG* and *Caprica* from its precursor *DS9* is their overt use of Judeo-Christian elements, which is still rather uncommon in the genre. At the same time, they never stop being science fiction—

they deal explicitly with the patterns and consequences of technological advancement and frequently comment on posthumanist ideas. They are truly religious sci-fi narratives. We will now assess in detail, how the series deal with the inherent contradictions of such stories and discover that the use and re-interpretation of gender stereotypes play a significant role in resolving them.

2

Saviors: Women Bring Salvation

In scholarship of religion and popular culture, savior-like figures are easily the most investigated characters. From Superman to Ripley from *Alien* (Ridley Scott 1979), characters who save the world and sacrifice themselves or important aspects of themselves in the process have been contextualized within the Abrahamic (predominantly Christian) concept of the messiah (Kozlovic 2002). However, few of these narratives possess an overtly religious context. Even in narratives as identified by Sofia Sjö, where messiah figures are "surrounded by a religious structure" (Sjö 2007, 60), saving the world and sacrificing oneself in the process is not understood in a religious sense. In other words, there is a difference between a savior or Jesus-like figure in a largely secular narrative and a savior figure in a religious one. When it comes to science fiction, as Sjö has established in another context, messiah figures are rarely connected to God (Sjö 2010, 3–4). Yet in *BSG*, a clearly religious narrative that is commonly understood as science fiction, messiahs are sent and guided by God. Significantly, the two characters that can most strongly be identified as saviors in the Christian sense are surprisingly passive and unaware of the plan God laid out for them.

BSG does not simply employ the stereotypical messiah trope. Instead, the series makes significant changes to the concept that go beyond the mere fact that messianic figures are female. An important tool for this change is the idea that salvation cannot be achieved by only one hero. We have already established that salvation can be defined as establishing a new life in the Promised Land which includes both humans and Cylons. This goal is not achieved through one unique savior. Salvation is instead a group effort that includes Cylons and humans, women and men alike. However, three characters stand out. These are the hybrid child Hera, Galactica's best viper pilot Kara Thrace, and politician Laura Roslin—all of them female. In this chapter, we will investigate the messianic character of these women and assess how their depiction changes the (traditionally male) character of the savior. To this end, we will draw on the ancient origins of messianism as well as its usage in contemporary popular culture.

Laura, the Davidic Messiah

The idea of one or multiple messiahs originated in ancient Judaism and was initially a rather political concept. Messiah (in Greek: christos) is Hebrew for "anointed one," referring to the traditional anointment of kings and high priests in antiquity. Scripture promised that a chosen leader would bring about redemption (Cohn-Sherbok 1997, 1). He would be a political leader, even a warrior; a king who would defeat the enemies of the Israelites and establish a kingdom of justice on earth (Sacchi 1990, 151–152; Collins 1995, 68). The messiah (in some writings also referred to as the "Son of Man") was this-worldly, chosen by God, but explicitly not a miracle worker (Novakovic 1997, 151). This leader would be a descendent of the Biblical figure David, king of Israel and Juda (also famous for defeating the giant Goliath). When the Davidic line[1] fell, it was believed that the house of David would eventually return to power to reunite Israel and Juda. Some asserted that this period of glory would be preceded by a series of disasters: the believers would suffer destruction, famine, exile, and pain. God would punish his people for their sins before he would redeem them through the anointed leader (Cohn-Sherbok 1997, 3–6). The idea of messianism was closely connected to the loss of land and power: at some point, God would return this lost land to the Jewish people through the savior.

In the narrative of *BSG*, Laura Roslin takes on the role of this political messiah, whose leadership is prophesied in the sacred scrolls. While her portrayal combines elements from several messianic and prophetic traditions, the concept of the Davidic messiah certainly fits her best. We first meet Laura Roslin in a doctor's office on Caprica, where she is informed that she has breast cancer. Shortly after, she attends the decommissioning ceremony of the Galactica as a governmental representative. She is a former schoolteacher, who has now taken the office of secretary of education. On her way back from the ceremony, the Cylon attack begins. Laura is left the only surviving member of the government and is sworn in as president of the colonies. She begins to gather survivors and guides them to the Galactica. Her political responsibility to keep the remaining 50,000 humans safe and find a new home for them, is soon complemented by a religious one. Influenced by the drug chamalla that she takes for her cancer, she has visions and relates them to the (female) priest Elosha. The priest is in disbelief at hearing these visions that she immediately identifies with the prophecies of Pythia from the holy scrolls. She recounts these prophecies that include a statement highly significant for our topic: "And the Lords anointed a leader. To guide the caravan of the heavens to their new homeland" (1.10 "The Hand of God"). The prophecies further state that this leader would suffer from a "wasting disease," and would die before entering the Promised Land. The prophecies thus relate to Laura very clearly.

Elosha explicitly uses the term "anointed" to describe this leader, which immediately creates a link between her and the Davidic messiah of ancient Judaism. According to Pythia, it is Laura's role to lead humanity to paradise and "rebirth." Her role, like that of the Davidic messiah, is connected to the loss of land (the 12 Colonies) and power (breakdown of governmental structures), and her coming is preceded by destruction and exile that is described as a precursor to salvation. Like the Davidic messiah, Laura is a political leader with a religious function. As such, she also needs to be caring and just. In scripture, the messiah is also referred to as a "shepherd," (Pomykala 1995, 27) a role Laura also fills—she is responsible for the well-being and survival of her flock, the remainder of humanity.

Laura Roslin is not originally a very religious person, but her visions and the events following them convince her rather quickly, especially when compared to *DS9*'s Benjamin Sisko who needs a few years to fully embrace his messianic role. When she has her first drug-induced visions, she immediately turns to the priest Elosha for guidance instead of searching for a purely scientific (or medical) explanation. While Gaius Baltar, who is in many ways a parody of the stereotypical sci-fi scientist embodied by Star Trek's Sisko, needs painful convincing and tangible proof for the existence of divinity and his role in a divine plan, Laura quickly accepts this premise. If the reality of divinity had not been accepted in the narrative, this would have proven once again that women are easily convinced by irrational explanations. Since divinity is real, women are instead quicker to recognize the truth.

In fact, the politician Laura Roslin is never naïve in her faith and recognizes the danger and power of religious rhetoric. She also argues strongly for the rationality of faith. This becomes very clear in the beginning of season two, when Laura is imprisoned on Galactica after having sent Starbuck to Caprica to retrieve the Arrow of Apollo against military orders. From her cell, she reveals her divine mission to the Quorum (governmental council) in a statement that is both political and religious. She condemns her imprisonment and the takeover of the military that accompanied it, and defends her actions as something that is utterly rational—on the basis of prophecy. When Colonel Tigh calls her crazy because she believes herself to be a prophet, she stays calm and explains her reasoning to the Quorum. She tells them that she believes to be the leader prophesied in Pythia and will lead them to the Promised Land—and manages to convince the Quorum with her calm reasoning.

The support she receives is of course a direct consequence of the dire circumstances. Everything has been destroyed, billions of people are dead, humanity is homeless and chased by a seemingly overpowering enemy. However, Laura is not presented as a power-hungry politician who takes advantage of other people's desperation. Neither is she presented as "crazy," although this is clearly what Colonel Tigh is hoping for. As Jones pointed out, the opposition between rational masculinity (as exemplified by Adama and especially Tigh) and irrational femininity is clearly established in this course of events, as Roslin is imprisoned because she acted "irrationally" by going with her religiously-motivated gut-feeling (Jones 2010, 176). Rational masculinity demands that she be punished. Significantly, she is able to convince the Quorum that everything she has done is "logical," thus challenging the essence of male rationale. Laura's belief is not irrational—it is based on experience and observation, as she saw her visions materialize and the course of current events described in the Holy Scriptures.

Because she knows that she will be dead soon, Laura can concentrate all her energies on her task of saving humanity. She can devote herself to the sacred scrolls while simultaneously fulfilling her role as a politician, which often requires her to make difficult and unpopular decisions. Laura Roslin can be calculating and callous—once even corrupt, when she tries to rig the presidential election. Laura is not a Jesus-like spiritual leader, who preaches love and forgiveness, but a politician who understands that she is at war and is in charge of the survival of the human race. Because she is a genuine believer, her religiosity does not seem fake, as if it were a means to an end. The series contrasts her with the two other (both male) presidents who are shown in the course of the series, Gaius Baltar and Tom Zarek. Both of them are entirely unfitted for the job. The series thus begins and ends with Laura as the political leader.

Laura is a middle-aged woman who is unmarried and has no children. Her ability to lead is frequently questioned, yet never on the basis of her gender, but mostly by pointing out her lack of political experience—after all, she is "only a school teacher" ("Women on Top" 2008, 157). She is juxtaposed with Bill Adama, commander of the Galactica and thus military leader. The conflict between military and politics is a frequent issue especially in the beginning of the series, as is the personal relationship that develops between Adama and Roslin. In slight contrast to the prophecies found in the scrolls of Pythia, Laura does enter the Promised Land in the end, but her highly advanced cancer kills her soon after their arrival. After Starbuck, she is the other major female character to die or disappear in the series finale, a fact that has especially disappointed critics. Laura Roslin's death (as well as Starbuck's disappearance which we will turn to shortly) has led some to argue that masculinity eventually triumphs in the series, while femininity is tamed and domesticated (Jones 2010, 177). There is certainly merit to this conclusion regarding the two most important female characters, though the case of the female Cylons as discussed in the next chapter will lead us to reconsider this position.

Interestingly, of the three female messiahs, Laura is the one who

2. Saviors: Women Bring Salvation

is not usually identified as a messianic figure, while both Hera and Starbuck have been called messiahs, either in or out of the series. Laura is instead referred to as a prophet or a leader. Yet her function, the words used to describe her mission, and her destiny, all point into the direction of the Jewish Davidic savior: she is anointed by the gods to lead humanity in a time of war, and her proclaimed goal is humanity's salvation. Of course she also exhibits Christological and prophetic traits. Indeed, Laura's suffering and ultimate death not only leans her towards the Christological savior, but also towards the fate of a prophet in ancient Judaism, as explained by Adela Yarbro Collins: "Suffering, rejection, and death were not part of the traditional picture of the role of the Messiah of Israel. But suffering, rejection, and even death were typically associated with the prophetic role" (Collins 2007, 24).

The conflation of the prophet and the royal messiah into a "prophet-messiah" was still rare at the time of Jesus of Nazareth, yet became increasingly common. For the period of Jewish apocalypticism (first century BCE to second century CE), Condra has found several biblical and extra-biblical precedents as well as "real-life" examples of prophet-messiahs (Condra 2002, 254–256). In the same manner, Laura shows some prophetic or Christological traits while simultaneously being firmly embedded in Ancient Jewish messianic conceptions (also noted by Butler, Winston 2009). There is of course also a strong connection to Greek mythology, as evidenced by the use of the name "Pythia" for the holy scrolls that announce Laura's destiny, invoking the ancient Greek oracle of Delphi (Maass 2007, 6–7).

The fact that Laura is not the only messiah is likewise not without precedent. Some messianic traditions in Judaism believed in a "division of labor" between two or more messiahs. Already in the 6th century BCE, writers like Ezekiel referred to two messiahs: the prince and the priest (Sacchi 1990, 152). In some cases, disillusionment with the house of David even transferred most messianic attributes to the priesthood. For Ben Sirach (second century BCE), for example, it is the priest, not the warrior king, who holds the key to salvation (Pomykala 1995, 151). In the rabbinic period (starting around the time of the Romans' destruction of the Temple in Jerusalem in 70 CE), a rather complex messianic scheme emerged: the Rabbis stated that not one, but three significant leaders would appear to bring about redemption: first Elijah would bring order to the legal world, then the "son of Joseph" would defeat Gog and Magog (and be killed in the battle), and finally the son of David would arrive to sit on the throne (Cohn-Sherbok 1997, 46–48). Such a "division of labor" between several messiahs is also characteristic of *BSG*, although they work simultaneously rather than in succession: Laura as the political leader is complemented by two other messiahs who play a different part in the series' salvation narrative. We will first turn to the child-savior, Hera.

Hera and the Role of Hybridity

In *BSG*, the child-savior's name is Hera, and (like Laura) she fulfills an important function in the series' salvation narrative. Hera, a human-Cylon hybrid, is the daughter of the human Karl "Helo" Agathon and his Cylon wife Sharon "Athena" Agathon, an Eight model. For the Cylons, their inability to reproduce naturally poses a religious problem, as "procreation is one of God's commandments" (Messenger-Six to Baltar, *Miniseries*). While present posthuman enthusiasts strive to replace, enhance, or alter the patterns of natural reproduction through technology (Squier 1995, 115), our religious machines desperately want to make "regular" babies. The conclusion they arrive at (scientifically) is that they can only reproduce naturally through hybridization with humans, and that love is a fundamental ingredient for successful reproduction. Overall, reproduction is associated rather strongly with the Cylons in the series, not with the humans—the subject is both technologized and feminized (Jowett 2010, 66). While most Cylon reproduction is technological and can be described as multiplication or a way of cloning, this kind of reproduction is unsatisfactory for the religious Cylons.

When they realize that their efforts of forced hybridization with humans go nowhere, they send an Eight model to the human Karl Agathon and instruct her to seduce him romantically. While the ploy is successful, Sharon also falls in love with Helo and eventually joins the Colonial Fleet as an informant and later a member. As Claudia Springer has noted, Sex often illustrates the fusion between human and technology (Springer 1999, 37). This is certainly the case for Helo and

2. Saviors: Women Bring Salvation

Athena and the subsequent birth of their hybrid daughter Hera. Hera's birth is highly improbable—to our knowledge she is the only human-machine hybrid ever to be born. She joins the ranks of Jesus (born to a virgin) and John the Baptist (born to a barren woman) (Strauss 1995, 83) as a miracle child whose birth should not have been possible. For the Cylons, Hera is a miracle because they see this possibility of hybridization with humans as an acceptable solution to their reproductive difficulties. The Cylons want Hera because they consider her to be their future, while humans initially fear her but hesitate to kill her because she is partly human.

The child of love, Hera, is considered innocent by both sides, and yet the Cylons stylize her as a messiah and the humans fear her as such. Her blood has healing powers and (temporarily) cures Laura Roslin's cancer, which reinforces her messianic role and connects her to the healer-messiah Jesus. Yet Hera's main attribute lies in her nature as a hybrid. As Shana Heinricy has pointed out, the main difference between humans and Cylons is their bodies (Heinricy 2008, 95). As a hybrid, Hera negates this boundary and thus the differences between the two species. Wetmore noted that she has "two natures" (human and cylon), which also relates her to Christ who was considered both human and divine (Wetmore 2012, 125). This is in fact characteristic for Christianity as opposed to Judaism and Islam, which are both built on the insurmountable difference between human and divine (von Braun 2010, 33). In this sense, Christ is also a hybrid who conflates humanity and divinity. Yet unlike Christ, Hera does not actively pursue the salvation of either human or Cylon—she is a child, and for the most part does not understand her importance at all. It is WHAT she is, rather than who she is that makes her important.

Hybrids are not simply mediators between the two aspects they merge. They are neither the one nor the other; they are both and thus more than either (Schumacher 2008, 33). The idea of composite beings is common in many cultures and existed at many points in time, and they always occupy a special, even extraordinary place in the imagined universe. In the Ancient Near East as well as Ancient Greece and Rome, hybrids were often composed of human and animal parts, understood as a sign of the divine. Christianity also has its hybrids, namely angels and demons that walk the earth looking like humans but outfitted with (often animalistic) signs of their true nature. Like Hera, such beings were always considered special and extraordinary, but also frightening. Hybrids always cross a society's boundaries and thus question the established order of things by simply being (Vallant 2008, 75), regardless of whether they only exist in the imagination or also in reality (mestizo children, for example, also fit this description). Of course Hera is a rather unrecognizable hybrid, which makes her all the more frightening because, as stated, she negates the difference between the two species.

Hera is nevertheless a rather untypical hybrid, as she is the product of natural reproduction and not artificial creation: sci-fi hybrids are usually made, not born (Vallant 2008, 14). More than that, her biological birth is the entire point of her messianic character. Hera is not, like Frankenstein, the creation of a "mad scientist" (Schumacher 2008, 95), but the product of traditional reproduction within a romantic relationship. Because of that, she is seen as a gift from God. When she is birthed, the doctor explicitly states that Sharon's Cylon body is not made for such a complicated process. She is the impossible: born naturally to a Cyborg woman. Whereas other hybrids overcome nature, Hera overcomes her mother's artificiality and returns the technological to the natural. The return of the natural is in many ways a theme in *BSG*: the artificially created beings see themselves as incomplete because they cannot reproduce *naturally*; the Cylons have to give up eternal life in order to permit *natural* death; the series ending suggests that we need to let go of our technological advancements and return to *nature*. Hera is the embodiment of this message: a naturally born human-machine hybrid. Through her, the Cylons are "naturalized."

By focusing on her birth, the series connects Hera to the Christian messianic tradition that can be traced to a period in Judaism that scholars call Jewish apocalypticism (first century BCE to second century CE). During this time, many movements proclaimed that the end of days was near and gathered around messiahs. One such group was the Jesus movement that had proclaimed a certain Jesus of Nazareth as their messiah. Eventually, this movement managed to become an independent religion, now called Christianity. After Jesus' demise, writings about his life and teachings surfaced, among them the Gospels that were to form the New Testament. The goal behind these writings was not sim-

2. Saviors: Women Bring Salvation

ply to teach the followers what it meant to be Christian and how the messiah had brought about salvation; they also tried to link their messiah to the Jewish tradition and thus legitimize him to prove that he was indeed the messiah prophesied in the Torah.

The so-called infancy narratives in the New Testament should be understood in this context. These stories concern the birth and childhood of Jesus and serve to confirm the nature of the adult Jesus as a messiah by relating his life story to the Old Testament, especially to the birth and infancy of Moses (Rodger 1997, 61; Hultgren 1997, 91). Naturally, the stories also emphasized his connection to the house of David (Strauss 1995, 76). Western tradition has frequently adapted the idea of relating a hero's journey to his birth and childhood, confirming his chosen or divine status by doing so. As a child, the heroes usually already show signs of future greatness, but they are also innocent and in need of protection until they become adults. They need to be protected so that they can fulfill their destiny.

Keeping Hera safe means keeping the idea of human-Cylon reconciliation alive. Both humans and Cylons are thus instructed from above to care for her, and these instructions are relayed through dreams and visions, in particular involving the place known as the "opera house." The first designated protectors of Hera are not her natural, but her surrogate parents: Gaius Baltar and Caprica Six. In the season 1 finale, God's angel, Messenger-Six, announces the arrival of Hera in the first opera house vision (1.13 "Kobol's Last Gleaming—Part II"). She guides Baltar to a cradle embedded in gleaming white light and tells Baltar that he is "the guardian and protector of a new generation of God's children." Later, several other characters share the opera house vision, including Caprica Six, Hera's mother Athena, president Laura Roslin, as well as the child Hera herself. With the exception of Gaius Baltar, the opera house vision includes only women—women are charged with protecting the hybrid child, whom God has designated as the future of both humanity and Cylons. While one could conclude that the (motherly) protection of a child is traditionally left to women—making this plot choice a rather stereotypical one—the issue has an additional dimension: The vision is transmitted to people who are inclined to take it seriously. This involves her mother, as well as the highly religious Caprica Six and Laura Roslyn. The men of Galactica are generally unbelievers, and likely would not have known what to do with this vision.

In the series finale of *BSG*, the human-Cylon alliance lands on our Earth, on the African continent, sometime far in the past. Hera is safe to grow up in this new paradise, together with her human father and Cylon mother. A look into the future, which is set only a few years from our own present, suggests Hera to be "mitochondrial Eve." Despite the fact that the science of this statement is a little off (Ryman 2010, 49–51), the suggestion is clearly that Hera is humanity's ancestor and that we are consequently all, to a certain extent, Cylons. The opera house vision is sent to ensure Hera's survival that will eventually form the basis of reconciliation. The vision is necessary, because both (some) Cylons and humans initially feel threatened by the child. President Roslin originally opts to have the child aborted, later to have her killed, until she finally decides to fake Hera's death and put the child in the care of an unknowing human woman. The threat posed by Hera is that of eroding boundaries, of erasing difference between the two mortal enemies (Rennes 2008, 72–73). Consequently Roslin needs Hera to remain different, other—meaning her personhood cannot be recognized. Without the opera house vision, Hera might not have survived.

While all Cylons are to a certain extent hybrids, Hera is a different sort of hybrid, since she is the product of "natural" reproduction. Nobody can deny that Hera is both human and Cylon. She makes it clear for anyone with eyes that humans and Cylons are not two completely different species—otherwise her birth would not have been possible. So I maintain with Gumpert that only Hera functions as Haraway's Cyborg completely, because she is the one who erases Cylon-human dichotomies (Gumpert 2008, 150–151). As Gumpert explains, the fear of being a Cylon, which haunts so many of the main human characters, already illustrates that no real difference between the two exists (Gumpert 2008, 150). While such fears can be compartmentalized and disguised in most cases, Hera makes them impossible to ignore.

Hera also differs from Haraway's Cyborg because she is both innocent and female instead of ungendered and without innocence. It is precisely this innocence that on the one hand makes Hera a messianic figure, and on the other refutes any interpretation of Hera as THE savior. While important children are certainly a well-known element of both religious and popular culture narratives, their significance lies in the fact that they will grow up to be someone of relevance—they will be either a hero-messiah or a villain in the future. This is certainly the case for Jesus of Nazareth, also frequently portrayed as a baby, or John Connor in *Terminator* (James Cameron 1984), as well as Anakin Skywalker from the *Star Wars* franchise, or Clark Kent aka Superman.

Yet we never see Hera grow up and there is no indication that she will do something extraordinary when she is an adult. Her messianic role is restricted to her nature as a hybrid, while her actions are irrelevant. Thus, if we remember our definition of salvation in the narrative of *BSG*, it becomes clear that Hera is only responsible for one aspect of salvation, the reconciliation of humans and Cylons. The second part—finding the Promised Land—is not her doing either directly or indirectly. In this respect, other characters are of central importance, reinforcing the idea of salvation as a group effort. Of these characters, Kara "Starbuck" Thrace fits the Jesus-like messianic role quite clearly, especially considering her resurrection. In a way, Kara complements Hera. We shall now see how.

Kara Thrace and Her Special Destiny

If Hera represents the aspect of innocence and purity in particular of the Christian messiah story that is frequently associated with the depiction of the baby Jesus, Kara "Starbuck" Thrace represents another aspect of the messiah, namely the role of a divinely inspired guide to salvation. The series gives much space to Kara's journey towards her destiny, associating her with both the "movie messiah" as well as comparable female television heroines. She must accept and find her destiny, sacrifice herself for the good of the many, and finally guide her people to the Promised Land as a resurrected spiritual leader. As "the harbinger of death" she leads both humans and Cylons to the end of their separate, "pure" existence and towards hybridization. To explore her role as a messiah, I will look for the parallels and differences between the Christian ideas of messiah and resurrection, and link her to the contemporary popular culture messiah.

As discussed by several scholars, humans are consistently coded masculine in *BSG*, in contrast to the feminized Cylons (Kirkland 2008, 133–136). While we will focus on the latter in the fourth chapter, Kara Thrace is the best example for the former. With her short hair, tough and impulsive attitude, and her incessant cigar-smoking, Galactica's best fighter pilot is a classical "butch" character. Matthew Jones has gone even further and described her as "the ultimate in masculinity" (Jones 2010, 173; see also Kirkland 2008, 342). Indeed, the character "Starbuck" was a man in the original series. Starbuck represents a world in which equality is such an integral part of society that female military officers and fighter pilots are frequent and unisex bathrooms the norm. As Sarah Conly observed, "Colonial society is less gendered than our own" (Conly 2008, 236). Starbuck is an officer who (initially) follows orders without question, but is prepared to punch the XO (Executive Officer) who she believes is a drunk who is not fitted for the job. Kara is also portrayed as overtly sexual and highly religious.

At first glance, Kara seems to support the stereotype of the masculinized female hero, which has frequently been reinforced by ambiguous names such as Max, Sam, Sidney, or Ripley (and was overtly challenged by the character Buffy in *Buffy the Vampire Slayer*) (Kirkland 2008, 136–139). As Samantha Holland observed: "Representing 'masculine' women is far from being feminist, as it fails to adequately deconstruct the basic dualism of gender constructed and sustained by the patriarchal order" (Holland 1995, 169). Yet as Kara's importance to the narrative—especially the religious narrative—grows, she is also feminized. She lets her hair grow and becomes more intuitive and driven by emotions. In accepting her religious role as a savior or guardian, she increasingly accepts her feminine side. However, like Buffy, she does not end up with a traditional feminine "happy ending." In a traditional narrative, she could have been expected to end up in a stable relationship with on-again off-again love interest Lee Adama; instead she disappears into thin air after finishing her task. While religion makes her more feminine, she is not "rewarded" with the traditionally female "goals" of marriage and children. As a savior-figure her goal is the salvation of others, which is frequently associated with self-sacrifice. Kara's feminization might seem like a step back (indeed, some critics have interpreted it as such), but for the female appropriation of the messiah myth it is essential. As Sofia Sjö pointed out, women are usually only allowed to be full-fledged saviors if they act like men (Sjö 2010, 3). Kara, however, is not "weakened" or otherwise lessened by her feminine side, but can only fulfill her role by embracing it. She is transformed from a traditional masculinized female hero (e.g., Ripley from *Alien*) into a more "feminine" savior.

Kara follows the established Christian pattern of a savior, starting with her birth. Messianic figures are frequently marked as different though a miraculous or mysterious birth or an unknown parent. For Jesus of Nazareth, the virginity of his mother as well as the divinity of his father mark his difference, while signs of his extraordinary status are sent to be recognized by a chosen few. More recent messiahs of popular culture were likewise conceived in extraordinary circumstances: Clark Kent aka Superman is the only son of Jor-El who is frequently allotted God-like status in the franchise's universe (Kozlovic 2002). He is born in the middle of an apocalypse and sent to earth, where the Kents find him and recognize that he is special. Luke Skywalker has to learn that his biological father is the evil Darth Vader (Anakin Skywalker), a secret revealed at a later point in the narrative and constructed as a mystery. Anakin's birth is likewise mysterious, a kind of "virgin birth" (Sjö 2010, 2) without a biological father. John Connor from *Terminator* actually meets his father in the future before he is ever conceived in the past, where his mother needs to be saved from persecution. These mysteries and exceptionable circumstances surrounding the origin of the messiah figure mark the characters as special and different.

For Kara, her origin story is closely connected to the mystery of paternity. Her father apparently left when Kara was a child, but their relationship had always been positive. He was an artist who played the piano and encouraged her to paint. In the last season, Kara is led by a character she initially does not recognize, possibly another angel in the likeness of her father, to remember a song that her father had written. This song finally contains the coordinates to earth. We never find out who Kara's father is and why he had written this particular song. Kara's mother is equally mysterious, as she seemed to know about Kara's destiny and tried to prepare her for it, telling her that she was different (3.17 "Maelstrom"). Thus for Kara, the issue of paternity is forever unresolved, while it is at the same time unclear how her mother knew what she knew. Divine inspiration—or even divine origin—is not impossible. A chosen few (her parents and the Cylon Leoben) are aware of Kara's destiny and try to encourage her in their own way.

While some commentators and fans have opted to see post-resurrection Kara as an angelic figure (Jones 2010, 175), others are more content with the messianic explanation, and a closer look confirms the latter as more likely, especially if compared to the messengers. Kara herself clearly understands herself in a different manner, as she tells Gaius Baltar in the fourth season that she might be a "dead chick" and does not understand what that makes her, but "one thing I know for sure: I'm not an angel" (4.18 "Islanded in a Stream of Stars"). While the following image of her in a bright light marks her as supernatural and divine, it does not make her an angel. Compared to the messengers, she clearly is something different. First of all, she is initially human, and not simply a mouthpiece of God without a back story. Second, she dies and is resurrected, linking her to Christ. Third, she is not only visible to one or two characters and otherwise immaterial, but instead returns to life in a very material body. Fourth, she amasses a group of believers around her that is significantly smaller than the group of misbelievers who eye her suspiciously—this is reminiscent of messianic movements, including the early Jesus movement, though in *BSG* this only happens post-resurrection. Kara is more of a spiritual leader; she never has any official function. In fact, she never appropriates the term "messiah" or even "leader" for herself. This also corresponds, at least according to some scholars, to Jesus' self-perception (Watts Henderson 2009).

Kara's messianic character is reinforced through her resurrection—a resurrection that is not permanent but limited in time. Like Jesus, Kara's resurrection has a specific purpose, and like Jesus she cannot stay longer than she must. Before she disappears she tells Lee: "I am done here. I've completed my journey and it feels good" (4.20 "Daybreak—Part II"). Yet there is one significant difference between Kara's and Jesus' resurrection. While both Jesus and Kara resurrect "in the flesh," Jesus resurrected in his original body. In the history of Christianity, the "empty grave" tradition has been highly relevant theologically: Jesus' empty grave was seen as proof for his return, or according to some created "false proof" of his resurrection in the first place (Theissen and Merz 1996, 416–417). The significance of the empty grave is the idea that lies behind it: that resurrection is always bodily resurrection in the *original* body. From a Christian point of view, the resurrected body would be transformed, but it would still be the original body (based on 1 Corinthians 15: 20–58).

Kara, on the other hand, resurrects in a completely new body—a lot like the Cylons, as we will see in chapter four. Kara does not need proof for her resurrection (and does not need to prove her resurrection to others), but instead needs proof for her death. She gets this proof on Earth I in 4.11 "Sometimes a Great Notion," when she finds her original body decaying in her original viper. While the resurrected Kara is material, her body is not the same: God has resurrected Kara in a new body. She even comments on this before ever knowing about her death on Earth I: "It's like everything seems so far away. The way things feel, the way they taste. Like I'm watching myself and I'm not really experiencing it, not living it. Like my body is just that alien thing that I'm still attached to" (4.03 "The Ties That Bind"). As Wetmore has noted, theologically Kara's death and resurrection are proof of eternal life (Wetmore 2012, 57). This is certainly how Baltar and others see it as well. This "proof" nevertheless remains vague, since Kara's state—like Christ's—is unique. On a more basic level, however, Christian ideas of resurrection have theologically always reinforced one thing: divine power (Bynum 1995, 2). If the resurrection of Jesus' body was a testament to God's power, than the creation of an entirely new body out of thin air certainly does the same.

The resurrected Kara is no longer Starbuck—her Self has been transformed considerably. Starbuck had never been particularly emotional and, although religious, she always showed a fair amount of reasonable skepticism when it came to spirituality and gut-feelings. The resurrected Kara is different. She "feels" where Earth is and is physically and emotionally distressed when Galactica keeps jumping in the wrong direction (4.01 "He That Believeth in Me"). She reminds Laura Roslin that back in the day (at the end of season 1) she had followed Roslin because the latter claimed to have had a vision—yet now Roslin refuses to place any faith in Kara (4.02 "Six of One"). From Laura's perspective, of course, the situation is quite different—Laura's role had been confirmed by scripture, while Kara's had not. Kara detaches herself from her old life in many ways, while she openly attaches herself to Leoben and his idea of her destiny and chosen status. She also embraces her artistic side more than she had done before—she paints and plays the piano.

Kara openly believes that a higher power is behind the events on Galactica and that she has a role to play. As so often in the series, the women of Galactica have to convince the rational men, in this case Lee Adama, that these "superstitions" are not irrational, but factual. When Kara's viper is the only one to pick up a distress signal, she tells a skeptical Lee that the signal might lead them to Earth. Were it not for his personal respect for Kara, Lee probably would have dismissed the entire notion of divine intervention. The scene is reminiscent of Laura's rationalization of her religious convictions in the beginning of the second season. Like Laura before her, Kara has to convince Lee that the religious interpretation is the only logical explanation and is not at all "irrational." Both Adamas—Bill and Lee—need women to find faith, while Kara and Laura can find faith on their own, by analyzing their own experiences. The three female messiahs challenge our traditional conception of the messiah, yet also embrace many of its traditional aspects. By doing so, they create a new messianic system that is nevertheless rooted in tradition.

Challenging the Myth of the Savior

The three saviors of *BSG* challenge traditional assumptions of the sci-fi messiah in various ways, as I will illustrate using Sofia Sjö's excellent analysis of the gendered messiah in sci-fi film and TV (Sjö 2007).[2] First, as Conrad Oswalt observed, apocalyptic films use religious language, but do not impose religious truth: the messiah is not sent by God (discussed by Sjö 2007, 61). Here, the *Battlestarverse* departs from typical sci-fi: The messiahs are indeed sent by a supreme being that has a clear goal in mind and guides the saviors' lives towards this desired outcome. The fact that Laura has cancer, Hera is born, and Kara resurrects are signs not only of their nature as chosen saviors, but also of divine agency. Laura's cancer triggers her prophetic visions through the drug chamalla (which she otherwise would not have taken) and

2. Saviors: Women Bring Salvation

opens her up to becoming not only religious, but also a religious leader. The birth of a human-machine hybrid seems impossible and is described as unique, which marks Hera as a miracle child. Kara's resurrection defies all scientific principles and is thus (like Hera's birth) a sign of divine intervention.

Second, salvation is not only brought by God, but also affected through women, which defies stereotypes. As Sofia Sjö has pointed out following E. Jane Via, traditional savior-stories confirm that women need to be saved, while men do the saving (Sjö 2007, 62–63). This basic message is reaffirmed through the role of the savior's mother, whose relevance is confined to giving birth to (and sometimes raising) the male messiah. *BSG*'s assault on the dominance of male saviors is illustrated by the birth of the child-messiah: a woman gives birth to a female messiah, breaking the traditional complementary "cycle" of gender roles in the messiah myth. *BSG* turns the entire notion of gendered salvation on its head: men need to be saved, while women do the saving. Since God not only exists, but is actively involved in human or cylon events, disbelieving men could never have hoped to find salvation without the guidance of the faithful women. Had the men not listened to these women, the Galactica would still be roaming the Galaxy or, more likely, would have been destroyed by an army of atheist Cylons long ago. Men need to be saved (mostly from themselves) and this can only be accomplished through women.

A third attack on the traditional messiah narrative arises from the question of uniqueness. Strong women in Film and TV (not just in the sci-fi genre) are usually presented as exceptional, meaning they are not surrounded by other strong women (Sjö 2007, 64). Through this narrative device, these women become less threatening: it is easier to accept that one woman can be so "special" that she assumes the traditionally male role of savior than to accept that women are generally as strong and "special" as any man. We can easily see that this interpretation does not work for *BSG*, a world where not one but three female saviors are surrounded by a broad variety of other strong women. This is not a world where one exceptional woman leads a group of heroic men into the apocalyptic struggle. Instead, these women lead both men and women.

The fourth re-interpretation of the messiah myth lies in the question of religious voice and authority. Sjö has pointed out that male messiahs usually hold a position of "religious" leadership, while female saviors are deprived of a religious voice. In narratives centered on female messiahs, this voice is instead given to a complementary male character. Religion is presented as a male space in which women might have a position (as savior), but not a voice (Sjö 2007, 66–68). This stereotype is most clearly subverted by Laura Roslin, who is not only a figure of authority in the political, but also in the religious sphere. She is a believer who stands firm in the face of (male) criticism and is recognized as a religious authority by the people. She remains true to her status as "hero-messiah" as she is neither crazy nor a megalomaniac. The religious voice is hers, as is religious authority. To a lesser extent, Kara Thrace also takes on a religious voice and leadership role after resurrection, though her voice is more mystical and less concrete than Laura's, and not as explicitly connected to divinity. In any case, Sjö found that female messiahs usually lack both religious voice and authority as a strategy of lessening the threat she poses to traditional conceptions of gender (Sjö 2007, 69). Laura Roslin illustrates this threat and is consequently met by male strategies to discredit her. The important point, however, is that these strategies are unsuccessful and presented as "wrong."

A fifth and last point concerns the question of the savior's character. Sofia Sjö found that one of the fundamental differences between male and female messiahs is the latter's lack of a journey towards their destiny. According to Sjö, female messiahs "are more or less already messiahs when we first make their acquaintance" (Sjö 2007, 66–67). While we could interject that part of their journeys in fact lie in the past, Sjö is correct in pointing out that the viewer is usually confronted with a rather mature female messiah figure, while male messiah figures are more frequently presented as regular people who only gradually grow into their role (for concrete examples see Stucky 2005; Kozlovic 2002). While the male figure needs to evolve and become a hero (usually through external factors), the female figure rather needs to find and understand herself better in order to fulfill her role. Sjö suggests that the "evolution of the character" is not as prominent in the narrative of a female messiah.

At least in Kara's case, *BSG* does not support this idea. The character can plausibly be positioned somewhere between the evolving

2. Saviors: Women Bring Salvation

hero who is changed by external factors and the mature messiah who needs to find herself. External factors clearly play a big part in her development. For example, at the end of the first season, Kara is sent back to Caprica to retrieve the Arrow of Apollo, which President Roslin believes will guide the fleet to Earth. This marks an important turning point for Kara, as she slowly starts to believe in her fate and begins to question her central authority (and father) figure, Bill Adama. Keeping with her personality, Kara is initially unwilling to act against the orders of "the old man" as Commander Adama is frequently called. Her faith, for her, is something she was raised with—she could not believe otherwise, but she would initially not find a role for herself in God's plan either. Roslin convinces her by telling her that she is dying of cancer and that she believes to fulfill the role of the leader who will lead humanity to the Promised Land. This simple piece of knowledge, in combination with the information that Adama had previously lied about knowing the location of Earth, helps Kara to make the first decision that will bring her towards her destiny. She goes to Caprica against orders and retrieves the Arrow of Apollo that really does provide a roadmap to Earth. In this plot, Kara is very much influenced by external factors to rethink her worldview and her own role in the religious narrative.

However, a better understanding of herself also plays a role in her development. After finding her dead body on Earth I—and realizing that the planet is a wasteland—Kara, like so many other characters on the show, becomes desperate again. Uncertain of her own place in the world, she explains to the mysterious piano player: "When I was leading the fleet to Earth, everything seemed so clear. For the first time in my life, I knew what I was doing and why I was here. Now I'm just adrift again." The piano player responds: "Sometimes lost is where you need to be" (4.17 "Someone to Watch Over Me"). Like Laura, Kara needs to lose faith in her destiny in order to regain faith in herself—which eventually leads her to fulfill her destiny as planned. Clearly, both internal and external factors play their part.

Both of our adult saviors—Laura and Kara—fall into desperation after the discovery of Earth I, where their entire belief system is shattered. Had the series ended on this note, we would have been stuck with a very typical case of female irrationality proven wrong by male rationalism. But the series continued—and illustrated that in the end, both Laura and Kara fulfilled their respective destinies by leading the human-Cylon alliance to Earth. They were right all along, because a higher power (whether singular or plural) did orchestrate all of the series' events and chose them to fulfill important messianic roles. Kara receives the coordinates to Earth II in the form of a musical sequence and becomes the "harbinger of death" for the human race, because humanity is no longer "pure," but mixed with the Cylons on Earth II. Laura is the political leader who saved humanity from destruction and made sure that all the necessary hints to the location of Earth were found and followed, thus leading humanity to "paradise." Hera, our child savior, is the link between the two races that ensures that humans and Cylons have a common goal and a shared future.

The series' ending admittedly erased much of the subversive potential created by these challenges to the traditional messiah myth. Two of our saviors—indeed the most active and thus "threatening" ones—die or disappear, after leading the religiously clueless men to the Promised Land. Power is returned to the men, while the women have fulfilled their destiny and become "sacrificial heroines" of an all-powerful (male) God. Scholars understandably criticized the fact that a large number of women die either before or during the series finale (Stoy 2010, 12–13). While this criticism is justified, I would like to advocate a more differentiated view. It needs pointing out that female irrationality in the form of religiosity is not discredited through male rationalism or science in the end. Laura and Kara were correct to follow their intuition, to believe in their destiny and into the divine. Proving religion wrong and explaining the course of events through rational (masculine) science (as expected and hoped for by both critics and fans) would have been the biggest blow to femininity in the narrative.

In conclusion, we should not disregard the centrality of female messianism as established in the series, where we can find at least three female characters that can plausibly be associated with salvation. We should remember that female messianism is not the norm either in religious history or in popular culture texts, especially not in the form presented by *BSG*. In addition, as we will see in chapter four, it might not be a coincidence that the only surviving messiah in the series is Hera, the human-machine hybrid. Indeed, in *Caprica* the role of savior

2. Saviors: Women Bring Salvation

was once again filled by a female Cyborg, reinforcing the franchise's commitment to the (female) religious machine. Before we delve deeper into the issue of religious Cyborgs, we will first assess how God communicates with humans and Cylons—and will find that this communication is likewise strongly gendered.

3

With God's Voice: Angels and Prophets

In *BSG*, God is never seen or heard directly—he communicates with humans and Cylons through intermediaries, namely angels, prophets, oracles and scripture. God has a plan; he has already determined the outcome of the story and its characters. This basic truth is reflected in the ubiquitous phrase "All of this has happened before and all of this will happen again," describing a circular vision of history as a constantly repeated story in which everyone plays their part. The idea of repetitive or cyclical history is of course nothing new. Before Zoroastrism and Judaism developed their linear perception of time, such worldviews pervaded ancient religions from Egypt to India (Cohn 2001). In *BSG*, the circularity of the world means that ultimately, there is not much room for choice—whatever has happened before will eventually happen again. This also means that the issue of free will is an implicit theme of the series (see Johnson 2008).

God communicates though scripture and guarantees that events will unfold accordingly through his messengers and oracles. God is a distant divinity, but involved in human events nonetheless. It is precisely this distance that calls for mediators. Historically, mediators between God and his followers were the result of a growing distance between believer and divinity (Läpple 1993, 80–81)—a distance that is also felt on *BSG*. While God is (for the most part) a "he," his mediums and mouthpieces are predominantly female. In this chapter we will place these women in the context of religious history and trends in popular culture. In the first two sections, we will look at the angel-motif on *BSG*, before we turn to the role of scripture and prophecy.

Terrifying and Beautiful

In many respects, the depiction of angels in the two series follows the biblical precedent more closely than other pieces of U.S. popular culture. The series even surpass the horror-fantasy series *Supernatural* in their reliance on biblical representations of angels (Wimmler and Kienzl 2011). This is all the more significant because the genre of science fiction does not usually feature heavenly angels, but rather angel-type characters or behavior (Gardella 2007, 228–231). This section and the next will take a closer look at the transformation of the angel motif in the two series. We will first compare the depiction of angels in *BSG* to Judeo-Christian scripture, focusing on the two most important angels or "messengers," Messenger-Six and Messenger-Baltar, before exploring their "mission" or role in the narrative, which will include a closer look at *Caprica* as well.

From the perspective of religious history, angels are a remnant of the polytheistic origins of Judaism: they were originally separate deities who were then integrated into the monotheistic system as servants of the single, all-powerful God. Although they were a potential threat to the uniqueness and authority of this God, the Bible had, as Tuschling put it, "sufficiently domesticated" angels (Tuschling 2007, 13–14). Angels are mediators and divine messengers, an idea that can conceptually be found in polytheistic religions as well. However, especially when coupled with their evil counterpart (demons), angels proper are characteristic of the Abrahamic religions (and, to a certain extent, the dualistic system of Zoroastrism, see Hutter 2007). In general, polytheistic systems have no need for angels, because the gods inhabit the entire natural world and are thus, in a sense, their own mediators. These gods can be structured hierarchically as well as regionally in a rather dynamic way: some gods may be subordinated to other gods , and this hierarchy can in turn vary according to region. A divine messenger in a polytheistic system would thus typically be a subordinate God (see, e.g., Schipper 2007, 1–5). Consider the well-known figure of Hermes in the Greek pantheon: he is the messenger of the God Zeus (his father)—but he is also a god himself. The angels of *BSG* and *Caprica* thus never appear in a polytheistic context. In other words, they are never messengers of Zeus or Hera (who, following the internal logic of the series, don't actually exist), but always of the one true God.

The New Testament described contact with angels as an uncomfortable experience. They are clearly otherworldly and terrifying. In Matthew 28, the appearance of an angel is described as follows: "And his appearance was like lightning and his clothing as white as snow. The guards shook for fear of him and became like dead men." While the appearance of the angels in *BSG* is much more subtle and does not involve "lightening" of any sort, the staging of the angelic body is nevertheless striking. Messengers are always beautiful and perfect, in contrast to almost all the other characters in the series. In one of the DVD-specials, director of photography Steven McNutt states that with the exception of Messenger-Six and President Laura Roslin, he was not supposed to make anyone look beautiful.[1] The idea behind this statement is that in this narrative, nobody really had the time or means to care too much about their appearance—the president being an obvious exception because she needs to represent. The only other exceptions are the angels.

Historically, angels were indeed understood as incredibly beautiful creatures, stemming from their close connection to God. When seen by humans, this connection to the divine is often expressed through a bright light that surrounds them (Ernst 2007, 682–683), an idea also taken up in *BSG* on occasion. Messenger-Six, for example, is frequently staged in a white light and often a white dress. She never trips, her hair is always perfect and she is never in any way out of order. Mirroring the Cylon model Six, the angel also often appears in a red dress, which evokes (not entirely by coincidence) the double connotation of evil and sexuality in the viewer's understanding. Red was actually associated with angels for a rather long time, while the devil usually appeared in shades of blue, purple, or grey. Angels, the early Church Fathers agreed, were made of fire, while the devil and his demons were made of air (Ernst 2007). Of course the cultural perception of this color has

3. With God's Voice: Angels and Prophets

changed significantly since then, and it is unlikely the authors were aware of this history.

Concerning the gender dimension, we can make note of the fact that the Torah as well as the New Testament present angels as male. Of course technically, angels do not possess any gender whatsoever because they are immaterial beings—but they appear to humans in male form. Any indications of female angels found in scripture, for example in Zachariah 5:9 are highly controversial. The Judeo-Christian tradition thus excludes women from being mediators between God and humanity: God delivers his messages through men. By focusing the angelic theme on Messenger-Six (and Messenger-Zoe on *Caprica*, as we will see later), *BSG* and *Caprica* turn the mediation between God and humanity into a female affair.

Of course much time has passed since the days of the Bible, and angels have since been feminized. If "modern" angels are depicted as female (which has become a popular motif in the 20th and 21st centuries, especially in advertising), the angel's sexuality frequently becomes an issue. Consequently, female angels often play the role of the weakling or seductress and sometimes even turn out to be Satan in disguise (e.g., *The Last Temptation of Christ,* Martin Scorsese 1988) (Gardella 2007, 148–149). Looking at the TV Series *Supernatural*, this trend of disregarding or discrediting female angels continues: the only female angel is a deserter. On *BSG*, the female angels surpass their male counterparts in screen time and (arguably) importance. Messenger-Baltar is the only male angel to receive much attention in the narrative. Two other male messengers appear in the guise of Leoben and the piano player (who we have seen might represent Kara's father), but neither of them is explored in much detail.

The main angel in *BSG* is clearly Messenger-Six, a woman. She follows the example of her predecessors and appears as a seductress. She takes the form of Baltar's former Cylon lover and is highly sexualized. She engages, encourages, and distracts Baltar with her femininity. At first glance, this seems like a rather stereotyped female role. However, the fact that she is not evil, but sent by God, and the related fact that she will turn Gaius Baltar into a hero for the story, contradicts such an interpretation. In fact, it is the nature of Gaius Baltar that is the issue here. Messenger-Six's mission is to guide Baltar, a narcissistic unbeliever, to heroism and faith. Her appearance is guided by his character—this is the angel Baltar needs to find his way. The story is further balanced by the appearance of a second angel (Messenger-Baltar) who visits Caprica Six. The Cylon Caprica Six needs a conscience—Messenger-Baltar provides a cynical and honest one. Her angel does not appear highly sexualized, but rather sarcastic, critical, and reputable (which the real Gaius Baltar never truly is).

Although Messenger-Baltar is not sexualized quite as obviously as Messenger-Six, his appearance also differs quite substantially from the human Baltar's. He wears a fitting suit and continuously looks assured and serious. In contrast, both Caprica Six (as well as other Six models) and Gaius Baltar are clearly imperfect. Baltar's flaws, which will be discussed in more detail in the last chapter, are also reflected in his physical depiction which is often comical. Likewise Caprica Six, while physically and psychologically more stable, can clearly be discerned from her angelic counterpart by her facial expressions, which reflect her doubt and insecurity. The fact that *BSG*'s angels come without wings is also worth noting: this corresponds more closely to an earlier image of angels that visualized them as ordinary men, without wings or other significant physical attributes (except for beauty).

The angels are depicted without any kind of discernible individuality—they are merely enhanced copies of Caprica Six and Baltar, and are tools God uses to guide his creations. This aspect of *BSG*'s angels is rather close to Jewish tradition and also distinguishes the series' angels strongly from much of popular culture, including *Supernatural*. As explained by Erik Eynikel, angels in the Torah or Old Testament cannot oppose God "because they are an extension of God himself" (Eynikel 2007, 112). The point here is that the angels of early Judaism lack free will and can only do what God wants them to do. This position was also espoused by the rabbis who dominated Jewish theology after the destruction of the second temple in 70 CE (Rebiger 2007, 640). Although interest in angelology and especially the hierarchies and names of angels increased significantly in the following centuries (Olyan 1993, 2–3), this remained the official Jewish position. The *Battlestarverse* constructs angels in the same manner, that is, without free will.[2] They are purely in the service of God and are never seen doubting anything. Since they appear as mysterious elements of the plot, the angels do not strike us as agents of their own plan. They clearly have a mission that originates elsewhere. The only time they are seen reflecting on God's plan is in the last episode, where they are nevertheless not represented as any kind of opposition to their "superior," God.

Consequently, the *Battlestarverse* is not plagued by demons—angels who decided (of their own free will) to rebel against God. Since there are no evil or "fallen" angels in this narrative, the series differ from stories based on Christianity (Piepke 2000, 54–55). In the *Battlestarverse*, angels do not fight each other and they certainly do not fight against God. This element of the plot is more Jewish than Christian in nature (Jung 1974; Schäfer 1975, 83–85) and is in direct opposition to current angelic traditions in the United States. In the past decades, American popular culture has increasingly pushed the issue of dissatisfied, disobedient, and doubting angels. In many narratives, they are also unsympathetic towards humanity (Gardella 2007, 168–199, 231–236). *Battlestar* angels, on the other hand, are truly angels in the Old Testament sense: messengers and agents of God.

... and They Have a Mission

Biblical angels are not only messengers, but also guardians and guides. They can even be described as agents of salvation. As such, the role of angels is comparable to the role of Christ (Tuschling 2007, 1). We have seen that the interpretation of Kara fluctuated between angel and messiah, which is hardly surprising considering how closely related these two concepts are. Yet like Christ, Kara has a birth narrative, while the angels (either in the Bible or in *BSG*) do not possess such a background. There is also an inherent similarity between angels, prophets, priests, and even oracles: Their primary function is that of mediating God's message. What distinguishes the angels from the other three is their origin: the angel is not of the earth, but of the heavenly sphere. In addition, the angel's personality completely fades into the background of its mission, whereas prophets and other human messengers always remain definable people (Eynikel 2007, 110–112) whose existence is moreover fixed in time. In the *Battlestarverse*, the angels are on a mission to guide humanity by steering certain humans and Cylons in a particular direction.

The idea of angels in *BSG* is of course an ambiguous one, especially since their identity as angels is only gradually established and not confirmed until the very last episode. From the beginning, the angel-motif is closely connected to the Cylon character Six, in whose form the angel chooses to appear. A copy of the Six model (later referred to as Caprica Six) is in a relationship with the narcissistic technophile Gaius Baltar, to whom she confesses her Cylon identity right before the nuclear bombs go off. Baltar survives the blast (presumably through her protection) and is able to flee the planet on a Galactica raptor. Messenger-Six appears precisely in this moment and seems to ensure that Baltar is saved. From this moment on, Messenger-Six is Baltar's constant companion, but can only be seen by him alone.

Since the main angel appears in Cylon form, *Battlestar* angels are inherently connected to the technological sphere. This connection is reinforced through her ambiguous identity: is she a Cylon plot or a divinely inspired messenger? Messenger-Six frequently transports Baltar to virtual environments, which connects her to the Cylons and their ability to "project" themselves into imagined realities. Messenger-Six navigates between the spirit and technological worlds of the series, constantly keeping the viewer (and Baltar) wondering who she really is. It is also worth noting that *BSG* fansites have re-named the angels after their identity was clearly revealed. While the characters were formerly known as "virtuals," pointing to a technological interpretation, they were later renamed "messengers," which implies a more spiritual nature. With the Six angel, the series investigates how close science and religion can become and how difficult it can be to distinguish one from the other. An angel could certainly lead Baltar into a sort of dream world—but so could a Cylon.

Until the appearance of Messenger-Baltar, the best explanation for the existence of Messenger-Six is indeed that she is part of the Cylon plot to destroy humanity. The notion that Caprica Six implanted a computer chip in Baltar's head seems to be the most logical explanation in a science fiction narrative. Baltar does not strike us as a very good person; he was in a relationship with a Cylon and is partly responsible for the near extinction of humanity. Messenger-Six, whose secondary mission is to plant confusion in both Baltar and the viewer, uses her Cylon appearance to relate Cylon positions on various subjects and frequently comments on anti–Cylon statements on the Galactica. Since the series' salvation includes the reconciliation between humans and Cylons, the angel must take on a Cylon perspective, while her counterpart Messenger-Baltar takes on a human perspective when dealing with Caprica Six.

Messenger-Six often uses violence and aggression to steer Baltar in the right direction. This is not without biblical precedent: The Old Testament or Torah also describes angels who deliver the punishment of God. Only in the more dualistic Christian system is this role of destroyer and punisher partially "outsourced" to the more independent figure of Satan and his demons (Eynikel 2007, 112–113). *Battlestar* angels once again lean towards the Jewish or Old Testament depiction: they are not only guides and protectors, but also effect God's punishments. Messenger-Six thus merges many traditional "angelic" aspects: Her mission is to turn Baltar into a believer and hero. She guides him, questions his opinions, and even abuses him at times, in order to convince the atheist of God's existence. To accomplish this she not only mediates and guides, but also punishes.

As soon as Messenger-Baltar appears on the scene in "Downloaded" (2.18) we can no longer pretend that Messenger-Six is part of a Cylon plot, making this episode a turning point in the series (Stoy 2010, 2–3). In this episode, the events from the beginning of the series, which the viewer witnessed from the perspective of the humans, is shown from the perspective of the Cylons, in particular Caprica Six and Sharon "Boomer" Valerii. Caprica Six dies protecting Gaius Baltar form a nuclear blast and is resurrected naked in a tub filled with white fluid, surrounded by some of her Cylon sisters and brothers. The flash of scenes from Caprica Six' life is a review of her actions and experiences that continues to inform all of her future decisions. Memory is important—it humanizes her and the Cylons in general (Holland 1995, 170).

While Three wants her to let go of her pre-resurrection life and "to cleanse," Caprica Six is unable and unwilling to let go—this event transforms her rather than guaranteeing a new beginning. It is the responsibility of God's angel to ensure that she remembers her pre-resurrection life and continues to relate to humans on a personal level. Messenger-Baltar is an advisor and a conscience, who guides Six throughout the episode to arrive at a rather significant conclusion: that Cylons and humans must end their war and work together. The angel does not allow her to forget, to "cleanse" or to let go of her guilt regarding the nuclear holocaust as Three proposes. Instead, Messenger-Baltar repeatedly reminds Six of the billions of people that were killed. The Cylons initially understanding death differently (Willems 2008), since bodily death is hardly ever final for them and life consequently eternal. Before they can reconcile with humanity, they have to learn what the genocide really meant.

The angel helps Caprica Six to recognize the value of a perishable body. When she is trapped with Boomer and Three after a human terrorist attack, she refuses to let Three kill her despite severe injuries and pain. Resurrection is not a solution for her. This marks a big change in the Cylon relationship towards the body that will eventually lead to the abolishment of resurrection. Apart from the appreciation of the body, the limits of resurrection, and the value of human life, Messenger-Baltar helps Caprica Six to value emotion, in particular love, as a key to personhood. In Cyborg film, the ability to feel pain and love is frequently seen as the biggest difference between human and machine, or between the "good Cyborg" (e.g., Robocop) and the "bad Cyborg" (e.g., the original Terminator) (Holland 1995, 163). In *BSG*, all Cylons (both male and female) are generally able to experience emotion—it is simply a matter of acknowledging and welcoming feelings, which not all Cylons are willing to do.

The change of Cylon policy towards the humans in the course of the second season is a product of divine intervention and is effectuated through women with help from a male angel. We should note that it only takes one episode for Messenger-Baltar to show an already God-fearing Caprica Six the way (though admittedly, the episode covers a larger time period). On the other hand, Messenger-Six has to work Gaius Baltar for four seasons (and several years) before he is finally ready to be God's willing agent and, in the end, a heroic figure. "Downloaded" makes us reevaluate the entire story of *BSG*, specifically the nature of the Cylons. With the help of the angel, Caprica Six finds the path God intended for her and her people. She already lays the groundwork for the future solution of the Cylon-human conflict: respect for the body, for life and death, and the triumph of "positive" emotions such as love or guilt.

Battlestar angels can also be described as guardian angels to a certain extent. As we have seen, *BSG* usually assigns individual angels to individual humans: Messenger-Six appears only to Baltar, Messenger-Baltar only to Caprica Six (later also to Baltar), Messenger-Leoben appears to Kara. However, they do no accompany their wards throughout their entire life as we would expect a guardian angel to do. Though guardian angels do not figure prominently the Old Testament or Torah, scholars have discovered that the idea was rather present in Judaism of the Second Temple Period (early 6th century BCE–70 CE) and was also espoused by early Christendom (Hannah 2007). Since then, guardian angels have been a staple especially of popular angelology and remain so today in both Christian and esoteric circles.

On *Caprica*, *BSG*'s personalized angels were transformed into such guardian angels. A messenger accompanies Zoe throughout her entire life. She first visits her as a child and from then on makes regular appearances. This makes her a constant presence and guardian of sorts. While the series seemed to rewrite much of the religious content of *BSG* in favor of technological explanations, the first appearance of the messenger in a flashback episode once again proved the *Battlestar-verse*'s commitment to the supernatural (1.12 "Things We Lock Away"). This episode revealed that the "real" Zoe Graystone had been visited by an angel throughout her childhood who took on the form of an adolescent version of herself. The angel had a protective as well as an encouraging function. It was this entity that encouraged Zoe, for example, to use her computer skills to create life. She also saved Zoe from a fire and thus served as a protector.

After Zoe's death, her avatar inherits this messenger. Messenger-Zoe first appears to Zoe-A (Zoe-Avatar) in a time of crisis: she is back in v-world, where the regular users of cyberspace are using her unique immortality for their own personal amusement by repeatedly stabbing and torturing her. Not only does the messenger help her to deal with this situation on a psychological level, she also guides her to the realization that she has to separate her own identity from the original Zoe's (1.12 "Things We Lock Away"). Zoe-A's emancipation from her creator is necessary to fulfill her destiny and thus God's plan for her. Again, a female angel is the mediator and guardian through whom this goal is achieved.

Although the angels of *BSG* and *Caprica* fully embrace their biblical role as messengers and mediators, they nevertheless lack an important traditional function that is still rather present in today's popular culture: the role of the warrior angel. The Old Testament angel Michael, for example, is the military leader of the heavenly host (Rosenberg 1986, 94). Yet in the *Battlestarverse*, angels do not have any military function whatsoever. They are sometimes portrayed as violent (especially Messenger-Six), and frequently offer military or political advice, but they do not engage in combat against disbelievers or obstructers of God's plan. When God punishes, the angel interprets the punishment and tells her protégé what God wants from them. This implies a direct line between the messenger and the divinity: God acts on what the angel observes. There are nevertheless some connections between the appearance of angels and war. First of all, the angels in *BSG* appear in the midst of war and attempt (in their own mysterious way) to mediate between the opposing parties. This appearance of angels in times of war and crisis is in fact rather traditional (Gardella 2007, 199).

While aspects of the warrior angel can be found in the series, this is clearly not their primary mission. The mission of angels in *BSG* and *Caprica* closely resembles that of their Biblical predecessors: they are messengers, advisors, protectors, and teachers. As immaterial beings, they cannot take action in the physical world—instead, they instruct humans to take action purely through the power of persuasion. Angels are God's messengers quite literally, but only very few characters ever have the "pleasure" of meeting one (and having one appear in their own likeness). Most people instead have to rely on other mediators, for example the Holy Scriptures.

Interpreting Scripture

We have already seen that the scrolls of Pythia play an important role in the religious narrative, especially regarding Laura Roslin's nature as a chosen leader. According to the polytheistic religion, Pythia was an oracle who lived 3600 thousand years ago (1.10 "The Hand of God"). By confirming Pythia's prophecies, Laura is the first, but not the last, to substantiate the authority of prophetic speech and writings in the narrative. Although prophecies and oracles are strictly speaking not the same thing, they are closely related and often appear jointly (Heller 2003, 534). In the *Battlestarverse*, the boundaries between these two concepts are sufficiently blurry to justify using them interchangeably.

Prophecy in *BSG* is both written and oral: the humans rely on sacred texts and oracles, while the Cylons try to decipher the word-salads generated by the so-called hybrids, human-machine combinations unable to be integrated into society. We will take a closer look at the hybrids shortly, but for now I am interested in the role of scriptures and oracles in the human polytheistic system. First, it is intriguing that the polytheistic humans are associated with Holy Scriptures that are usually connected to monotheistic religions.[3] On the other hand, the monotheistic Cylons rely on oral prophecy, and do not believe in the scriptures, at least not completely. However, humans do not rely entirely on scriptures, as the written word is complemented by oracles. This is an intriguing approach from the point of view of religious history that can also help us contextualize the relationship between gender and religion in the series.

The conflict between the oral and the written transmission of God's word is not a necessity, but can easily arise. The history of early Christianity is a case in point. Early Christians were influenced equally by two religious and cultural systems: Judaism with its reliance on scripture, and Greek thought that preferred the oral over the written transmission. Initially, they opted for a middle position where the oral word was preferred but respect given to the written transmission. Things began to change once Christians established their own canonic text, called The New Testament (Baynes 2012, 6). Gradually, the written word gained authority, until it finally took over completely. During the first centuries CE, Christians still believed in prophecy (the transmission of God's word through the Holy Ghost), but late 4th century writings already indicate a growing conflict. In many writings, the word "prophet" was gradually replaced with "priest," or even "bishop" (Jensen 2003, 261).

There was a reason for this change. The emerging church struggled for authority that had been challenged by several prophetic movements. These movements created their own structures and hierarchies that conflicted with that of the Church. They also challenged the Church's monopoly of interpreting God's word, in particular through prophecy. Prophecies could "update" scripture and charismatic prophets could threaten the power of the bishops and other church officials. The Church proceeded to persecute the movements and argued that the time of prophecy had ended either with Christ or the apostles (Jensen 2003, 344–352). Anyone who claimed otherwise was considered a heretic. The (officially sanctioned) position of the charismatic leader, who had previously often been a prophet, was now taken over primarily by martyrs and saints. The seemingly inherent contradiction between scripture and oral prophecy was thus in fact a result of the professionalization of Early Christianity's religious structures.

Returning to Judaism, we should note that this religious system always accorded a central place to scripture, but also valued the continuing comment on scripture. Although the Torah was understood to be complete and eternally valid, its meaning constantly needed to be re-established in order to fit the times and circumstances. Theologically, the idea was that God had transmitted the Torah in two forms: one written, the other oral, to be passed from one generation to the next (Neusner 1990, 1). Both transmissions were considered equally important—they complemented each other.[4] Interpreting scripture was furthermore not understood as a domain of certain learned experts. Every male Jew should ideally study the scriptures at one point in his life, while the synagogue service always included communal readings of the Torah. Although this does not mean that Judaism did not possess hierarchical structures or struggle with establishing authority over charismatic leaders (as seen in the case of Jewish apocalyptic movements), the issue was ultimately less pronounced in the Common Era, especially considering Judaism's status as a scattered minority religion. Judaism nevertheless shares one important aspect with the emerging Christian Church: the access to God's word was largely restricted to men: Women were to remain silent in the Christian Church, and they were not supposed to study the Torah the way men did in the Jewish system. In both cases, this was the result of an active process, and not

3. With God's Voice: Angels and Prophets

inherent in the religious systems themselves. Due to these processes, the transmission of religion was vested in men.

Let's see how the *Battlestarverse* deals with these issues. *BSG* takes the position that scripture can never stand alone. The series favors transcendence and direct oral communication with the Devine over the written word that is portrayed as imperfect, though not entirely incorrect. This is illustrated in *BSG*'s second season, when Laura Roslin goes rogue and decides to find the Tomb of Athena on the planet Kobol without military help (but with quite a large following). According to the scriptures, the Tomb will lead humanity to Earth. This scene once again illustrates how gendered religion is in the series: Elosha and Laura Roslin argue that they should act against Adama because they attribute authority and truth to the Holy Scriptures, while their male co-conspirators make a calculated political decision and complain about the women's reliance on "superstitions."

The scriptures also include clues concerning the location of the Tomb, but the humans are unable to decipher the references. Roslin enlists the help of the Cylon Athena-Sharon, who has just recently joined the Galactica as a prisoner. Her help is allowed because, as the priest Elosha explains, "The scrolls of Pythia speak of a lower demon who helped the people in a time of crisis" (2.06 "Home—Part I"). This is one of only two references to a demon in the entire series and is actually not consistent with the rest of the narrative that neither portrays demonic characters nor implies their existence. The fact that the "demon" is a Cylon supports the idea that there is actually no such thing, since the Cylons are clearly constructed as God's children in the series. This reference to a demon probably results from the general prominence of Christian concepts in popular culture and seems a little displaced in the narrative.

On the planet, the Cylon Athena Sharon illustrates her knowledge of scripture that seems to be more accurate than that of the humans. Sharon uses this talent to lead Laura to the Tomb as instructed (2.07 "Home—Part II"). She implies that there is some truth—or rather some facts—in the scriptures, but as a monotheist she rejects the idea that the Lords of Kobol are actually divine. Messenger-Six had previously convinced Baltar that the scriptures are a lie, a "cover up" for savagery, though it is unclear whether she is communicating a Cylon position or the word of God in this instance. Apparently, the scriptures constructed Kobol as a paradise, where gods and humans lived peacefully before the exodus. Messenger-Six explains to him that eventually humanity's true nature "asserted itself," which led to death, human sacrifice, "barbarism."

The idea that Holy Scriptures contain a certain amount of truth while simultaneously being the products of humans—which makes them flawed—is of course not original. Historical bible criticism has long pointed out that the Bible was the product of various (human) authors and thus reflected the needs and values of their authors' times and societies (Kee 1997, 32–39). Whether their words were inspired by God is not actually the issue in this discourse. *BSG*'s position seems to be that the scriptures at least contain the possibility of access to God or gods, though they contain many imperfections that make them misleading. The basic idea of truth behind them is illustrated by Baltar in the fourth season, when he tries to find the road to Earth using a mixture of the scrolls and science.

The use of the scriptures is overall highly feminized in the series, because the polytheistic faith is both communicated and mediated by women. To start with, Elosha—the priest and Laura's religious guide in the first and early second season—is a woman (though it is noteworthy that the writers originally conceived of this part as male, planning to cast the "original" Apollo, Richard Hatch, who would end up playing Zarek) (Vallant 2008, 133). Throughout the series, Laura is most strongly associated with the scriptures. She is frequently portrayed reading them, consulting them, and generally holding the Holy Book in her hands. In 4.11 "Sometimes a Great Notion," Laura burns the scrolls of Pythia, which she now believes never to have been correct in the first place. Considering that Laura had previously taken considerable solace in the scriptures at various difficult stages of her post-genocide life, this decision is a clear indicator of her desperation and frustration after finding the wasteland that had been the original Earth. Wetmore proposes that at this point, Laura and Kara experience a "transformation of faith" that represents humanity's rejection of the old religion in favor of the Baltar cult's monotheism (Wetmore 2012, 131). Considering that neither of the two women ever espouses monotheism, I propose that this transformation is of a different nature: Laura begins to rely less on the scriptures and more on her visions. She switches from depending on the written word to trusting her own experiences.

The imperfections of scripture in human religion are balanced by the oracles, who are again exclusively female. As discussed, the parallel use of scripture and prophecy is intriguing, since a prophet or oracle can easily invalidate scriptures by claiming that God communicated something entirely different to them. Significantly, women played an important role in the abovementioned prophetic movements of early Christianity. For example, the "New Prophecy" movement (today misleadingly known as Montanism) that emerged in the 2nd century CE was condemned and prosecuted because they believed in contemporary prophets. At least two of the main prophets (and according to recent research probably the most significant ones) were women by the names of Prisca and Maximilla. The struggle of the Church was thus not just about the challenge to their authority as the sole interpreters of scripture, but also one against female religious authority as such. If women were supposed to remain silent in the Church, they clearly were not supposed to prophesy (Jensen 2003, 268–352). Prisca and Maximilla also wrote some of their prophecies down, but most of their writings were later destroyed. The remaining writings are known as oracles, reinforcing the close connection between prophecy and oracles. Like the prophets of the New Prophecy movement, the oracles in *BSG* are female, linking the feminine to the spiritual. However, unlike Prisca and Maximilla, they do not have to assert themselves in a male-dominated world, but are acknowledged and accepted as mediators of God's word in the human religion. In the polytheistic religion of *BSG*, the spiritual world is constructed as an inherently female space unchallenged by male authority.

Monotheistic religions usually speak of prophets, while the concept of oracles is more closely associated with Greco-Roman Antiquity, where oracles were asked for advice with certain problems or questions in mind. The oracles—usually women—tended to answer these questions in riddles. To decipher these riddles, religious experts such as priests or seers were consulted.[5] In contrast, the polytheistic oracles of the humans are fairly easy to understand. An oracle tells D'Anna very explicitly that Hera is alive, and that "you will hold her in your arms and you will know for the first time [what love is]" (3.03 "Exodus—Part I"). The message for Kara is likewise rather straightforward: Leoben will help her to find her path (3.17 "Maelstrom"). These oracles communicate rather clearly—the same cannot be said of the Cylon oracles, the hybrids, to which we will now turn.

Technological Prophecy

So far, we have discussed prophecy in the context of the human polytheistic religion, a system that is described as ancient and thus bereft of advanced technology. The Cylon religion, on the other hand, is utterly technological. This is to be expected, since the Cylons are themselves technological beings. *BSG* never completely explains how the Cylons communicate with God. We know that they do not believe in scripture and initially seem to have no other medium of contact. Both oracles (the hybrids discussed in this chapter) and angels only appear on the scene in the course of the story. It is unclear what the Cylon religion is based on and how it is filled with content in the first place. The prequel series clarifies these issues to a certain extent. It seems that the Cylon religion is based on the teachings of Clarice Willow who communicates the human monotheist religion to them. Although one of the monotheists, Zoe Graystone, is inspired by an angel, the religion itself already exists before this event. The origins and principles of the "original" monotheist religion remain obscure. However, we know that Clarice Willow's teachings are fundamentally connected to the subject of the Cylons' personhood and include the prophecy that the Cylons will someday rise up against their creators and destroy them. The Cylon monotheism we meet in *BSG* can be traced back to Clarice's teachings, although we cannot be certain how much of this teaching is in return inspired by God.

It seems that *BSG*'s Cylons have not had mediators in between Messenger-Zoe and Messenger-Baltar. The discovery of the hybrids as prophetic oracles also falls into this time of crisis: they take over the role of mediators and fill this gap. Before that, the Cylons seem to believe in a direct connection to God that also distinguishes them from the humans who still need mediators. Leoben suggests in the first sea-

3. With God's Voice: Angels and Prophets

son that this may be the case when he tells Kara that he sees parts of the universe that are inaccessible to her: he sees patterns and is, in a way, God (1.08 "Flesh and Bone"). Leoben seems to have a certain access to the divine, and might even have visions—a fact that calls for closer investigation (chapter seven). However, it seems that a direct way of communicating with God (including the possibility of asking him questions and, possibly, having them answered) is only established with the hybrids. Since Cylon religion is technological, it is hardly surprising that their oracles are not "regular" oracles, but technological ones.

Hybrids are humanoid Cylons that are restricted to the resurrection tubs and spend their lives connected to this technology, unable to function in "regular" Cylon society. They control the Cylon baseships and their functions, but are unable to communicate with the other Cylons in a verbal manner. They are described as constantly aware of everything, embedded into the Cylon collective consciousness, yet clearly imperfect. Their imperfection stems from a technological "overdose" that overpowers their organic elements (Heinricy 2008, 101). They nevertheless speak, almost constantly. While initially most Cylons believe that the hybrids have "simply gone mad and the vocalizations we hear are meaningless," other Cylons (especially the Leobens) believe that God speaks through them and that every word they utter has meaning and is, in a way, prophetic (3.06 "Torn"). The hybrids are usually understood as gender-less, but through the actresses and actors who play them we perceive them as gendered. In addition, while they are mostly referred to as "it," some Cylons distinctly refer to them in a gendered manner, as "she." Most hybrids we see are indeed coded female. Their permanent position in the gooey resurrection tubs, their chaotic speech, as well as their utter defenselessness have been seen as further evidence for this feminization (Jowett 2010, 70–71).

The mutterings of the hybrids that are often only heard in the background of other conversations, but are sometimes the scene's center, indeed have prescient qualities. Occasionally, the writers used the hybrids for some amusing meta-discourse, having them state, for example: "Throughout history the nexus between man and machine has spun some of the most dramatic, compelling and entertaining fiction" (3.10 "The Passage"). Very true. Like the ancient Greek oracle, the hybrid knows not only the future, but also the past and present (Wiesehöfer 2010, 337). Yet for the most part, their rants have a prophetic overtone. Sometimes they also provide moral statements. In their conduct, they are reminiscent of ancient oracles of Greco-Roman antiquity as described in the last section. This imitation of Greek religious customs should not surprise us, considering the gods of *BSG*'s humans are based on the Greek pantheon.

According to tradition, oracles were not in themselves comprehensible to an ordinary person, but needed to be translated. In *BSG*, only few people can successfully translate the hybrid's advice. If they attempt this, they need to take care to approach the hybrid-oracle carefully, mirroring Ancient Greek oracles, where the connection between God and the oracle was regarded with reverence (Maass 2007, 7). When D'Anna reveals to Gaius Baltar that she is searching for the Final Five humanoid Cylons, they decide to ask the oracle for help or information. Baltar immerses his hand in the hybrid's resurrection fluid and the hybrid—who usually pays little attention to her surroundings— grabs his hand, looks at him, and then offers information: "Intelligence. A mind that burns like a fire.... Find the hand that lies in the shadow of the light. In the eye of the husband of the eye of the cow." While D'Anna believes that the oracle speaks nonsense, Baltar is able to decipher its speech. He deducts that the eye of the cow is Hera, her husband Jupiter (the Roman version of Zeus), and the hand stands for the Final Five. D'Anna then makes a connection to the scriptures that mention the eye of Jupiter (3.10 "The Passage"). Once again, the series suggests that the scriptures have authority, but this authority can only be accessed in a meaningful way through additional oral prophecy. It also introduces a man as an interpreter between oracle and woman.

Baltar is able to interpret the oracle because of knowledge and intelligence—but also because the hybrid wants to be understood in this instance, and she relates information that Baltar can decipher to accomplish this. The man Baltar as a mediator for the female oracle is rather reminiscent of the Greek case, where the oracle was usually female, whereas the interpreter (priest or seer) tended to be male. Baltar is the first to decipher the hybrid oracle. After this has been accomplished, the female Cylons begin to listen to her and increasingly understand her meaning. Hal Shipman has suggested that the initial inability of the humanoid Cylons (which the exception of the Leobens) to understand the hybrids stems from their failure to acknowledge them as sentient. He sees this as a strategy of dehumanizing the Cylon ships in order to see them purely as tools (Shipman 2008, 160). Indeed, Six explains to Baltar that "[the hybrid] is the baseship in a very real sense" (3.06 "Torn"). As a human with definite pro–Cylon tendencies, Baltar is more open to recognizing those that are different as sentient. He is also an outsider to Cylon society who has no precast opinion about their (dis)function.

It is noteworthy that the oracles originally appeal to men: Leoben is the first to realize that the hybrids' vocalization is not meaningless, while Baltar is the first to decipher an oracle. However, after this first initialization, the female Cylons are the ones who continue to listen and translate, while the men are only initiators. The special connection to Baltar might also stem from the fact that the hybrids are not simply religious institutions but also technological ones—the hybrid controls the baseship and its technological functions. The idea that the oracles are connected to God is likewise not simply a religious statement, but also a technological one. Something is different about them technologically, they can see things that "regular" Cylons cannot, let alone humans.

This is of course a major notion of posthuman ideology: technology brings us closer to knowledge, spirit, and thus God—in a way becoming ourselves divine (Zimmerman 2008, 351, 358). The connection between the hybrids and God is consequently both spiritual and technological. This technological aspect is also enforced through the hybrids' language, which is infused with scientific words and phrases. This scientific approach to the prophetic oracle essentially implies that God is accessible through technology. For example, the oracle that informs the female Cylons that the Final Five will be found in the human fleet uses mostly technological terms to describe the circumstances: vibrational relaxation, atmospheric nitrogen, cut the fuse, rise and measure, data-font-synchronizations—these are all technological, not religious terms. The hybrid also states that "transformation is the goal," she hints at the posthuman message of hybridization that needs to be accomplished (4.02 "Six of One").

After it has become clear that the oracles can indeed be consulted, various characters try to get information from them, but only few succeed. Laura Roslin, for example, is completely unable to gather anything from them. This might stem from her lack of association with technology or Cylon myth. Laura is very clearly not a religious figure of the Cylon. Kara, on the other hand, is heralded by Leoben as a person of import for God's plan. So while she initially seems likewise unsuccessful, she eventually receives the clearest hybrid message of the entire series: "Thus will it come to pass. A dying leader will know the truth of the Opera House. The missing Three will give you the Five who come from the home of the Thirteenth. You are the harbinger of death, Kara Thrace. You will lead them all to their end. End of Line" (4.06 "Faith"). Overall, the hybrids and oracles provide much clearer and "truer" prophecies than the scriptures, reaffirming the series preference for the oral transmission of God's word. It should also be noted that as soon as the women discover that the hybrid makes sense, they no longer need a translator to receive a message from the oracle. The only ones who are able to decipher the full meaning of the message (for example in the quote above) are in fact the female Cylons.

In the movie *Razor*, which aired between the third and fourth seasons, we discover that the hybrids were the first botched Cylon attempts to "evolve" from pure robotic to organic bodies. When we are introduced to the (chronologically) first hybrid in *Razor*, his (!) statements are comparatively coherent and he is able to acknowledge the people around him and almost have balanced conversations with them. This implies that the hybrids might not have been "mad" from the beginning. While Hal Shipman proposes that the hybrids' madness might derive from their connection to the FTL-jump drive (the faster-than-light capacities that are used to transport ships quickly over long distances) (Shipman 2008, 160), we could also interpret their insanity as a consequence of their relationship with God. We are reminded of Leoben's frequent statement "To know the face of God is to know madness" (1.08 "Flesh and Bone"). The hybrids' knowledge of God makes any return to sanity impossible.

This chapter continued to illustrate the major tendencies regarding the feminization of religion in both series and provided the first clues to their connection with technology. First, the messengers walk the fine line between both spheres, in particular through the most

3. With God's Voice: Angels and Prophets

prominent angel, Messenger-Six. The female angel who is also, in a way, a Cylon, unites religion and technology in her (female) person. Similarly, women are dominant in interpreting and mediating the divine: they are connected to scriptures and function as human and technological oracles. Only very few men have this kind of direct access to the divine: male prophets or oracles are rare to non-existent, our male angel is comparatively absent and only Baltar and the Leobens take the hybrids seriously. These men are exceptions: mediators of God(s) are usually female. However, the most significant connecting element between technology and religion in the series is the female Cyborg to whom we will now turn.

4

The Religious Machine

Cyborgs have become a staple commodity of both science fiction and scholarship. Both employ the human-machine hybrid as a metaphor to explore the human condition. Cyborgs have become a utopia for many, be it Donna Haraway's vision of a post-gender world (Haraway 2004) or posthumanism's wish to escape the confines and limits of the human body (Benford, Malartre 2008, 195–255; Clark 2004). Yet this utopian vision is frequently reversed in popular culture, as Cyborgs are often excessively gendered, suffer from their less-than-human status or are portrayed as evil killer machines. The typical sci-fi Cyborg will be male, violent, near indestructible, and utterly rational.[1] Thus in 1999, Anne Balsamo could reasonably state: "Cyborg images reproduce cultural gender stereotypes" (Balsamo 1999, 148). Balsamo also recognized that female Cyborgs—rare as they are—have more potential of challenging these stereotypes than their male counterparts, as Western culture's traditional femininity is at odds with science, technology, rationality, and artificiality. Since masculinity is not typically associated with nature, Balsamo concludes that the male Cyborg supports the assumption of a "natural" difference between human and machine, nature and technology. Female Cyborgs blur that boundary, because women are associated with nature, body, irrationality, and maternity—none of which seem to compute with technology (Balsamo 1999, 148–149; Jordanova 1989, 21). The female Cyborg is thus highly ambivalent: both mechanical and "natural," rational and irrational at the same time.

Of course in most sci-fi narratives, the disruptive potential of female Cyborgs is thwarted by a narrative that presents her as evil and in need of destruction, or simply as a minor character. While Susan George has proposed that in *BSG*, a fear of technology is once again coupled with fear of the feminine (which she interprets as misogynistic), she also acknowledged that the important element of a final destruction of these dangerous women is missing, which in her opinion changed the stereotype slightly (George 2008, 167). I will go even further, proposing that the female Cylon in *BSG* and *Caprica* makes constructive use of the culturally established opposition between femininity and technology, as well as the gender stereotypes associated with this opposition by constructing female Cylons as the ultimate navigators between technology and religion. Of course for Donna Haraway, the Cyborg is a utopian metaphor because, among other things, it has no religion, no belief, no innocence or sin. If it did, it would be subject to a patriarchal system and thus not feminist (Haraway 2004; Graham 2002, 211–213). In this chapter, I wish to explore how the religious dimension changes the role of the female Cyborg. I will begin by analyzing how and by whom the first Cylon is created, and then take a closer look at the creation of the humanoid Cylons in *BSG*, before assessing the female Cylon's attitude towards death and the otherworld, ending with the re-interpretation of Lilith as God's avenging angel.

Zoe Graystone and the First Cylon

Creating artificial life is a male task. Scholarship usually connects this endeavor to a male "envy" of female reproductive powers—by developing artificial intelligence, men can actively create life. Women—who have already monopolized natural reproduction—are consequently not welcome in this enterprise. We witness a connection between fear of technology and fear of the feminine, which is conveyed both through the depiction of out-of-control man-built female Cyborgs and through problematic female creators (Corea and Bradish 1988, 237–246; Doane 1999, 24). Springer has analyzed the film *Eve of Destruction* (Gibbins 1991) concerning this subject and has come to the conclusion that science fiction narratives punish women who indulge in technological creation for assuming this "unnatural" role. While women are encouraged to engage in biological reproduction and to take on motherly roles for their offspring, they are eyed suspiciously when creating life outside of their physical bodies (Springer 1999, 50–51). Yet in *BSG* and *Caprica*, women are associated with both biological and technological reproduction. The entire system of creating life is firmly in the hands of women, while men only assume assisting or hampering roles. Women take leading roles in the traditionally "male" creation of artificial intelligence (see also Wimmler 2014).

In *Caprica*, we learn that the creation of the first Cylon was an accident, based mostly on unpredictable circumstances and grief. Zoe Graystone had accomplished what her father and others had long failed to do: she created a self-conscious artificial being. She took information from the internet—dental records, personality profiles, emails, report cards, and so on—and fed it into a database that would become her virtual double, Zoe-A (Zoe-Avatar). Zoe had a plan for Zoe-A which included bringing her to the planet Gemenon, where incidentally, the monotheistic religion has its religious as well as military base. Zoe's unplanned death at the hands of her suicide bomber boyfriend throws all of that out of order. Zoe-A is discovered by Zoe's father Daniel Graystone, who is fascinated both by his daughter's genius and by the prospect of bringing her "back from the dead." With the help of a stolen metacognitive processor from a rival company, he transfers Zoe-A from cyberspace to a robot body, thus creating the first self-conscious Cylon.

It might seem at first glance that Daniel is the one who accomplishes the creation of the Cylon, once again invoking a debate described by Toffoletti "where the machine is equated with the feminine while remaining the exclusive domain of the masculine" (Toffoletti 2007, 20). When looking more closely, however, it becomes evident that Daniel has little control over the entire process. Zoe-A was created by his daughter and the necessary processor by a rival company (which later creates significant problems when this processor needs to be duplicated). The only thing Daniel brings to the table is the robot body, which had so-far failed to fulfill even the most basic expectations. In addition, it is later revealed that Daniel "stole" the concept of the Cylon Centurions (the robots) from one of his daughter's childhood drawings (1.12 "Things We Lock Away").

4. The Religious Machine

Daniel is fully aware of his minor role when he tells his acquaintance Joseph Adama: "I didn't do it. Zoe did" (1.01 "Pilot"). Daniel is never in control of Zoe-A in her Cylon body either: the transfer from cyberspace appears to fail, and Zoe-A keeps Daniel unaware of her presence in the robot body. Daniel is always a step behind, until he decides to give up what little control he has. According to Toffoletti, the assumption that technology is patriarchal needs to be challenged in order for women to gain something by engaging with it (Toffoletti 2007, 22–23). In *Caprica*, patriarchal forces (as represented by Daniel) are portrayed as negative powers that need to be overcome, while Zoe represents Donna Haraway's ideal of female appropriation of technology for feminist purposes, escaping victimization (Haraway 2004, 23).

Looking at Zoe as a creator, the religious dimension of her task is immediately evident. Zoe creates in a completely religious setting: She is inspired by an angel, who first appears to her during childhood and looks like an older version of herself. She consequently understands her computer skills as a divine gift, and Zoe-A as an important tool in religious renewal, in changing the world for the better. Other female characters on the show also understand Zoe-A in this manner, namely STO-leader Clarice Willow and Zoe's best friend Lacy Rand, who explains already in the first episode: "There's good and there's evil. Only the one true God can tell the difference. Zoey knew God. He gave her the ability to create life itself" (1.00 "Extended Pilot"). Technological advance through divine intervention is not a new thought in posthuman circles—the idea of co-creation or *creatio continua* is frequently used to counter religious accusations that posthuman endeavors interfere with God's creation (Isherwood and Stuart 1998, 35). The idea is that God creates through humans, making human-made creations divinely inspired. This is essentially the idea promulgated in *Caprica*.

Nevertheless, Zoe's role in creating the first Cylon is already over— she dies before the task is completed. What happens next was clearly not her plan, yet because of her untimely death she has absolutely no influence on the remaining process. Her death is brought about by a man and a masculine trait—violence—and her technology is appropriated by another man and turned into something else. In comparison with the fictional female Cyborg creator Eve from *Eve of Destruction*, it is nevertheless noteworthy that Eve's Cyborg—who like Zoe's is created in her own image and shares her name—is a monstrous and out-of-control creature, who some scholars have identified as the creator's Freudian id (Holland 1995, 161–162). Zoe-A is nothing of the sort—and unlike Eve, she must not be destroyed. Still, were Zoe the only female character of relevance in the narrative, her death and the appropriation of her technological knowledge by a male character would be troubling from a feminist point of view. Fortunately, other women are ready to take her place as leading mediators between the spheres of technology and religion, namely Zoe-A and Lacy Rand.

Lacy also illustrates the conflation of technology and religion through women. Because she is Zoe-A's only contact to the outside world, the first Cylon becomes particularly attached to her, which has wide ranging consequences. When Zoe-A returns to the virtual world, she leaves an improved robot body behind. Graystone industries is finally able to copy the processor that had made Cylon-Zoe-A unique and the warrior Cylons go into mass production. These Cylons are gradually evolving from mindless followers to independent thinkers, as both viewer and characters soon discover. When Lacy meets them again on Gemenon, where she attends an STO training camp, she discovers that the Cylons respond to her commands although they are not programmed to do so. While the STO-leaders only see them as tools, the Centurions receive affection and recognition of their sentience from Lacy (see also Wetmore 2012, 185). Because of this unique bond, Lacy will overthrow the monotheist leadership and reorganize the STO. She will become the leader of the monotheistic religion (also referred to as "the mother") because of her connection to this technology, which arose from her friendship with Zoe-A. Again, women are involved in the religious and technological spheres at the same time.

Yet by far the most interesting case study is the first Cylon herself, Zoe-A. The character challenges various sci-fi stereotypes about the connections between femininity and technology, while her depiction simultaneously shows great awareness of traditional associations. In the beginning of the story, Zoe-A seems very passive, as she strongly relies on other people, especially her creator Zoe. When Zoe dies, this creates a crisis for her that is only partially resolved when she attaches herself to Lacy. Lacy can only be a friend and supporter, and not a guide or mother figure as Zoe had been. Zoe's death was necessary for Zoe-A to come into her own. Yet just as she is trying to gain control and to establish herself as a person in her own right, Daniel traps her and forces her into a robot body against her will. In the first half of the series, her body is exploited and controlled. As she remarks to Lacy: "I'm trapped. I get man-handled and ordered around" (1.02 "Rebirth").

In these scenes, the morally troubling exploitation and objectification of female bodies by men is quite clearly linked to the exploitation and objectification of machines. Zoe has to do as she is told and is confined by restraints while the scientists experiment on her. The two scientists Daniel charges with working on the Cylon approach her differently, but ultimately they are both suppressive forces. The first scientist is most obviously dubious. He refers to the Cylon as an "it" and a "tool" and does not acknowledge the possibility of sentience. The other scientist, Philo, seems to be a more positive character at first. He treats the Cylon gently and refers to her as "she." He also considers that she might be sentient. Zoe-A then tries to interact with Philo in the virtual world in order to include him in her escape plan. Yet as soon as he finds out that she is the Cylon, he turns on her. In the end, he is fine with a sentient female Cyborg as long as she depends on him and can be formed according to his wishes. However, if she is more powerful and independent than he imagined, he sees her as a threat. In the heat of the moment, Cylon Zoe-A kills Philo and escapes from the lab. Philo cannot handle the powerful and independent female machine and is punished for it. The objectification of the female or machine body is portrayed as unjust and patriarchal, while Zoe-A is the exploited victim whose actions against her oppressors seem justified.

Yet the situation is more complicated than that. Zoe-A is not simply a passive victim who finally manages to escape from her prison with one heroic act. In reality, Zoe-A is never without power throughout these entire events. Her first act of rebellion is against her father, who—though a grieving parent—is still presented as controlling and authoritative. She refuses to comply with his plans by keeping him ignorant of her presence in the robot body. When Daniel becomes suspicious and tries to expose her, she resists and finally diffuses his suspicions. Her lack of bodily resistance against her father (and later the scientists), is strategic: she knows that her escape from the research lab needs to be prepared in order to be successful. Since her robot body is clearly superior in strength, she could use violence against the men at any time. She opts against it and instead plays the passive machine. In the end, she is able to escape from exploitation through her intelligence, knowledge of technology, and religious belief.

While the robot body is forcefully retrieved, Zoe-A's consciousness is again transferred to the virtual world, where she is even more powerful. As she observes: "In here I have power, out there I am broken" (1.18 "Apotheosis"). She feels the restrictions of an easily recognizable and obviously different body and finds herself more at home in the artificial world that she can influence through sheer power of mind. She re-appropriates previously male virtual space and creates her environment in a way that defies all the computer programmers and their imperfect virtual realities—a process Daniel consciously compares to divine creation (1.17 "Here Be Dragons"). She single-handedly takes charge of cyberspace or "v-world," thus changing the virtual world men have built. Wetmore introduces the intriguing idea of Zoe-A as a kind of Gnostic demiurge: she is an immortal being with the power to create matter and affect miracles, yet she is still trapped in this created world and is consequently not identical with the actual divinity (Wetmore 2012, 187). The demiurge Wetmore describes by using the name Ialdabaoth is the "evil" creator of all material things, rejected in "Gnostic" circles that wish to overcome his creation. In contrast, it seems that there is a true connection between Zoe-A and the "actual divinity," God.

For the purposes of our topic, the point is that Zoe, Lacy Rand, and Zoe-A are extraordinary women who are not only strong and brave, but also religious and technologically skilled. Their knowledge and power over technology merge with their ideologies and morals with the intention of creating a better world. They do not need to be destroyed in order to re-establish male dominance and a patriarchal order. Quite to the contrary, they need to take charge. As a monotheist, Zoe creates a likewise monotheistic Zoe-A, which explains why the Cylons in *BSG* are also monotheists. Because of their belief, the Cylon Centurions will strive to be more human and will eventually succeed in building humanoid Cylon models. This creative process is once again left to a woman.

4. The Religious Machine

"Skin jobs" and "Bulletheads"

The image of the Cyborg in *BSG* and *Caprica* is an ambiguous one, primarily because there is more than one type of Cyborg. On *BSG*, we meet humanoid Cylons, Centurions, and Raiders, while *Caprica* adds virtual space as a "natural habitat" for artificial intelligence. A Cyborg is traditionally defined as a human-machine hybrid that incorporates biological and technological elements. Following this definition, only the humanoid Cylons and the Raiders clearly qualify as Cyborgs. The humanoid models, though mostly biological, can intersect with machines and create virtual environments. They are not born but built, and are able to transfer their consciousness (software) to new bodies (hardware). The Raiders are primarily machines, but cannot function without biological elements (they need air supply, for example). The Centurions, on the other hand, are problematic because they do not possess biological components—they are really just robots infused with consciousness and sentience. Zoe-A is likewise simply an artificial intelligence who then inhabits either a robot body or the virtual world. Significantly, the robot body (a military "tool") is the only part of the Cylon that was created by men. We have seen that sentience and consciousness were created by a woman (Zoe), and the same is true for the biological components that make the Cylon a true Cyborg.

Before we go in more detail, a few words on the Centurions are in order. The Centurions (sometimes referred to as "bulletheads") are frequently ignored in *BSG*-scholarship, despite the fact that their image graces practically every scholarly book on the series (see the covers of Eberl 2008a; Steiff and Tamplin 2008; Potter and Marshall 2008; Kaveney and Stoy 2010). Paradoxically, the Centurions most obviously transgress gender boundaries, as they appear physically masculine but are coded feminine both because of their "irrational" religious belief and because of the origin story told in *Caprica*. The Centurions are frequently pushed to the background in favor of their humanoid counterparts. Nevertheless, their central importance is often established through the narrative. After all, the Centurions want to create humanoid Cylons, because their belief dictates it. They approach the Final Five for their reproductive technology, yet they never transform themselves. Instead, they remain true to their original purpose as soldiers. In *BSG*, it seems as though the Centurions are being exploited, as noted by Gaius Baltar in a one-sided conversation with one of them: "I can see a real hierarchy around here. And I have to tell you, you're on the lower end of the scale, my friend.... Which is odd when you think about the Cylon God.... They told you about God, didn't they?" 04.09 "The Hub"). Baltar assumes that the Cylon God originated with the humanoid models, which we later learn to be incorrect. He also makes assumptions about their place in the Cylon hierarchy.

The Centurions aim to create humanoid models because they believe that their creators—humanity—were created in God's image. For the humans, the humanoid Cylon models who they also refer to as "skin jobs," are particularly threatening because they are so much like humans that the boundaries between human and machine are completely unclear and eventually erode. The creation of these humanoid models was, however, a long process. The Centurions unsuccessfully attempted to create "skin jobs" for many years, and these attempts also led to the accidental creation of the hybrids. Things change when they meet the Final Five, who belong to a different species of Cylon. Since the series stipulates that "all of this has happened before and all of it will happen again" it is feasible that other humans created other Cylons at a previous time and place—the Final Five are the last survivors of this Cylon race. The Final Five decide to help the Centurions to create humanoid models—with unforeseen consequences.

Season Four's search for the last member of the Final Five comes to an end with the revelation that the deceased (but of course resurrected as discussed shortly) Ellen Tigh is not only the last humanoid Cylon, but also the creator of the current humanoid models. Ellen is the wife of Colonel Tigh (revealed as one of the Final Five in the finale of season three), and had been killed by her husband after collaborating with the Cylons during the occupation on New Caprica. She was originally depicted as something of a trouble-maker, promoting her husband's drinking habit and hitting on Lee Adama while her husband was in the room (1.09 "Tigh Me Up, Tigh Me Down"). She is a middle-aged woman without children, known for cheating on her husband on several occasions. Ellen does not exactly meet the criteria of a "good" wife and woman.

When she resurrects, she remembers her true identity and takes on a somewhat different role. She describes the humanoid Cylon models as her "children," and indeed becomes a motherly figure in the series which she had not previously been. She is in conflict with her oldest "son," the number one model we know as Cavil. Cavil—our "evil" male Cylon—had poisoned the Final Five and placed them amongst the humans, making them unaware of their Cylon identity. He despises his mother Ellen for loving his brother more and, most of all, for confining him to the limitations of a human body. As Lorna Jowett notes, Cavil tries to hold Ellen in subordination (Jowett 2010, 69), putting an oedipal twist on the story through his previous sexual relations with her—at a time when she was unaware of her true nature, while he was certainly not. Cavil is the morally (and emotionally) unstable character in this plot, and Ellen tries to calm him with words both of wisdom and of love. Ellen is portrayed as a pool of knowledge for both Cavil and the viewer, as mothers frequently are (Doane 1999, 31). She informs us, for example, that monotheism came from the Centurions, and not the Final Five—a process we are already familiar with from our discussion of *Caprica*.

While Ellen is surely presented as a mother figure, she is also calculating and intelligent—her knowledge extends to science and technology. She and the remaining members of the Final Five worked in a research lab together before their planet was destroyed—and Ellen was the leading scientist. Ellen Tigh is transformed from a negative stereotype (which turns out to be deceiving) into a central character of our story. While this transformation is in many ways accomplished through motherhood, we should note that she is never a "natural" mother who gives birth. She is always a mother in the sense of a creator of artificial intelligence. This is, once again, the kind of creative process that women are usually punished for in sci-fi narratives. Ellen is neither punished nor destroyed, but instead rewarded with existence in paradise with her husband Saul. Unlike the human women discussed in chapter two, the female Cylons are allowed to survive the series ending. Hera lives, and so do Ellen, the Sixes, and the Eights.

Ellen Tigh not only provides information valuable for the plot, she also reminds us of the Centurions' importance. When she resurrects, the first words she speaks are a general thank you to a Centurion who helps her exit the resurrection tub. Ellen sees the belief in God as a

"Centurion value" as opposed to "human ideas" such as vengeance and murder (4.15 "No Exit"). In a way, it seems that the Centurions are uncorrupted by these human traits, which the Final Five combined with "Centurion values" in the humanoid models. Similarly uncorrupted are the Raiders (the Cylons' space fighters), who are equated with animals or pets, in any case sentient beings.

Although the humanoid models appear "superior" and in charge of both Centurions and Raiders (as evidenced by Baltar's statement above), these machines can occasionally access information that is inaccessible to the "skin jobs." In the fourth season, for example, the Raiders realize that the Final Five live amongst the humans and consequently refuse to attack the fleet, crippling Cylon war efforts. While the male humanoid Cylons see this rebellious behavior as a technical flaw and vote to lobotomize them in order to bend them to their will, the female Cylons call on the Centurions for help. The women remove the piece of technology restricting higher functions in the Centurions, and the Centurions then proceed to butcher the male Cylons for their actions against the Raiders (4.02 "Six of One"). Female traits (emotions) guide the otherwise male (warrior) Cyborgs for religious purposes (the search for the Final Five). Of course this implies that the Cylons' "humanization" led to a loss of certain cognitive abilities (which Cavil actually states repeatedly). Yet instead of proposing that the key to these abilities are reason and science, the series suggests that traditionally female traits (namely "irrational" intuition, emotion, and religion) can serve as a conduit.

And yet in *BSG*, the Centurions' story is always somewhat unfinished. It is worth noting that not a single Centurion is allowed to join the human-Cylon alliance in the Promised Land. The humanoid models leave their baseship to the Centurions, who are now free to roam the galaxy (to do what, exactly?). By choosing to end the series on prehistorical earth, the writers made the Centurions' continued existence on this planet impossible. So once again, they disappear from view. The Centurion is so recognizably different—un-human—that she is no more welcome on Earth than the male Cylons who refuse to compromise. In *BSG*, the Cylons need to become as human as possible in order for this compromise to work. They thus have to give up much of what makes them machine.

4. The Religious Machine

Jennifer Stoy realized that making the last one of the Final Five—and indeed the most important one of them—a middle-aged woman was a statement in itself (Stoy 2010, 9). The same can be said for the choice to make a 16-year-old girl the creator of all Cylon life. Mary Ann Doane has suggested that stories concerned with "artificial femininity" are frequently coupled with an investigation into the maternal, especially the opposition between natural and artificial reproduction (Doane 1999, 21, 24). In this argument she follows Andreas Huyssen who proposed that the female machine serves a double function: obviously, she couples fear of the feminine with fear of the technological—but she also represents the male wish to create a woman. Huyssen sees not only sexual desires at the heart of this wish, but also the ideal of creation without a mother. Creating a woman, Huyssen further explains, is an attempt of reconciling technology (artificial creature) and nature (woman) (Huyssen 1987, 70–71). While this association is maintained, the content of the debate shifts significantly in *BSG*. First, the female body is not fetishized by the scientific and analytical male mind—and if it is (as was the case with Zoe-A in the research lab), this is portrayed as unjust exploitation. Instead, women build women without ever reproducing naturally. Ellen is a mother without being a natural mother, her reproductive power stems purely from the mind, not the body. The women "blaspheme" even more by also building men, reinforcing that men cannot exist without the reproductive power of women—reproductive power that is not necessarily natural, but can very well be artificial.

Concerning gendered reproduction, we should also mention the episode "The Farm" (2.05), where predominantly male Cylons harvest female humans for their reproductive organs in an attempt to find a way to Cylon reproduction. I would argue that this reinforces my thesis: clearly, this attempt to control female reproduction is presented as negative and (not coincidentally) we mostly see male Cylons in the facility. The attempts are unsuccessful and the facility is ultimately destroyed. *BSG* strongly identifies this kind of exploitation of female reproductive capabilities as evil, and ultimately unfruitful. While the creator-men of other Cyborg stories struggle for control of the artificial woman (and thus for control over female reproductive capabilities), control is never theirs to begin with in *BSG*. Without women, neither humans nor Cylons would exist.

Ellen and Zoe are not simply technologically versed women, they are also religious. There is certainly a danger of reinforcing gender stereotypes by proposing that women are irrational, insofar as they are openly and faithfully religious. Critics of the Goddess movement or "thealogy" have pointed out that coding everything that is masculine "bad" and only feminine qualities such as maternity, emotion, or irrationality as "good" means that women could never hope to venture into science or technology, these "patriarchal" masculine domains (Graham 2002, 214–215). Yet by associating the female Cylon with religion, *BSG* and *Caprica* create an immediate connection between technology, woman, and religion. The narratives introduce female creators of technology, which automatically links them to science and rationality, while at the same time evoking stereotypical female irrationality through their religious convictions. Through this double association, the feminine is rescued from inferred backwardness, as well as exclusiveness. Religion—and hence irrational femininity—is also the motor behind the Cylon reinterpretation of death, as we will see in the following section.

Finding God in Mortality

Posthumanist elements pervade both series. This is particularly evident when it comes to discussions of "eternal" life or technological resurrection. Originally, Cylons are described as immortal. Sure, a Cylon body can be destroyed in such a manner that can be considered "death." The humanoid Cylons in particular die in the same way as humans, their bodies are as susceptible to bullets, knives, or loss of air as any human body. Yet what distinguishes Cylons from humans is that Cylon consciousness or self is practically immortal. When a body dies, the "software" as posthumanists would call it, is simply downloaded to a new body and the person lives on ("resurrects"). For the humans, this makes the Cylons even more "unhuman," and positively scary. For Cylons and humans to move closer together, the Cylons eventually have to learn to die. And as some of them find, technological resurrection in fact keeps them from God instead of bringing them closer to him.

Most proponents of posthumanism strive for immortality in one

4. The Religious Machine

way or another. Merging with machines becomes a sort of salvation from death and from the vulnerabilities and limits of the body.[2] For Christian theologies, this posthuman goal is extremely problematic, not only because they believe it tampers with God's creation and elevates technology to divinity, but also because it inhibits resurrection. In a Christian religious mindset, death is necessary for salvation, because humans are resurrected in a flesh and bone body (Campbell and Walker 2005; Murphy 2002, 203; Isherwood and Stuart 1998, 52–77; Peters 2002, xv). I would also suggest that posthuman ideas of immortality and salvation are in competition with comparable Christian goals—we saw in the first chapter that posthumanism can also be seen as a quasi-religious ideology. If technology becomes our savior, then what need would we have for God?

On *BSG*, resurrection is understood in rather posthumanist terms, at least where the Cylons are concerned (Starbuck's resurrection, on the other hand, is of a more Christian nature). I completely agree with Wetmore that Cylon resurrection is not Christian resurrection (Wetmore 2012, 135–136). Although the Cylons of *BSG* also "resurrect" in a flesh and bone body, the process is otherwise more technological than religious. It is highly reminiscent of the posthumanist division between hardware and software—body and "self." The body is replaceable and seems rather unconnected to the self—posthumanists would assert that the body is no more than a machine, while the self consists only of the information stored in that machine (Krueger 2005, 83). Could we separate the information from the body (as the Cylons do), we would be free of the constraints of this machine. However, without the body, there would be no existence for the Cylons, so it is not completely dispensable to them, as suggested by posthumanists. In addition, their belief dictates that God wants them to be embodied.

Initially, resurrection in the sense of downloading the self or mind into a new body is connected to God in the Cylon mind. In the first season episode "Flesh and Bone" (1.08) this belief is introduced through the Cylon character Leoben, who does not fear bodily death but is afraid that "his soul won't make it to God." The concept of the soul is of course part of our Western understanding of the self. Although it was incorporated into Christian doctrine, the soul actually has its origins in Greek philosophy (and not Jewish belief) and was only gradually adopted by

Christians (Russell 1999, 24–25). Originally, the Greeks believed in a dual soul, namely the free soul (a person's self) and the body soul that infuses a body with life. While the body soul perishes when a person dies, the free soul departs to the netherworld (Bremmer 1983, 13, 15, 18). Leoben is referring to this concept of the free soul that would be freed from the body once he dies. But where does it go afterwards?

When Leoben expresses the fear that his free soul might perish instead, Leoben means that he might be too far away from the next resurrection ship and thus not able to download into a new body. In that case, he (not just his body) would effectively die—the free soul would be lost. So we can see that the Cylons are actually very afraid of real death and differentiate between bodily death and complete death, only the first of which leads to resurrection. It is curious that their faith in God (and his power to resurrect without technology) seems to be weaker than their faith in technology—although this technology is of course always associated with God. In opposition to the posthumanists who wish to escape the confines of the flesh in favor of virtual space, Cylons actually cling to the body as a storage unit for the information that constitutes their identity. That storage unit is, however, replaceable.

Cylon resurrection differs from both Christian resurrection and posthuman resurrection in its lack of an "otherworld"—be it heaven or cyberspace. Cylons do not resurrect in order to live in paradise or in a virtual bodiless world, but in order to continue living in this reality, in a body familiar to them. The resurrection process is thoroughly feminized, as it takes place in the so-called "resurrection tubs" that are filled with white amniotic fluid. In these tubs, the Cylons resurrect in new, naked bodies that are seemingly identical to their previous deceased bodies. The tubs are rather similar to those occupied by the already discussed hybrids. Significantly, the series only shows us the resurrection process of female characters, never of male ones. It is a rather feminized process: the "goo," the nakedness, the emotionality of it (Jowett 2010, 70). None of this computes with masculinity.

As the series develops, we find an increasing number of Cylon characters who seek real death without resurrection. This is especially the case for tortured or suffering characters. Most notably, the Six-character Gina Invière, whom humans on the Battlestar Pegasus repeatedly raped and tortured, expresses a strong wish to die without the possibility of resurrection. While she initially rejects suicide on religious grounds, she later sets off a nuclear bomb outside a resurrection ships' reach, effectively ending her own life. Eternal life would mean eternal pain—a new body would not help her psychological suffering. This is also one of the issues raised by Mark Coeckelbergh in his critique of the posthuman concept of invulnerable immortal bodies (Coeckelbergh 2011, 4–5): Suffering is not just a bodily experience, but also a psychological one. On *BSG*, only the female Cylons acknowledge these negative side effects of resurrection—we do not see a male model suffering from resurrection pains or questioning the practice altogether. Cavil only states once that every resurrection is worse than the last (3.03 "Exodus—Part I") and Leoben's repeated resurrections in season 3 are much more harrowing for his prisoner Kara than for Leoben himself (3.01 "Occupation").

Other (female) Cylons begin to realize that technological resurrection is a barrier between them and God. In violation of Cylon law, the three model D'Anna is on a mission to find the Final Five in season three, who are thought to be more closely connected to God. She discovers that she can access otherwise hidden information in the time between bodily death and download into a new body that can help her find the Final Five. She repeatedly orders a Centurion to kill her in order to have more visions. She later explains to the other Cylons that "there's something beautiful and miraculous between life and death" (3.08 "Hero"). D'Anna taps into something that the Cylons had lost through their resurrection capability: the connection between death and transcendence, meaning access to something beyond this life, in this case something divine. The Cylons have lost this connection because of their resurrection capabilities. Trying to evade the uncertainties of death, they continue their individual earthly existences in a never-ending circle, never truly changing or transforming themselves. D'Anna's experiences help to raise the idea amongst some of the Cylons that eternal life in this world might not be God's intention after all. This realization is fundamental for the progress of the series, as it facilitates Cylon-human reconciliation.

In season four, the Cylons split into fractions and fight a civil war amongst each other. Fraction one is the rational, pragmatic, masculine one including the male models One (Cavil), Four (Simon) and Five (Doral), as well as one woman, a renegade Eight (Boomer). The second coalition is the religious, peaceful, feminine one including the female models Six, Eight (Sharon), as well as one male model, Two (Leoben). The religious fraction allies with the humans—and the first order of business is the destruction of the resurrection hub, which would effectively end Cylon resurrection capabilities. One goal behind this plan is to assure the humans that their offer of collaboration is sincere, another one the rescue of the female model Three (D'Anna) who has been "boxed" (her consciousness frozen) because she has looked upon the faces of the Final Five during her near-death experiences. The search for the Final Five is a religious goal that supersedes any quest for immortality. However, the realization that death is an important aspect of life is an equally strong motivation for this step. The Six model Natalie explains that the Cylons came to the conclusion that death is necessary in order for life to have any real value (4.07 "Guess What's Coming to Dinner?").

Not only does the series suggest that death is important in order to value life. Through D'Anna's visions, it also proposes that there might be something beyond death that is inaccessible through technological resurrection as practiced by the Cylons. Through resurrection, the body becomes replaceable. By questioning resurrection, the body emerges as something precious, and something that cannot be replaced. The moral message behind this narrative strand is closer to Christian criticism than to posthuman ideology: embodiment is a precondition for salvation. Since the Cylons who realize this are still machines, are still "built, not born" (Lee Adama in 3.07 "A Measure of Salvation"), it seems inappropriate to see this message completely in contrast to posthumanist ideas. All the more so since another boundary between human and machine breaks down once they are all able to die. Accordingly, an Eight remarks after the Resurrection Hub has been destroyed: "And it's a good thing. Because now there's no difference" (4.09 "The Hub"). And this, after all, is another way of becoming posthuman, by breaking down boundaries between "us" and "them." More than anything, the narrative reestablishes the supremacy of the body with all its flaws, including mortality. It implies that only a body can lead to salvation through God, whose will it is for this body to be mortal.

This shift in Cylon self-understanding is brought about by women—more precisely, religious machines, and is interpreted as morally "good." The men (especially Cavil) have an entirely different view of the body, namely that it prohibits them from fully experiencing the universe. It is rather stereotypical that the rational male Cylons who are markedly less religious should espouse a more posthuman ideology regarding the body. After all, the body is traditionally associated with women, while the mind is the domain of men. They thus want to let go of the body and search for a disembodied future in which they are God-like and cannot die. We will discuss the male position in more detail later, for now it is sufficient to say that the women are advocates of the body and associate death with access to God. The stereotype is nevertheless undermined through the conclusion, which is that the women are both "good" and "correct" in their assessment, while the men are both "bad" and "wrong." By describing the female Cylon in such a manner, the series also reinterprets the idea of the female demon, namely the notion that powerful and independent women are evil—we shall now see, how.

Lilith Strikes Back

On *BSG* and *Caprica*, the oppressed fight back. The woman, the machine, the believer—they are all marginalized in the science fiction genre. Since their exploitation is interpreted as unjust, their revolt seems justified to the viewer, at least eventually. The oppressed are embodied by the dangerous woman: the sexualized femme fatal (Six on *BSG*) and the independent creator and religious leader (Zoe or Zoe-A) who can both be identified as variations of the mother of all dangerous women, Lilith. The image of the dangerous woman was quite consciously employed by the series' creators: Tricia Helfer aka Six as the classical femme fatal was the center of *BSG*'s promotional campaign in her red dress and platinum blonde hair, while Alessandra Torresani aka Zoe seductively graced the posters of *Caprica* with a red apple in her hand. Of course this was also part of a marketing scheme: sexy women sell. Yet it was more than that.

Miniseries begins with various stereotypes that are gradually and effectively dismantled, not the least of which is the hyper-sexual female Cyborg in the form of Caprica Six. As the story progresses, it introduces the viewer to the Cylon position, and humans become less sympathetic, while our Cylon sympathies grow. By the time we watch *Caprica*, the subjugation of the machine is clearly portrayed as an injustice, and the connection between the exploited machine and the exploited female body is obvious. Yet the female machine refuses to be a victim. She becomes the wrath of God, the "avenging angel" who fights against her oppressors, but does not lose sight of what is morally right. The stereotype of the dangerous woman was used only to be transformed into something else: namely retaliation against those who would stylize her as evil. Using Six and Zoe as examples, this section will illustrate the process of transforming the dangerous woman from "evil" to "good," using Lilith as a point of reference.

The night demon Lilith has her origins in the Ishtar and Lamashtu traditions of the ancient Near East. Extra-biblical Jewish traditions (namely from the Talmud) gradually established her as Adam's first wife, who reportedly refused to be subjugated by Adam because she was created from the same material (not from his rib, as was later the case for Eve) and consequently understood herself as equal. Lilith fled from paradise to escape subjugation and was rejected by God, who condemned most of the children she would bear to die. As an act of revenge, she became a demon who seduced men and kidnapped or even murdered children. Lilith is a sexual fantasy, a woman of intense beauty, who is morally perverted (Strauss 1995, 37–42). Lilith is in many ways the "original" female demon, a creature of the night. She has traditionally embodied male anxieties towards female sexuality and power (Hurwitz 1992, 87–88). Jewish feminists have since turned this interpretation around: Lilith was proof that God created men and women as equals and Adam demonized her (especially in front of his second wife Eve) to keep his relationship to God exclusive and Eve subjugated (Tuschling 2007, 31–32). Of course Eve was likewise a model for a traditional image of dangerous women: in 19th century literature and art, she emerged as the original femme fatal who brings destruction to the world, often because she seeks revenge (Menon 2006, 3–4).

On *BSG*, we find that the Cylon model Six shares many characteristics with Lilith (Rolufs 2008, 353–356), but also with Eve's femme fatal tradition. Six, who is in many ways the most significant model, is the first Cylon we meet. She appears in the first scene on the armistice station in a red dress, leather boots, and platinum blonde hair, kissing the confused colonial officer before and during the Cylon attack on the station, muttering, "It has begun" (*Miniseries*). From the very beginning, Six is the embodiment of femininity, a classical femme fatale who seeks revenge while being both enticing and highly dangerous. As mentioned, she reflects both a fear of female sexuality and of technology. Her image is further stereotyped when she snaps a baby's neck at the market on Caprica, becoming the antithesis of motherhood and protection. Like Lilith, Six seduces men (Baltar), kills babies (*Miniseries*), and kidnaps other women's children (Hera).

And yet Caprica Six is ultimately chosen by God, and not a demon. She has an angelic likeness and a divine mission. Like Jewish feminist texts, *BSG* turns the negatives positive from the very beginning. After murdering the baby on Caprica, for example, the Six model walks away from the scene in pain—she clearly did not enjoy that experience. She is motivated by the impending Cylon attack on the colonies that would have led to a more painful death for the child. She does not murder the baby because she revels in the pain of the innocent, but instead sees this as an act of mercy. From the beginning, Caprica Six believes in God's plan and consequently in the justice of her actions. She represents the suppressed who have decided not to be victimized any longer. Her wrath is subtle, but uncompromising. After her death and subsequent download into a new body, God sends her an angel in order to convince her that humans and Cylons need to reconcile. Her initial desire for revenge and justice is now replaced by the thought of reconciliation.

Caprica Six also illustrates that she can be a competent and caring mother, thus preventing complete demonization as had been the case for Lilith. She takes on a motherly and protective role for the hybrid child Hera—a role that is divinely inspired. She is also impregnated with the first possible Cylon-Cylon baby as a consequence of her relationship with Tigh in season four (4.08 "Sine Qua Non"). Of course this development supports the criticism that the series increasingly reduced women to traditional female roles in the third and especially the fourth season (Stoy 2010, 13–14). Focusing on Caprica Six as a

"Lilith-like" character, however, I find it more interesting hat her baby is never born. We are instantly reminded that God cursed most of Lilith's children to die. In Jewish tradition, this is Lilith's punishment for refusing to bow to Adam. The Cylons are equally cursed—they are obsessed with natural reproduction which they see as one of God's major commandments, yet fail to accomplish.

Indeed Hera is the only baby ever birthed by a Cylon—and she is half human. Considering that the Cylons in *BSG* are commonly understood as strongly feminized, it is intriguing that these women fail to fulfill their most traditional role: that of giving birth. The Cylons themselves see this failure as their biggest flaw. There is certainly a stereotype to be found here: women who cannot give birth are incomplete, flawed, broken. And yet Caprica Six is allowed to enter paradise—by fulfilling a motherly role without being a natural mother, Lilith is reconciled with Adam, Cylon is reconciled with human.

The one difference between Lilith and Caprica Six lies in their relationship to God, which is also an indicator of their morality: Lilith is evil, while Caprica Six is good; Lilith's connection to God is broken, while Caprica Six' is strong. Caprica Six' role throughout the narrative is guided by her faith—she believes in a loving, all-knowing God and his plan, she believes that Hera is the future of human and Cylon, and she believes that she has a role to play. Caprica Six is the ultimate irrational machine, guided by emotions such as love, guilt, and pain. In a traditional sci-fi narrative, she would have to be destroyed, her authority undermined, her belief exposed as wrong. None of it is the case. Caprica Six is correct to believe in God, she is right about Hera, and her authority as a source of knowledge and truth never disappears. In the end, she is pleased to have fulfilled God's plan for her and is rewarded for her troubles with a kind of paradise, establishing a peaceful society without conflict or hatred.

Although the prequel series does not introduce such a fitting personification of the mythological Lilith, her wrath is also felt on *Caprica*, where Zoe-A and Tamara-A embody independent women with God-like powers who are re-interpreted as angelic. As the "avenging angels," the two girls make it their mission to cleanse v-world from sin. The girls who cannot die and are able to manipulate the code that holds v-world together clean up immoral night clubs in New Cap City. Their wrath is directed at the immorality of the virtual world that is filled with death, sex, and drugs. Finally, they decide that they are done being a tourist attraction for those from the "real world," and destroy New Cap City in order to build their own paradise on its ruins. After being abused by this space they were forced into by their fathers, they decide to use their powers and assert their independence. Adam had demonized Lilith to remain in an exclusive relationship with God—in *Caprica*, God is complemented by technology in this instance. Daniel wants to control technology just as he wants to control his daughter; he does not want to share or cooperate. The "avenging angels" re-appropriate male space—like the feminist version of Lilith, they refuse to be subjugated and enter into their own exclusive relationships with God (and technology).

Another factor we should take into account when discussing the re-interpretation of traditional gender roles is the use of violence. As Cylons, Zoe-A and Caprica Six possess the kind of enhanced bodily strength that makes them threatening on a physical level. Marilyn Maxwell has pointed out that violent women in postmodern fictional texts are usually less comfortable with their own violent behavior than men (Maxwell 2000, xii). While male violence is portrayed as acceptable and even necessary, women need to be apologetic about using force to reach their goals. We could of course question whether violence should ever be portrayed as justified, but the fact of the matter is that male heroes of popular culture (especially in science fiction) are usually violent in one way or another. While women are made to rely on and admire male violence, they are not allowed to be at ease with their own violent behavior, which is certainly a double standard: men are entitled to violence, while women are not.

We have seen that Zoe-A accidentally kills the scientist Philo while escaping from the research lab. The scene is fascinating because it lacks a clear moral implication. Had Zoe-A killed the less likeable scientist, this act could have been subsumed under typical revenge. Philo, on the other hand, was neither "bad" nor unlikeable, so there is no perceived justice at work. Yet Zoe-A does not spend much time thinking about this murder and does not mourn this man she had come to know and like. The viewer is likewise not given much time to concern themselves with this issue. Zoe-A neither apologizes, nor does the narrative punish her for the action. Neither does Caprica Six apologize for violent behavior (except of course the general genocide of humanity, which is a completely different kind of violence) or for her physical strength and superiority. Our metaphorical Liliths refuse to be held to this double standard, where violent men get to be heroes while violent women get to be sorry. Lilith is not to be tamed in order to conform to her society's image of femininity—she is to use her abilities to redefine that image.

The female machines we have met in this chapter can navigate the waters between religion and technology in a way that male machines cannot. Caprica Six and Zoe-A are united in their strong sense of justice and morality that they associate with the divine, though this does not mean that they are peaceful and passive "angels." They are thoroughly religious, but also inherently connected to the technological, since they are themselves technological creations. Their creators are women, the middle-aged Ellen Tigh and the teenage genius Zoe Graystone. Both these creators and their creations conflate the rational and the irrational. The stereotypes of objectified female bodies and dangerous murderous femme fatals are employed and eroded at the same time, as the religious machine takes matters into her own hands and fights for justice. Because her cause is just and she is morally stable, she does not need to be destroyed like so many of her predecessors, but instead is welcomed in paradise (Caprica Six) or allowed to create her own (Zoe-A). Not all women are that lucky—some less stable characters are indeed denied salvation.

5

"Fallen" Women: Razors and Delusions

The traditional Judeo-Christian understanding is that evil originated with man's first sin: eating the fruit of the forbidden tree of knowledge in paradise. Mankind's sin was to want the one thing they were not allowed to have. They lusted after it because the snake told them that the fruit would make them God-like. This is the original sin from which all evil was born (Krochmalnik 2003, 14–16). While traditions exist within monotheistic religions that associate evil with the supernatural—for example in the Book of Watchers with its story of fallen angels and their destructive children (Horsley 2009, 54)—the conventional view is that humans brought sin to the world. The idea that women are especially susceptible to evil emerged with the story that the snake could convince Eve more easily than Adam. This tradition, which is both a Judeo-Christian and a long-standing European philosophical one (Krochmalnik 2003, 34–35), has continued to inspire popular culture narratives.

The *Battlestarverse* brakes with the idea that women are "naturally" more prone to evil. In the *Battlestarverse* "evil" women are consequently less frequent, but some examples can be found. To the series' credit, these characters are usually rather well-rounded and their positions are often explained to the audience to a certain extent. I describe these women as "fallen" rather than "evil," because they all chose to stray from the righteous path following a major event or conceived betrayal. Some of them are also consumed by misguided delusions of grandeur. I will first investigate fallen masculinized women without a clear connection to the religious or technological spheres, with a special focus on the character of Admiral Cain. I will then explore Boomer before discussing *Caprica*'s Clarice Willow in the remaining two sections, which includes an in-depth analysis of the series' understanding of heaven. This chapter thus serves as a counterpart to the association of technology and religion with heroines by looking at this connection in "fallen" women.

Female Masculinity and the Razor

The aptly named Admiral Helena Cain is unquestionably the best example of female evil in *BSG*. Like Starbuck, Cain was a male character in the original series and represents female masculinity rather than femininity. Judith Halberstam has alerted us to the fact that we often falsely understand white male masculinity as "normative" masculinity, and argued that alternative forms of masculinity, such as female masculinity, are more helpful in understanding the concept of masculinity itself (Halberstam 1998, 2). Female characters in *BSG*'s military are usually masculinized, strengthening the connection between masculinity and war, which is typically associated with aggression, rationality and physical courage, and as such connected to normative masculinity (Hutchings 2008, 389–391; Higate and Hopton 2005, 434). The depiction of Admiral Cain is thus best seen as a comment on the masculine that is made more accessible through the characters' gender. Ewan Kirkland has stated that Cain "perversely [represents] the worst excesses of militarized masculinity" (Kirkland 2008, 143). She does not seem to possess any traditionally feminine qualities, but is portrayed as an aggressive military strategist who is callous and cruel, lacks empathy, and refuses any compromises.

Cain appears on the scene in the middle of the second season, when the Galactica unexpectedly encounters another Battlestar that had survived the initial Cylon attack (2.10 "Pegasus"). The Battlestar Pegasus is commanded by Admiral Cain—and because she has a higher

5. "Fallen" Women: Razors and Delusions

position in the military hierarchy, Commander Adama is displaced as the prime military leader. The Pegasus (and her commander) is a negative mirror image for the Galactica in a variety of ways. Like the Galactica, the Pegasus started out as the protector of a civilian fleet. Because war and retaliation was Cain's primary objective, she decided to abandon the fleet and to raid their ships for spare parts and valuable personnel. When Cain's first officer refused to comply with her orders, she killed him. Like the Galactica, the Pegasus has a female Cylon prisoner. The Pegasus prisoner is repeatedly tortured and raped. The Pegasus illustrates what would have happened to the Galactica without the leadership of Laura Roslin and Bill Adama (who initially was not thrilled to leave the war behind either), and also confirms the heroism of the entire Galactica crew, who (we hope) would not have complied with Cain's orders.

Cain is considered "evil" for various reasons. She is unable to see Cylons as people and represses opposition. When two of the most moral male characters on the show (Helo and Tyrol, who are discussed in the next chapters) rush to save Galactica's Cylon prisoner from being raped by some of the Pegasus crew, Cain orders them to be executed. Her actions against the moral males define her status, and also illustrate the danger of "pure" and unchallenged masculinity. Cain also abuses power. She uses her position as an Admiral and unchallenged military authority to control and dominate others. This is much in keeping with the Christian idea of evil, where power is coupled with the temptation to do evil (Häring 2003, 74). Similar to Kirkland, Rikk Mulligan suggests that gender is the least of the issues here, as he rather sees similarities between Cain and then-president George W. Bush in the criticism of powerful leaders who overstep their authority (Mulligan 2008, 53, 57). I would again stress that Cain is overall more masculine than feminine, while her biological gender only becomes an issue when we are confronted with her homosexuality (Burrows 2010, 200–203, 208–209).

Various commentators have pointed to the lack of challenges to heteronormativity in the form of lesbian or gay characters on the show (Jones 2010, 166–169; Stoy 2010, 14). Although Ronald Moore attempted to remedy that in *Caprica*, where Sam Adama is introduced as a traditionally masculine Mafioso-type who is happily married to a man, the issue remains problematic in *BSG*. In the series itself, homosexual relationships are completely absent. Outside of the series, two characters are revealed as homo- or bisexual: Felix Gaeta in the Webisodes *The Face of the Enemy* and Admiral Cain in the movie *Razor*. Both cases are troubling. Cain is seen in a romantic relationship with Gina Invière who turns out to be a Cylon (a Six model). After this revelation, Cain orders her to be imprisoned and tortured, and does not stop her (male) crew from repeatedly raping Gina. This is certainly part of the explanation offered for Cain's cruelty—she was betrayed by her own emotions. And yet she shoots her first officer before she finds out about Gina, which illustrates that something was wrong with her morality to begin with.

Gina later murders Cain—a convenient move that relieves our primary characters from this inevitable action. Laura Roslin had previously suggested to Adama that Cain needed to be killed, and he later orders Kara to shoot her (2.12 "Resurrection Ship—Part II"). Instead, our evil lesbian is shot by her former lover. Of course this is also a valuable comment on the illegitimacy of torture—Cain's callousness spirals back to her: the tortured victim kills the woman who ordered her torture. Yet their romantic back-story leaves us with a homophobic aftertaste. In a similar manner, Felix Gaeta, originally an idealist with a tendency to choose the wrong side, is court-martialed in season four, leaving the second homosexual character dead (4.14 "Blood on the Scales"). That the lack of a proper moral compass is associated with non-heterosexuals is certainly a troubling cliché.

Razor explores the fate of the Pegasus crew and her commander more closely. It attempts to make Helena Cain more accessible by giving her a back-story. Yet although we are provided with a more thorough understanding of the situation that led to the events recounted in 2.10 "Pegasus," the movie ultimately fails to make Cain's actions comprehensible. She is not seen as overwhelmed or ill-equipped to face this extraordinary situation, but instead makes a conscious decision. This leaves the viewer with the feeling that she simply lacks morality. Or, as Cain-actress Michelle Forbes put it: "She's lost perspective" (Storm 2007, 211). Admiral Cain is not, like many evil women in religious traditions and popular culture, simply evil—nor is she evil in a distinctly female fashion. She is "fallen" in that she lost her way and started to make bad decisions that led to a constant downward spiral. One could argue that a complete break with any "female qualities," in particular empathy and any kind of positive emotion marks her descent. It is also noteworthy that Starbuck sees Cain as a role model and mentor for quite a while, even though she will, in the end, always take her orders from Adama.

Razor also introduces an additional female character, Kendra Shaw, to the story. Kendra is revealed as Cain's protégé and finally as the woman responsible for carrying out Cain's orders against the civilian fleet. Cain had ordered the civilian ships to be stripped not only of spare parts, but also of valuable personnel. When the selected civilians refuse to abandon their families, Cain orders her officers to shoot the families of those who refuse. While this certainly supports the idea that the women on Pegasus are "fallen," if not fully evil, the story is also a testament to the inadequacy of the ship's men. As one commentator remarked, only women are "razors" in this movie, while men are altogether weak (This Razor's Edgy 2008, 260). The new first officer Colonel Fisk is hesitant and clearly overwhelmed by the situation, so Kendra steps up. In addition, Fisk is not a heroic character, as the viewer already knows from further events of the second season. Kendra and Cain are thus not opposed by heroic male characters. Kendra is still more of a hero than Cain. Cain conditioned her to be "a razor," and Kendra consequently numbed her guilt and pain with drugs (Livingston 2008, 149). In the finale of *Razor*, she sacrifices herself to save the Galactica crew (notably Starbuck), and clearly sees her death as penance for her actions. When alone with a hybrid, he asks her, "Do you wish to be forgiven?" Kendra's clear answer is "Yes."

I consequently agree with Mulligan that the stories of Cain and Shaw do not portray the danger of women in charge. He noted that "the world of Galactica is not ours" (Mulligan 2008, 57), meaning that women are never understood as less capable or unqualified for any position based on their gender. This differs from contemporary discussions about women in the military that often include such accusations (Higate and Hopton 2005, 437). Women are not "confined by patriarchal structures" (Halberstam 1998, 17), they are not victims of a gender-biased system. I would again add that both Cain and Shaw are rather masculinized women, so their depiction tells us a lot more about the series' interpretation of masculinity than it does femininity. However, this leads to another relevant gender issue, notably how the series ultimately deals with female masculinity.

While Starbuck is increasingly feminized as she accepts her religious role (religion feminizes), Cain has no such possibility. She stays thoroughly masculine in the worst sense of the word: she is the patriarch. It seems that masculine women are either "brought back" to femininity (Starbuck) or die (Cain and Shaw). In Starbuck's case, even feminization cannot stop her eventual demise. Although the series presents many masculinized women, it ultimately disposes of them in favor of their more feminine counterparts. Female masculinity seems to be somewhat doomed, while femininity is ultimately the goal to salvation. I would argue that the often criticized feminization of *BSG*'s women in the course of the series is not so much a crusade on the previously established dominance of women in the narrative (which in many ways existed even after the series finale), but rather displays discomfort with female masculinity. Certainly this is not the case if we only take the first season into account—but the overall trajectory seems to penalize at least the more obvious forms of female masculinity. This does not mean that women are not allowed to exhibit masculine traits or cannot "act" male (remember our discussion of the "Liliths," Caprica Six and Zoe-A), nor does it indicate that women are portrayed as weak—far from it. Yet these are usually otherwise feminine women who also come with (feminine) religion.

Overall, Cain and Shaw are counterpoints to characters such as Starbuck, Roslin, or Caprica Six on the one hand, and men such as Cavil or Fisk on the other. In this world, both men and women can be faulty. Portraying a masculinized female military leader as an "evil" lesbian who is then killed is clearly the real gender issue here. Cain is not "personified evil," since she is portrayed as a real person who has made some bad decisions and has consequently lost perspective. She is not even irredeemable. After all, she stands down from her previous decision to have Adama and Roslin killed in "Resurrection Ship—Part II" (2.12). Cain does evil, but she is not fully evil. Evil is rather described as morally faulty or perverted action. Significantly, none of this is associated with either religion or technology. Cain, Shaw, and their crew are fully secularized human evils.

5. "Fallen" Women: Razors and Delusions

Traitors and Lost Identities

With the exception of Cain and Shaw, *BSG* offers surprisingly few examples of female evil. Of course some women do not make a very good first impression and indeed suggest stereotyped female evil—most notably the Six model in the first season (just think of her portrayal as a baby-murderess). The Cylon Three (D'Anna) does not strike us as particularly likeable either. Yet in the course of the narrative, they both become heroines. Two of their fellow Cylons are not that lucky. Sharon "Boomer" Valerii mutates from an unwilling Cylon sleeper-agent and proponent of human-Cylon reconciliation to a humanity-hating minion of Cavil who betrays her fellow Eights and joins the (male) anti-human alliance. She also betrays her former lover Galen Tyrol, kidnaps Hera, and pretends to be Hera's mother Athena to sleep with her husband Helo. Boomer is somewhat redeemed in the series finale when she decides to hand over Hera to Athena, but her alter ego shows no sign of forgiveness and kills her. Cylon Tory Foster also ends up dead (at the hands of a man) after handling her own identity crisis badly and committing serious crimes. Instead of becoming heroes, Boomer Sharon and Tory Foster turn into traitors and become fallen women.

In *Miniseries*, Sharon "Boomer" Valerii is established as a human pilot who is thoroughly integrated into the Galactica crew as a friend of her fellow pilots and the lover of deck Chief Galen Tyrol. The plot has her crash-landing on nuked Caprica where she rescues a few survivors and leaves Helo behind in favor of Baltar on Helo's request. *Miniseries* ends with the shocking revelation that Boomer is, in fact, a Cylon—a major plot twist that successfully establishes suspense. During the first season, it becomes clear that Boomer is a sleeper agent who has no knowledge of her own Cylon identity. Boomer thinks she is human. Unwittingly, she performs acts of sabotage on Galactica and finally ends up shooting Bill Adama (who had trusted her completely) in the finale of season one. Boomer has us (and the characters) wonder what constitutes identity and from the beginning creates Cylon sympathy in the viewer. While the other Cylons originally seem evil or ambivalent at best, Boomer evokes compassion. However, once this compassion is established and has transferred to other Cylons as well, Boomer becomes less important and her position in the narrative changes. She becomes an almost psychopathic traitor who can, in the end, only find redemption through death. To understand her story, the consequences of failed human-Cylon reconciliation on New Caprica are vital—and a comparison between her and Caprica Six provides answers.

The compassion we feel for Boomer makes her the ideal protagonist for our first real glimpse at the Cylon side of things in the already discussed episode "Downloaded" (2.18). Boomer bonds with Caprica Six who is established as a second sympathetic figure of the Cylon and together, they decide to change the Cylons' trajectory by proposing reconciliation with humans, which leads to the colonization of the newly established human settlement on New Caprica. After this experiment fails, Caprica Six is able to move past this disappointment while Boomer is not—here, their stories part ways. Both characters conducted a sinful act: Caprica Six bore much of the responsibility for the initial genocide, while Boomer almost killed Bill Adama and committed various severe acts of sabotage on Galactica. Overall, it would seem that Caprica Six is the bigger sinner—her act had harsher consequences and was successful, while Boomer's ultimately was not. Is it fair that Boomer becomes the fallen woman, while Caprica Six gets to be a hero?

When discussing Boomer, scholars have usually focused on her identity problems. Since she was unaware of her Cylon nature, George Dunn noted that Boomer does not have a purpose she can identify with—whatever she believed in was unmasked as programming (Dunn 2008, 131). Daniel Milsky further noted that Boomer lacks an intelligible life story or "emplotment," making it impossible for her to write a cohesive narrative for herself (Milsky 2008, 3–4). Heather Rolufs has compared Boomer to the Bible's Eve: She commits sins (acts of sabotage and finally an attempt on Adama's life) that end with her expulsion from "paradise" (human life on the Galactica), but like Eve she does not comprehend her own actions until after they are committed (Rolufs 2008, 350).

A comparison with her "better" self, Athena Sharon also comes natural. While Athena always knew she was a Cylon and could make her own decisions, Boomer was forced to develop a split identity: one of them is a human pilot, the other a Cylon agent. In addition, Athena's mission is to create life; Sharon's is to end it. The difference between Boomer and Athena is also obvious if we compare their behavior while imprisoned on Galactica: Boomer seems confused, frightened and

5. "Fallen" Women: Razors and Delusions

helpless, Athena self-contained, strong and confident. Athena chooses to side with the humans—Boomer never had any choice. Boomer's inferiority to Athena is also illustrated in her awkward contact with Hera. Forced to take care of her while the child is on the Cylon basestar, Boomer shows that she lacks any maternal skills whatsoever, which is clearly coded as negative. Finally, Gaius Baltar is able to calm down the child (3.11 "The Eye of Jupiter"). When Athena returns to the baseship to retrieve her daughter, Boomer even threatens Hera. Caprica Six—whom God had put in charge of protecting Hera—turns against Boomer and helps Athena escape. By turning against Hera, Boomer shows that she can no longer be trusted, that she has "turned to the dark side" (3.12 "Rapture").

The comparisons with Athena or Eve do not, however, explain why Boomer is not allowed full redemption (including entry into paradise). We always return to the problem that Boomer was initially an unwilling Cylon agent, while Caprica Six knowingly conducted genocide. A look at religious history can be helpful in understanding this seemingly unfair treatment. Scholars of the medieval Judas tradition have found that it was completely irrelevant to stories of sin and betrayal whether the guilty person acted consciously or accidentally—what mattered was how they reacted afterwards. Judas, constructed as the product of incest in medieval legends, does penance for his parents' sin by turning to Jesus and is thus redeemed (from a sin that from today's perspective is not actually his own). By turning against Jesus, Judas falls back to sin and is now unable to pull himself out of his desperation which finally leads to suicide. His real sin is not the betrayal as such—it is desperation which is, essentially, a lack of faith in God (Dieckmann 1991, 30–31). Against this background, the difference between Boomer and Caprice Six becomes clearer: Boomer despairs at her betrayals and failings, while Caprica Six can pull herself out through her faith. Boomer's real sin is her lack of belief in God. Like Judas, her "original" sin is not actually her own fault and she tries to repent by turning towards Cylon-human reconciliation. When this fails, she gives in to her desperation instead of trusting God. For this reason, she is never awarded full redemption, while Caprica Six is. Since she lacks faith and resigns to desperation, the series also forces Boomer to subordinate to patriarchy as represented by Cavil.

By the fourth season, Boomer has completely fallen from grace. She is in a relationship with the One Model Cavil (as we shall see, one of the big male evils), and has turned her back on the religious Cylons, including her fellow Eights. The abuse of her identity is staged in a way that reminds the viewer of patriarchal exploitation of women. Cavil refers to Boomer as "my pet Eight" who has "seen the light of reason" (4.09 "The Hub"). In this man's club, Boomer is on the lowest end of the hierarchy—she is told what to do and where to go and allows Cavil to make these decisions for her because she cannot deal with her emotional trauma. It is just easier to hate humans and take orders. She tells Ellen that Cavil is teaching her "to be a better machine, to let go of my human constructs."

Boomer has been exploited from the very beginning. Effectively, Cavil always held her in submission—he programmed her as a sleeper agent and is responsible for her split identity in the first place. Cavil stole Boomer's identity; he controlled her and took her freedom of choice. Afterwards, she fails to assert herself and finds it easier to adhere to exploitative structures: she "voluntarily" subjects herself to patriarchal control. As a victim, her portrayal especially reflects on the nature of the male Cylons (in particular Cavil) and the negative effects of patriarchal exploitation. Boomer's fall is never complete—she helps Ellen escape from the baseship and, as already stated, eventually turns against the male Cylons and hands Hera over to Athena: she puts the savior into the hands of a "better" version of herself, sacrifices her own existence in favor of a stronger, independent woman. As she understands it, this is the first choice she actually makes by herself (4.20 "Daybreak—Part II"). Athena nevertheless kills her, proving that full redemption is no longer possible for this particular fallen woman.

While Boomer has allowed herself to be restrained and subordinated, another "traitor" Cylon does the complete opposite and frees herself from all restraint and places herself above the social and moral norms of society. Tory Foster, who replaced Billy Keikeya as Laura Roslin's presidential aid after his death, was revealed as one of the Final Five in the finale of season three. When she believed herself to be human, she was—for the most part—a moral character, committed to her society's values. Although she rigged the presidential election in favor of Laura Roslin (which might be considered less than moral), she did so with explicit permission from the president or dying leader herself. Like Boomer, Tory experienced an identity crisis after she realized her true nature, but her crisis took a different turn. For Tory, this revelation freed her from the restraints of the norms of a society she was not a part of. Her "elevated" status amongst the Cylons as one of the Final Five fueled her delusions of grandeur. Her first "evil" act was to kill Tyrol's wife Cally who had found out about the Final Five (4.03 "The Ties That Bind"). Some people act morally only when confined by normative values, while their behavior can change radically once these confinements are lifted and this moral and social context is gone (Scarre 2010, 589). Tory is one such person. Although she claims to have killed Cally for the good of the Cylons, her motifs are ultimately self-serving, especially since she does not bother to ask anybody else for their opinion on the matter.

Tory convinces herself that guilt is unnecessary (4.04 "Escape Velocity") and becomes a "racial purist": For her, the survival of the 13th tribe "in its purest form" is the ultimate goal (4.16 "Deadlock"). She is finally killed in the series finale by Galen Tyrol after he finds out about Cally's murder (by the way, that's another two women dead). Unlike the other members of the Final Five, Tory feels that moral standards no longer apply to her—she understands herself to be better than humans. She does appropriate religion for herself at that juncture, in particular Baltar's monotheist message. However, she only accepts those elements of Cylon belief that suit her: the idea that, as a member of the Final Five, she is special, and that as God's creation she does not need guilt. While Boomer illustrates the danger of abandoning the self and subordinating it to patriarchal structures, Tory embodies the threat of elevating the self above and against the good of the community. Her arrogance and delusions of grandeur mark her actions as "evil" and prevent her entry into paradise. A very similar definition of (female) evil is found in *Caprica*.

A Virtual Heaven

Caprica is really all about dealing with death. We have seen that the creation of the Cylons was fundamentally connected to Daniel

Graystone's inability to let go of his dead daughter. After (apparently) failing to bring Zoe back, Daniel proceeds to develop his daughter's technology further and tries to market it on a commercial level. His pitch to potential investors begins with an alleged "cure for human grief"—a way of "resurrecting" deceased loved ones and avoiding the pain of their loss. Although Wetmore maintains that Daniel only proposes resurrection for those left behind—and thus no resurrection at all (Wetmore 2012, 182), the implications actually go further. Daniel states that his technology could "end death and disease" and "demolish our very conception of mortality" (1.14 "Blowback"). Since Daniel is a scientist, his ideas are "rational" and "scientific"—and connected to financial gain. This virtual solution to death that is suggested on the micro-level by Daniel Graystone is put on the macro-level by Clarice Willow, who introduces a religious dimension to the subject. She wants to create a virtual heaven based on Zoe's technology. In this heaven, the faithful would live eternally. With the help of technology, she proposes, God's promise of eternal life after death for the faithful (for which there is really no proof) can be made a measurable reality: "An afterlife that we can see and touch" (1.06 "Know Thy Enemy"). In this section, I will contrast Clarice and Daniel's use of Zoe's resurrection technology before I interpret Clarice as a "fallen" woman in the final section.

When Clarice speaks of "life everlasting" in virtual heaven, she refers to conventional Judeo-Christian ideas. Heaven as a physical space inhabited by God entered Judaism during the Second Temple period (6th century BCE to 70 CE), when the idea of a separate living space for the divine in Jewish thought emerged due to the growing distance people perceived between themselves and their God (much like the idea of angels as mediators; see Vorgrimler 2008, 83).[1] Of course images of celestial realms also existed in Ancient Near Eastern religions, but these realms where usually the domain of the gods and, with occasional exceptions, could not be accessed by humans. Instead, humans went to the netherworld after death. Only the Egyptians imagined heavenly spheres that were approachable for humans after death, an idea that would later dominate Judeo-Christian thought. However, access to the dwelling place of the gods was not granted for the morally righteous, but could be achieved by performing the proper rites (Wright 2000,

5. "Fallen" Women: Razors and Delusions

16–19, 24–25, 50–51). Judaism first adopted the general Near Eastern idea that understood heaven only as a dwelling place for God, whereas deceased humans went to Sheol, the netherworld, from which there was no return (Wright 2000, 96–97). Sheol later developed into an intermediary stage where the dead waited for the last judgment (Vorgrimler 2008, 88–89; Jezler and Altendorf 1994, 41). Another influence came from the Greco-Roman world with their visions of Hades and Elysium. In late antiquity, interest in the concept of celestial realms increased in all of these cultures, which some scholars proposed to be a result of the imperial structures of that time: individuals felt lost and unguarded in these systems (Boustan, Reed 2009, 3). Regardless of whether this was the case for all authors, it is clear that the Judeo-Christian view of heaven was the product of this time.

The connection between heaven and resurrection (strongly employed in *Caprica*) is one case in point. Although individual or collective resurrection was untypical for Jewish thought, the rise of apocalypticism from the fourth century BCE onwards gave birth to the idea that God would reward the righteous by accommodating them in his residence, a thought that was probably also influenced by Zoroastrian ideas. The only apocalyptic text included in the Hebrew Bible, the book of Daniel, hints at this idea of resurrection: "Many of those who sleep in the dust of the ground will awake, these to everlasting life, but the others to disgrace and everlasting contempt" (Daniel 12: 2–3). Christianity further developed the idea of resurrection for the righteous and the reward in heaven, a place that was seen as any Christian's true home (Vorgrimler 2008, 125, 141). In heaven, Christians would dwell with Christ and, in a way, become one with him.

Clarice employs the notion of resurrection as reward for the righteous when she introduces her idea of an artificially created heaven. She proposes her plan to the monotheist leaders through the holoband that provides access to the virtual world (and was invented by Daniel), showing a terrorist attack on a stadium that would lead to the resurrection of the chosen few—the monotheist suicide bombers. Like Daniel, she announces that this technology would conquer death and lead to eternal life. However, her proposal has a strongly religious tone. The chosen few would be transferred to heaven, while the others would simply die. After seeing that heaven is a real place and eternal life is an achievable reality, many people would convert to the monotheist religion. Clarice paradoxically employs the enlightenment ideal of reason and the superiority of science for religious ends when she states that "myth and mystery have been replaced by reason, science." She calls this "a religion of certainty," and refers to it as apotheosis—the process of becoming God-like (1.10 "Unvanquished"). There is no hell in this notion (just like there are no demons)—life on earth and inevitable death are the punishment for "the others" as the book of Daniel calls them.

Obviously, Clarice is taking the Judeo-Christian idea of heaven and resurrection to a new level—she does so by incorporating posthumanist concepts. What looks like futuristic science fiction has actually been a scientific discussion for many years now. Whether you can "upload" a person into a computer—be it a robot or a virtual presence—and thus release them from mortality is one of the linchpins of posthuman thinking. The question is, whether the uploaded person would be the same as the original. Some would argue that this is the case, because all of the relevant information persists—and humans are really no more than data. Others interject that something essential would be missing—and explicitly call this a soul (Walker 2011). And a soul clearly cannot be uploaded. *Caprica* reflects the discussion very clearly. When Daniel introduces Joseph Adama to Zoe-A, he exclaims: "Who's to say that her soul wasn't copied, too?" Adama replies: "You can't copy a soul." This is really the essence of posthumanist debate. And when Leoben asks in *BSG*, "What if God decided to give souls to another creature" (*BSG Miniseries*), he also hints at an actual discussion within this ideology: some argue that machines might have souls, although these souls could not have been "copied" from humans.[2]

Most posthumanists would not be pleased to be called religious, although their ideology is clearly influenced by Christological motives. Yet they still employ the concept of the soul quite frequently. Likewise Daniel Graystone appropriates Zoe's technology in a clearly posthumanist manner. He does not openly believe in God or the gods and consequently does not see that kind of technology as a blasphemy. This does not, however, preclude him from discussing the idea of a soul—and the possibility of copying a soul. Seeing as most posthumanists are indeed male, Daniel embodies this ideology quite nicely. Clarice, on the other hand, is a posthumanist with a clearly religious agenda. According to her interpretation, Zoe's technology is divinely inspired, and her goal is to create a heaven—albeit one that is more scientifically viable. I discuss the differences between the male and female use of technology in *Caprica* more fully in my article "Masters of Cyber-Religion" (Wimmler 2014), but we can already see a clear difference here, though the series constructs neither Daniel's nor Clarice's approach as positive.

Caprica delves deeper into the problem of uploading, both from a scientific and a moral perspective. Clarice's husband reflects on both when he points out the flaws in Clarice's plan to open up virtual heaven to the martyrs: "They're not actually going to heaven, their scanned avatars are. And with the push of a button I could transfer them right now. The death of the original, it's just showmanship. It's totally irrelevant" (1.16 "The Heavens Will Rise"). The issue is whether uploading is simply a copying process or an actual transfer. The answer given by the series is by no means simple, but it could be summed up as follows: an avatar is distinct from the original—the original's death is consequently final, and they do not continue to live in the virtual world. Instead, a conscious copy (quite possibly infused with a soul) can be created who might believe they are the original. In any case, this being would be sentient. This is partially a blow for posthumanists, as it implies that we (humans) cannot cheat death. On the other hand, this thinking reinforces the idea that machines can be persons. *Caprica* discusses what Mark Walker calls the "no-branching" argument (Walker 2011). In this argument, the possibility of uploading a person more than once—as well as the possibility of retaining the original while simultaneously uploading—are taken as evidence that the uploaded person is not the original: If there can be two of me at the same time, then clearly the scan is just a copy. At least this is how Clarice's husband sees things. For Clarice, however, there's always the dimension of faith that needs no scientific explanation.

The image of heavenly life as corporeal reinforces its Judeo-Christian background: Heaven is not, as some posthumanists (and sci-fi texts) would have it, a place of immaterial existence and disintegration in the digital code. Souls or code do not merge into one—they remain separate, embodied beings. The "scanned avatars" are identical to the originals not only in essence, but in form: they appear in heaven in a digital version of their real-life bodies. While Clarice tells us that everyone would be able to create their own version of heaven after their initial arrival (effectively producing several separate heavens), she never suggests that heavenly existence would not be embodied. We have already discussed that the body is central for the process of resurrection as understood by Christians, who only adopted the concept of an immortal soul gradually from Greek philosophy. Even then, the soul was only allowed to accompany the body to the next world—without the body, the soul was nothing.

In this, the early Church differed markedly from the Gnostics who saw the body as the evil prison of the immortal soul. This is one of the issues where the similarities between Gnosticism and posthumanism become evident, and where the series tend to favor the traditional Judeo-Christian interpretation. Clarice also insists on the importance of corporeality, although she goes into a slightly different direction with the destruction of the original body and the creation of a completely new one in heaven. We have seen that a similar idea of resurrection was put forth in *BSG*, where new bodies always accompanied the process (e.g., Starbuck, or the Cylons). In both series, the original body is not important, but corporeality surely is.

Clarice's proposal for virtual heaven is clearly understood as blasphemy by the monotheist leadership, though their interventions remain fruitless due to the strong support Clarice enjoys within the movement. In the end, Zoe-A frustrates Clarice's plans and destroys virtual heaven for moral reasons: "If people think they'll go to heaven no matter what, they're gonna lose control over themselves" (1.18 "Apotheosis"). In her (and the show's) opinion, heaven needs to remain mysterious and based on faith instead of a scientific reality in order for it to work as a motor for moral behavior in this world. Again, we can draw a clear parallel to the Judeo-Christian tradition. We have seen that antique concepts of heavenly realms or netherworlds usually had nothing to do with righteousness and wickedness. Yet the idea of punishment and reward became closely connected to this concept in Judeo-Christian thought. To quote Wright, the goal behind it was "to inspire people to live an ethical or moral life" (Wright 2000, 183). Clarice's heaven does not do that anymore. Zoe-A finds her purpose in destroying Clarice's vision—

a vision that is not only considered blasphemous, but also morally unsustainable and scientifically flawed.

Another issue that can be raised concerning Clarice's plan is that of judgment: who decides who the chosen ones are? In the traditional Christian concept, the ascent to heaven is preceded by the divine judgment, imagined as a sort of middle station between earth and heaven (or, alternatively, earth and hell). Clarice's proposal erases the need for divine judgment or, even more problematic, places it in her own hands. Where Christ judges the worthiness of Christians, Clarice decides who is worthy to be uploaded and thus effectively turns herself into the messiah whose job is both salvation and judgment. Incidentally, this is also one of the most critical issues with both the posthuman concept of uploading and Daniel's proposal: this process is a question of access to technology, which in turn is a question of money. Whoever controls the technology controls who is chosen for eternal life. In the end, Clarice's appropriation of Zoe's technology for religious reasons is as misguided as Daniels' for financial gain. This mostly stems from Clarice's dubious moral status as a "fallen" woman, which we will now explore.

Clarice and the Messiah Complex

In *Caprica*, Clarice Willow is portrayed as the most prominent foe of our "chosen" women, the two Zoes and Lacy Rand. Clarice believes herself to be in a special relationship with God. She proclaims that God has chosen her to change the world and bring salvation to such an extent that some insinuate a "messiah complex" (1.10 "Unvanquished"). As mentioned in the introduction to this chapter, Christian tradition sees pride and lust for the forbidden as the origin of human sin and evil. Clarice certainly fits those categories. She attempts to build a virtual heaven, because salvation should be touchable and not filled with uncertainty. By doing that, she turns herself into a god, and very consciously so. As Wetmore observes, Clarice uses religion for power (Wetmore 2012, 179). Is she, then, simply a villain?

The character of Clarice Willow stands in a long tradition of female evil in religious history. Quite frequently, independent and powerful women were accorded a low moral character in order to show that women could not handle power, which effectively justified their subjugation. Feminist theologians of both Christianity and Judaism (certainly also Islam) have tried to rescue many of the women found in scripture from this patriarchal interpretation. They have re-assessed what "evil" means in this context and why certain women were perceived as such at all. Most of the time, they found that these were simply independent women who refused to adapt to the patriarchal order and escaped male control. The stories of evil women thus frequently re-affirmed a traditional gender hierarchy. However, scholars also cautioned against seeing all women as suppressed victims of patriarchal structures and thus as ultimately "good" (Bieberstein 2005, 8–9).

Clarice is the personification of biblical stereotypes of women: she is promiscuous and deceitful, dangerously calculating and murderous, proud and self-involved. She stylizes herself as a prophet-messiah but, unlike Kara or Laura, is not actually either. She leads believers out of conviction but also out of selfishness, she is a learned woman who attempts to use education for her blasphemous goals. Clarice's case is nevertheless different from biblical precedent, because she does not exist in a patriarchal world. She is not confined by men, but by other independent and powerful women. In biblical stories, "evil" women are usually pitted against heroic men who have to keep female immorality at bay. Yet on *Caprica*, this job falls to women: the Zoes and Lacy need to contain female monstrosity: they decide how far female power can go and when it needs to be checked. As we will see in this section, this changes the role of the "evil" woman considerably.

Sister Clarice Willow is first introduced to us as the headmistress of Zoe and Lacy's school and an Athenian High priestess. Clarice masquerades as a polytheist, but is in fact not only a monotheist, but also the leader of several STO terrorist cells. She lives in a group marriage that seems to be an accepted practice within the polytheistic as well as (obviously) the monotheistic religion. Her family is portrayed as rather loving and comfortable, and aware of Clarice's involvement with the STO, although some are more involved than others. Two of her husbands act as her "lieutenants" in a way and follow her orders, while her wives and other husbands seem to be more detached from these activities. In her position as headmistress, she recruits teenagers for the

5. "Fallen" Women: Razors and Delusions

STO and plans terrorist attacks. Clarice sees Zoe Graystone as a savior, the "mother of life everlasting" because of her resurrection program, which she is nevertheless unable to get her hands on during Zoe's lifetime. Clarice's evil is a misappropriation of science, which she uses to blaspheme.

She constructs herself as a kind of savior, or at least a religious figure in an attempt to justify her violence. As one of the monotheist leaders (who would shortly after be dead) tells her: "You're not a religious leader, you're STO. Technically a terrorist" (1.10 "Unvanquished"). Her "evil" nature is also confirmed by her actions against Lacy, whom she locks up in her attic as a punishment for her allegiance to the competing terrorist leader Barnabas (1.12 "Things We Lock Away"). She later sends Lacy to the STO training camp on Gemenon. Significantly, Lacy does not object to her presence in the training camp—as discussed, she eventually becomes the supreme monotheist leader. However, Clarice's methods are clearly evil in Lacy's (and our) eyes. Like Clarice, Lacy is a believer and even a terrorist—but her morals are stable and she is neither narcissistic nor overly fond of violence (Wetmore 2012, 184–185 comes to a similar conclusion). Clarice and Lacy are two sides of a coin: one has to be stopped, the other put in charge.

Through Zoe-A, we learn that the original Zoe did not trust Clarice. Quite likely, she suspected that Clarice's plans with her technology were unsavory. It is difficult to ascertain what religious role Clarice ascribes to herself. Possibly, she sees herself as a prophet or an executor of God's will. On the one hand, her messiah is clearly Zoe, because "she was the one who talked to angels" (1.17 "Here be Dragons"), and she states that God speaks to her through Zoe and her mother Amanda Graystone (1.07 "The Imperfections of Memory"). On the other hand, she wishes for a statue of herself to be erected in the entrance hall of virtual heaven, while she says nothing of a statue for either Zoe or Amanda (1.15 "The Dirteaters"). When a monotheist council member asks whether she wants to serve God or BE God, this question is certainly apropos.

Clarice is ruthless when it comes to religion and does not shy away from murder to accomplish her goals. She goes so far as to murder her own wife who had just given birth when she suspects her to be an informant for the police. Clarice sees the murder as a necessity, though she never revels in this action. The murder of the "good woman" is tragic because it turns out to be completely unjustified—Amanda Graystone is the real police informant. After realizing her mistake, Clarice is truly distraught. While she would do anything for her faith, she is not without conscience. She is a murderer with a clear motif, and not one without cause. Even in the other acts of murder Clarice commits—notably that of several of her young followers who had allied with Barnabas and of course the murder of Barnabas himself—she is never portrayed as a psychopathic serial killer who enjoys killing. Rather, she is a leader of a fundamentalist religious group seeking to maintain order in her cell. Her actions (though we do not condone them) are at least comprehensible.

Clarice is thus not personified or absolute evil. We learn much about her background in the course of the series that helps us comprehend her personality. Clarice was recruited for the STO at a rather young age, which raises questions of brainwashing or at least negative socialization. On top of that, she is a drug addict, though the series never puts her over the edge. We should also note that Clarice clearly has a place in God's plan that is unrivalled by characters such as Barnabas. Her actions might be morally questionable, but she serves an important function that cannot be easily explained away as purely "evil." It has even been suggested by fans that the final showdown with Zoe-A changed Clarice's faith, because she had not anticipated a confrontation with her "messiah."[3] This may or may not be the case—since the series was cancelled after one season, we cannot be certain of Clarice's path in the future, which might very well have included redemption. Significantly, Zoe-A only foils her plans for virtual heaven, but does not kill her—while the fate of *BSG*'s prime male villain (the unreligious Cavil) is destruction, Clarice gets to live. In this, her fate is also rather different from the powerful women in Judeo-Christian scripture, who are usually killed by men (Müllner 2005, 37).

The last episode (1.18 "Apotheosis") includes an extended "flash forward," which shows Clarice preaching to the Centurions. She then visits the new mother on Gemenon to plead for her support for the "differently sentient," which also brings her into a submissive position vis a vis Lacy (now the new "mother"). Clarice preaches to the Cylons that they are sentient, that they are God's children, and not humanity's

5. "Fallen" Women: Razors and Delusions

servants. She prophesies that there will be a savior and that the Cylons will rise up against humans in an act of revenge. In the grand scheme of things, Clarice is the preacher who frees the Cylon mind and initiates their rebellion—a rebellion that was necessary and wanted by God. It is impossible to assess whether her intentions were pure or tinged by some ulterior motif. However, Clarice clearly represents interests that are coded "positive" in the series when she defends the rights of the enslaved machines. Her (and the show's) posthuman ideology shines through rather clearly: sentient beings can be artificial.

It seems to me that Clarice is in many ways reminiscent of Baltar, who also occupies a position in between good and evil, divine election and insanity. But unlike Baltar, Clarice does not have to renounce technology in order to embrace her religious destiny. In fact, her allegiance to technology makes her religiously relevant: she recognizes machines as divine creations. Though this is also true of Baltar, his reasoning is exclusively scientific, while hers is also religious. Significantly, Clarice is the only religious female whose morality is instable in the entire *Battlestarverse*. Belief usually codes women in a positive way in both series, while morally problematic characters such as Helena Cain or Kendra Shaw mostly come without religious conviction. This is where men and women differ in both series. Female religiosity is usually "good," while male religiosity is either "bad" or simply non-existent. Overall, men simply do not believe. Her religious belief rescues Clarice from being a completely negative character altogether.

In the same manner as feminist bible scholars have cautioned against re-interpreting all women in scripture as originally "good," we also need to be careful about rescuing Clarice from her "evil." She is certainly portrayed as a villain, though arguably a more nuanced one than Cavil, as we shall see in the next chapter. Yet her moral failings are not put in the service of patriarchy and do not reflect on the general immorality of women as such or the danger of female power and independence. Instead, she shows that women are not born moral and that belief does not guarantee ethical behavior, while simultaneously confirming the superior morality and power of other women. The men she struggles with are not morally superior—in fact, quite the opposite (e.g., Barnabas). If they are, they are too weak to stand up to her (e.g., her husband who questions her plans for virtual heaven).

Clarice only bows to women and in the end, only women can contain her. Clarice also illustrates that sometimes, the right thing can be achieved by the wrong people and (possibly) through the wrong means: she effectively liberates the Cylons from slavery, which in theory is portrayed as a positive action. In practice, the violent nature of this liberation might be a result of Clarice's character, though the series is not clear on this issue. Paradoxically, Clarice supports the same religious worldview as the heroes—effectively, this is a struggle for the correct interpretation of God's word. It can also be argued that Clarice is another "masculinized woman," as she is calculating, violent and appropriates female reproductive technology in an inmoral way (see Wimmler 2014, 140, 154). As was the case in *BSG*, her masculinity needs to be curtailed in favor of more feminine "submission"—the intriguing point being that she needs to submit to (more feminine) women. In the end, Clarice is certainly an ambivalent villain, but a villain nonetheless—a female one that is defeated by female heroes.

We have seen in this chapter that religious "evil" women are rather rare in the *Battlestarverse*. "Evil" or rather "fallen" women are usually not connected to religion at all. The big exception here is Clarice (on a smaller scale, maybe also Tory), who navigates between the religious and technological spheres for "bad" purposes. She instrumentalizes both religion and science, and yet never seems false in doing either. There can be no doubt that Clarice is a true believer as well as technologically apt, although she certainly displays an unhealthy amount of narcissism when it comes to her own role in God's plan. Still, her shock at being opposed by her messiah, Zoe-A, is genuine. To support my argument that Clarice is an exception that confirms the rule, I will discuss the men and their relationship with the divine and the artificial in the following chapters.

6

Men Without God(s)

It would be a complete misrepresentation of both *BSG* and *Caprica* to state that there are no good men in these narratives. In fact, we find many highly moral male characters whose heroics we can admire. However, only very few of them are religious, and even fewer have a religious function within the narrative. Compared to women, men are surprisingly "secular." This corresponds to the connection between masculinity and rationality as opposed to femininity and irrationality, emotion, and religion. Enlightenment thought created a causal connection not only between men and rationality, but by extension also between men and morality, because morality was understood to be derived through rational means (Seidler 1996, 111). Rational morality was supported by objective science, and emotion was considered as the source of irrationality which in turn led to faulty morals. We have already seen that *BSG* and *Caprica* breech this connection by combining "objective" science and "irrational" religion in the feminine and coding this connection as "correct." Following enlightenment logic, men would have to be connected to science, rationality, and consequently morality. Yet the series breech this connection as well, as we shall see.

While characters are generally depicted very balanced and realistically—and can thus hardly be described as completely good or completely evil—we can definitely distinguish roughly between heroes and villains in both narratives. We have already seen that women can be either, and the same is true for men. In this chapter, I will deal with male heroes and villains who do not believe in God or the gods, but are instead thoroughly secularized. I will discuss their morality or immorality and the categorization of good and evil as depicted by these characters. I will start with human heroes, focusing on the examples of Bill Adama and Karl Agathon, and then move to the depiction of idealists, namely Lee Adama, Tom Zarek, and Felix Gaeta. The third section will discuss the atheism of the Cylon Cavil, while the last section will look at the leading men in *Caprica*. In the end, we will be able to conclude on these men's relationship towards religion and technology.

Humanity, Morality, Masculinity

As a responsible Battleship commander, Bill Adama is a natural candidate for heroics. He has to deal with an impossible situation and manages to lead his people out of it. He is nevertheless not perfect. In *Miniseries*, his strained relationship with his son introduces us to some of his flaws as a father, while the first season frequently puts him in disagreement with the civilian government (and Laura Roslin), which he does not always respect. Especially when seen in comparison with Admiral Cain, it is clear that in deciding to accept this government and to not impose martial law he is showing considerable restraint. Based on George Lakoff's family models, Sara Livingston has described Adama's leadership as the "nurturing parent" style, while Cain represents the "strict father" style (Livingston 2008, 144–146). In contrast to Cain, he represents the ideal of leadership that is not authoritative and does not cross the line, although he admittedly comes close at times. As Roz Kaveney pointed out, Adama is not a chosen leader like Roslin, but "a man at the head of a structure" (Kaveney 2010, 121)—a structure that might be strongly familial, but hierarchically organized nonetheless.

Adama initially has no regard whatsoever for religion. In *Miniseries*, he proposes to the demoralized human fleet that he knows the way to the mythical planet Earth mentioned in the scriptures, but quickly confesses to Laura that he has absolutely no idea where it is (or if it even exists). Adama himself remains a realist suspicious of irrational belief. When Roslin wants to send Starbuck back to Caprica to retrieve the Arrow of Apollo, Adama refuses and tells her that he does not want to mock her faith, but "these stories about Kobol, gods, the Arrow of Apollo—they're just stories, legends, myths. Don't let it blind you to the reality that we face" (1.12 "Kobol's Last Gleaming—Part I"). Especially the last sentence sounds rather patronizing: the notion that the scriptures might offer concrete advice for current life or death decisions seems ridiculous to him.

How can we read Adama's attitude to faith? After all, it was Adama who set the survivors of the 12 colonies on their path to mythical Earth described in the scriptures. Adama instrumentalizes religion—he uses it to give his people hope and purpose. He acknowledges the power of faith and respects religion as long as it either remains a personal affair or serves "real life" politics. He sees religion as *Schwärmerei*[1]–something that is opposed to reason but may be espoused in private for sentimental purposes. He does not propose that religion needs to be abandoned altogether, but sees its sole function in maintaining order in the population. The political and military structures, on the other hand, should ideally remain free of religious influence.

In a similar manner, American revolutionaries like John Adams or Thomas Paine saw religion as important in mobilizing political enthusiasm, while at the same time seeking to limit the influence of clergy and theologians on state matters (Kelleter 2002, 451, 454–455). Adama himself is not a believer: he does not believe in the truth of the scriptures or the existence of Earth. He tries to remain diplomatic and politically correct when talking to Laura, but he would never order a military operation based on religious goals and ideas. On the other hand, he will certainly use religious myths to support military strategy if the situation calls for it. The series illustrates the potential conflict in this outward "marriage" of religion and politics: Adama's religious rhetoric ends up having a life of its own. The myth of Earth that he had instrumentalized in order to provide hope becomes an actual religious quest that influences political decisions.

Yet the narrative has Adama's secularism exposed as "incorrect" in the end and Adama is eventually reformed by the dyeing leader. When Laura decides to go back to Kobol to find the Tomb of Athena, she invites the other ships to accompany her. Adama is sure that nobody will and describes her appeal as "religious crap" (2.05 "The Farm"). Of course one third of the fleet (24 ships or 18,000 people) end up following

Roslin. In a way, rational masculinity is defeated by this third of the fleet that chooses to follow irrational religion. Adama has to recognize that a large number of humans believe in Laura Roslin as their chosen leader. Whatever he may believe, he is responsible for all of these people. Since he is a good leader, he decides not to abandon these 18,000 people after all, no matter how irrational their cause seems to be. He concludes that staying together is more important than winning an argument.

Of course there is something else going on here, namely Adama's relationship with Laura Roslin. In the course of the series, Laura turns Adama into a believer. His faith is first in Laura (who insists on her religious role), and finally also in a higher purpose. When Laura and Bill meet again on Kobol, he tells her that every day since the attacks has been a gift. When Laura adds "from the gods," Bill interjects, "No. From you" (2.07 "Home—Part II"). In his opinion, it is not the gods who are responsible for the survival of the human race, but Laura. Since he believes in her, he will eventually believe in her cause—he consequently tells Laura, "You made me believe" (4.06 "Faith"). It is through a woman that Bill finds his way to the gods, though his belief is never as obvious. It is also completely irrelevant for the story whether he believes in the gods or not, as long as he believes in Laura (and does not get in her way).

We should also note that Bill Adama is often led by emotion rather than reason. His feelings for his son and "adoptive daughter" Kara quite frequently lead to "unreasonable" behavior on his part. Particularly noteworthy in this regard is the episode "You Can't Go Home Again" (1.05), where Bill and Lee Adama are prepared to risk everything to rescue Kara until Laura Roslin points out their foolish behavior. Bill Adama also shows emotional distress in several other situations. His despair at finding out about Boomer's real identity is later multiplied when his first officer and best friend Saul Tigh turns out to be one of the Final Five, at which point we even see Adama crying heavily in his son's arms. He is also emotionally attached to his ship, as evidenced towards the end of the series when the Galactica begins to fall apart. Although he is otherwise a rational military man, his emotions actually affirm his heroism when compared to the cold Admiral Cain, and also guarantee eventual support for Laura Roslin's religious journey.

6. Men Without God(s)

Bill Adama's emotional connection to his antiquated ship opens him up to nostalgia for a bygone era. Initially, he absolutely refuses advanced technologies on his ship for the very good reason that the Cylons might be able to hack it. Things have changed by the end of the series, when he reluctantly accepts Cylon technology in order to save the Galactica from breaking apart. However, this attempt of rescuing nostalgic, antiquated technology with an "update" is eventually abandoned in favor of complete destruction. Overall, Bill Adama remains uncomfortable with advanced technology, so the series' ending with its return to a "traditional" way of life clearly suits the character more than an enhanced Galactica.

The second moral male we should consider is Karl Agathon, also known as Helo. Married to a Cylon and father of the first (and to our knowledge only) hybrid baby, he is necessarily an advocate of hybridization. While his personality originally depends on his relationship to his wife and daughter, season three also establishes him as a highly moral man outside of these relationships. In "A Measure of Salvation" (3.07), the humans have the possibility to wipe out the Cylon race with a virus, which both Laura Roslin and Lee Adama are in favor of. Helo calls this "a crime against humanity." When his plea falls on deaf ears, Helo manipulates Roslin's plan. Interestingly, both Lee Adama and Laura Roslin are usually seen as moral pillars of the show. Neither, admittedly, has ever had much appreciation for the Cylons. That's why they need someone with an in-between status to do the right thing that they are unable to conceive of at the moment. Helo's position as a defender of human or Cylon rights is confirmed in the episode "The Woman King" (3.14). In this case, Helo is confronted with a genocidal doctor; this time the victims are not Cylons, but humans deemed "unworthy" of saving. Initially, nobody believes Helo's suspicion, but he continues his investigation and finally proves the doctor's guilt. Helo is the advocate of equality and moral behavior not only towards those belonging to the same community, but especially towards outsiders and others. To him, genocide is always wrong, and every sentient being has a right to live.

Unlike his wife Athena, Helo does not seem to have any religious belief—or if he does, he does not show or discuss it. Helo is, for the most part, motivated by his love for his wife and daughter and his understanding of right and wrong. Religion does not seem to play any role for him. Neither is he particularly associated with technology—except, of course, that he is married to a machine. His wife Athena, on the other hand, is more strongly associated with both religion and technology. When the Galactica is hit by a Cylon "logic bomb," for example, she connects her body to the ship's wires to stop the virus (2.09 "Flight of the Phoenix"), illustrating this overt bodily connection. She is also seen resurrecting and dealing with machines on various occasions, and illustrates in-depth knowledge of human scripture and faith in the Cylon God, as we saw in chapter two. Bill Adama likewise lacks both—he can even be described as a thorough technophobe, because he does not allow enhanced technology on his ship. Men tend to lack both the connection to religion and to technology.

The general morality of Galactica's men is confirmed through the comparison with Pegasus, which we have already met as a negative mirror for the Galactica. The crew's distorted idea of right and wrong becomes more than obvious with the attempted rape of Galactica's Cylon prisoner Sharon (mother of Hera). When some of the Pegasus crew brag about their repeated rapes of their own Cylon prisoner, the Galactica crew is clearly offended and disgusted. When they discover that the Pegasus' Cylon investigator Lieutenant Thorne is about to do the same to Sharon, Tyrol and Helo rush to save her, accidentally killing Thorne in the process. Cain court-marshals them and plans to have them executed, which almost leads to a battle between the Galactica and the Pegasus. In the meantime, some of the Pegasus crew beat Tyrol and Helo until Colonel Fisk intervenes. When Tyrol and Helo thank him and then defend their actions against Thorne, Fisk simply states: "You can't rape a machine." Of course the episode illustrates that rape says nothing about the victim, and everything about the offender. Whether Cylons are really people is insignificant in this case—the action itself is evil. Corrupted morality goes as far up as Fisk, who is otherwise portrayed as one of the most uncorrupted Pegasus crew members. The failure of the Pegasus crew to see the evil of rape as well as the personhood of the Cylons marks their faulty morality, and confirms the heroism of Helo and Tyrol.

It is noteworthy that the *BSG* military—both male and female—is largely decoupled from advanced technology. According to scholarship on the connection between war and masculinity, one of the typically "masculine" traits of war is "technological mastery, excitement operating machines" (Hutchings 2008, 393). While the *BSG* military is strongly coded male in any other way, this lack of a connection to advanced technology is noteworthy. The only male Galactica crew member to be associated with technology is Gaeta, and he is morally problematic, as we shall see shortly. Good men like Bill Adama and Karl Agathon are dissociated from technology, even display a certain amount of technophobia. While technology as "mastery of nature" is coded male in "our" world (Döge 2001, 128), men in the *Battlestarverse* shy away from it. Of course there is something "primal" about the kind of technology that is used on the Galactica. It's old technology, evocative of early 20th century military equipment, indicating a certain nostalgia for bygone markers of masculinity. "New" technologies and technological advancements—that's clearly the domain of the feminine. Does this theory hold up when we look at other male characters on the show? Let's turn to the idealists and see.

Being an Idealist

From the very beginning, *BSG* plays with the image of the idealist—the man who believes strongly that the world should be a certain way and will do anything to support this belief. While the idealist was a typical character in modernist narratives (including sci-fi), the postmodernist worldview criticizes idealism as it does any ideology that imposes a monolithic explanation of the world. Idealism is indeed a marker of modernity and now seems as naive as the grand narrative that proposes that the complex world we live in follows a simple pattern. This is the case because idealism requires the reduction of complexity into simplicity.[2] It should not surprise us then, that idealism and rationalism are critiqued at the same time, as they are both expressions of the modern. The postmodern popular culture text tends to be filled with ambiguities and bereft of easy answers to complicated questions. *BSG* is one such text, as can be shown clearly by the way it handles the issue of idealism. However, the text once again does not abandon the notion completely. By confronting the "good" idealist Lee Adama with the "bad" idealists Felix Gaeta and Tom Zarek, we will find that the series' paradoxically couples its critical attitude to easy answers with a remnant of modernist hope regarding the integrity of morals.

As is the case with many other moral males, Lee Adama's faith is never actually an issue. He has an exceptionally strong moral compass and stands up for what he believes is right—without being compelled to do so by his faith. Yet the series suggests that characters like that are rather rare by confronting Lee with other, less morally stable idealists, namely Tom Zarek and Felix Gaeta. This section thus explicitly explores the series' depiction of non-religious idealism. We are first introduced to the difficult position that idealists can be put in, when Lee Adama supports president Roslin's authority over that of his father in *Miniseries*. Lee believes that the military must always bow to the political leadership and considers Laura the lawful president. Essentially, this is a matter of principle, though Lee also finds that Laura is competent to fill the position. The decision in favor of Laura and against his father and the military is thus a comparatively easy one that does not put Lee's principles (and thus idealism as such) into question. In the course of the story, things will get more complicated.

It does not take long for the series to attack Lee's high regard for principles. In the episode 1.03 "Bastille Day," we meet political idealist Tom Zarek for the first time. In this episode, the fleet has to deal with an imminent water shortage (a result of Boomer sabotaging the water supply). Although water has been found, mining it would be extremely dangerous—which is why some propose that the inmates of the prison transporter The *Astral Queen* should be allowed to exchange their labor for "freedom points," eventually leading to their release. However, the prisoners are united under one of the inmates, Tom Zarek, who refuses the offer on their behalf. While some refer to him as a terrorist, others interpret Zarek as a prisoner of conscience, because he tried to stop his planet Sagittaran from being exploited by the other colonies.

Despite the fact that Zarek's appearance in this episode introduces us to some aspects of the colonies' historical and political controversies, it is also noteworthy that from the very beginning Zarek is paired with the other major idealist of the show, Lee Adama. Lee decides to approach Zarek to convince the other prisoners to help the fleet. Zarek confronts Lee with some of his political ideologies, for example by referring to Lee as a "master" and himself as a "slave," highlighting the exploitative nature of the prison system. Lee in turn reveals that he had actually read Zarek's (prohibited) book as a college student and agreed with many of this assertions. Yet it is easier to have principles than to survive in a harsh reality based on these principles. Tom Zarek and Lee Adama differ in this regard: Lee is also a realist. In contrast to Zarek, Lee understands the reality of the situation: the remainder of humanity is running out of water and will soon start dying. This situation does not call for idealism.

Zarek refuses the offer to earn freedom points based on a matter of principle, which has nothing to do with the harsh reality. After taking over control of the *Astral Queen* (and holding several Galactica crew members prisoner), Zarek demands the resignation of the "illegitimate" government and free elections. As Lee later points out, these demands are not unreasonable—they actually make a lot of sense if you subtract the rhetorical tone of the request. Lee will later promise free democratic elections and will hold Laura Roslin to this promise. In addition, Lee will not allow Zarek to be killed and turned into a martyr. He knows that Zarek is right in theory, but questions his methods as well as his intentions. Lee knows that extortion and terrorism are not the right way to go. At the end of the episode, Lee's pragmatic idealism wins over Zarek's radical idealism.

Yet Zarek's story is far from over. He later becomes a rather important political figure, first representing the people of Sagittaran, then becoming vice-president under Gaius Baltar and finally—for a very short time—president himself before power is returned to Laura Roslin. Because of his ideology, Zarek originally chooses Baltar as a presidential candidate in order to destabilize Roslin's popularity and authority. He is an idealist who will use any advantage to achieve his goals—even if this means teaming up with someone like Baltar. He later realizes that this was a mistake. We don't know exactly how it happens, but in the beginning of season three, during the Cylon occupation of New Caprica, Laura and Tom find themselves on the same prison transport, and on the same kill-list. Tom Zarek could not in good conscience support the Cylon occupation, and was prepared to die for that belief. He later voluntarily turns over power to Laura, but not before signing a very questionable executive order.

Again, this is something Lee Adama never would have done. Had he known about it, he would have stopped it. Zarek's executive order legalizes the activities of "the Circle"—a group of a few former resistance fighters who hold secret trials to determine who collaborated with the Cylons during the occupation and after the (very likely) guilty verdict murder them by throwing them out of air locks. Zarek proposes that this way, Laura Roslin can "come into office clean"—Zarek would do her dirty work (3.05 "Collaborators"). Of course this is not Laura's way; reminiscent of Nelson Mandela's policies in South Africa, she instead implements a Truth and Reconciliation Commission and issues a general pardon. Since Zarek is zealous in his idealism, and is willing to sacrifice many other moral values for his ideology, he will not find a very happy ending. Neither will Felix Gaeta.

Comparing Lee Adama to Felix Gaeta is illuminating, as these two characters are remarkably similar on the outside. Felix is an idealist who always does what he believes to be right. However, his knowledge of human nature leaves something to be desired, and this also clouds his moral compass. He is an enthusiastic follower of Gaius Baltar, for example, and becomes his aid when Baltar wins the presidential election. While other, more heroic characters can see very clearly that Baltar is not fit for the job, Felix cannot. During the Cylon occupation, he becomes a source of information for the resistance in an attempt to compensate for his involvement in Baltar's election. In the midst of human rebellion on New Caprica, he finds a depressed Baltar in his presidential office who, incidentally, had just proclaimed, "I just want to sit here and die" and threatens him with a gun. His desperation becomes clear when he tells Baltar that he had believed in him and the "dream of New Caprica" but turned out to be nothing but an idealist (3.04 "Exodus—Part II").

While Baltar responds that being an idealist is not a sin, Gaeta clearly cannot deal with the destruction of his ideological world-view. He feels betrayed by Baltar and later seeks revenge, which even leads him to lie blatantly in Baltar's trial. He states that Baltar willingly signed the assassination orders for a variety of humans (including Laura Roslin and Tom Zarek), while the viewer knows that Baltar literally had a gun to his head (3.20 "Crossroads—Part II"). Meanwhile Lee decides to join Baltar's defense council, reminding people that Baltar cannot be held responsible for all that has transpired. Felix' feeling of being betrayed later fuels his hatred for the Cylon-human alliance, leading him to initiate a mutiny on Galactica (together with fellow idealist Tom Zarek), for which both of them are finally court-marshaled.

Felix' involvement in the mutiny is explored in more detail in the Webisodes *The Face of the Enemy*, which focused on him as a character. The Webisodes reveal that Felix was involved with an Eight Model on New Caprica who betrayed him, which he only finds out after the discovery of Earth I. After informing him about her betrayal, she tells Felix, "You have to open your eyes. You have to see what the world is really like" (*The Face of the Enemy* 08). At this point, Felix starts to understand that his idealistic nature has completely blinded him to reality. Once again, he has been betrayed by someone he trusted and believed in. Gaeta is not an "evil" person, as is evident when Zarek orders the members of the Quorum to be assassinated during the mutiny. He is completely desperate upon discovering the scene, complaining to Zarek that this is not right (4.14 "Blood on the scales"). Yet he is moral and idealistic to such an extent that disillusionment and betrayal will finally destroy him.

Lee, Felix, and Zarek have principles and an ideological view of how the world should work, but Lee is by far the most realistic and down-to-earth. Unlike Felix, he is never blinded by his ideology. In addition, his morals are always dead-on, which is more than can be said of either Felix Gaeta or Tom Zarek. These characters show that being an idealist can also be dangerous. Felix clearly believes he is doing the right thing by mutinying—but in this series, the alliance with the Cylons is considered "good" and any opposition to it must be identified as "wrong." Because hybridity is the goal and not the enemy, Felix and Tom (as "racial purists") must be eliminated. The problem is not that Gaeta lacks morality, but that his morality is tragically outdated or slightly off. He is also "too idealistic," as he loses sight of reality in order to maintain his ideal version of reality.

The series is clearly opposed to uncompromising idealism, which it constructs either as naive (Gaeta) or as deceitful (Zarek). The only accepted form of non-religious idealism is Lee's realistic variety that keeps the big picture in mind and allows for a certain amount of compromise. Here, the series again shows its commitment to the postmodern: it breaks down certainty in favor of ambiguity (e.g., Dallmayr 1997, 33). Lee does not choose an ideological side and then sticks to it no matter what; he assesses the situation and then decides on a course of action: his idealism is flexible and is constructed by a commitment to morality. Felix, on the other hand, is reminiscent of Boomer who also gives in to desperation. Before the mutiny, Felix states: "The world is frakked. It's upside down and somebody's gotta turn it right side up" (4.13 "The Oath"). Yet his idea of "right side up" is simply wrong. Had the Cylons been trying to trick the humans with the alliance (as was the case in the original series) Felix Gaeta would have been the hero who saved humanity from destruction. The goal of hybridization defines what is morally right and wrong. As we will see, this is also why Cavil is a villain.

Cavil and the Plan

Compared to the female Cylons, male Cylons are notoriously unreligious in the narrative of *BSG*, and also tend to be either "evil" or insignificant. Cavil and the other male Cylons are nevertheless not stereotypical (good or evil) sci-fi Cyborgs. The series' "big bad" is certainly the Cylon model One, better known as Cavil. We have already seen how he manipulated the memory of the Final Five because he was jealous of his brother and angry at his makers. The movie *The Plan*, which aired after the series finale and attempted to explain some of the mysteries still left open after the conclusion, clarifies that Cavil was the driving force behind the genocide and especially behind the various Cylon plots and terrorist attacks conducted on Galactica during the first two seasons. The series finale had already portrayed him as a negative force that needed to be destroyed in order for Cylons and humans to achieve salvation. Cavil is thus the out-of-control machine that needs to be destroyed in order to re-establish social (and gender) order—a role we have seen is usually assigned to female Cyborgs. If there is an evil in *BSG*, Cavil is certainly it. I will consequently put this character in the context of male evil in religious history, relating him especially to the Christian figure of the devil. The central questions will be whether Cavil is a personified evil, and how his relationship to technology and religion is coded.

The Christian devil, also known as Satan or Lucifer, has its origin in the Jewish tradition of an angelic "accuser" who tests humans on God's behalf. Because angels have no free will in Judaism, Satan cannot be evil—he is an instrument of God. As Henry Ansgar Kelly has shown, Satan actually remained an accuser in God's service in the New Testament, while post–Biblical traditions (notably the early Church Fathers) identified him with the serpent in paradise that caused humanity's fall because of jealousy. In the third century CE, Origen of Alexandria then laid the groundwork for Satan's new role as God's supreme enemy (Kelly 2006). The issue of jealousy is certainly at the heart of Cavil's evil as well. While Satan is jealous of humanity and especially God's preference for humanity as opposed to angels, Cavil's jealousy is directed at his brother Daniel, who his mother-creator Ellen preferred. Satan's reaction is to persuade Adam and Eve to eat from the tree of knowledge, expelling them from paradise. Cavil reacts by killing Daniel and then wiping out the memory of his creators.

Cavil's rebellion is not directed against God (whose existence he refutes), but against parental authority. There is nevertheless a connection to the divine, because his "parents" are also his creators. In Cavil's opinion, they have limited him by creating him in human form. Time and again he insists that the Cylons are machines and as such don't have souls or a god to watch over them (e.g., 4.03 "The Ties That Bind"). A human body, Cavil explains to his mother-creator Ellen, is limiting. Human eyes cannot see gamma rays, the nose cannot smell dark matter, and ears cannot hear x-rays. He concludes: "I'm a machine. And I could know much more. I could experience so much more, but I'm trapped in this absurd body, and why? Because my five creators thought that God wanted it that way" (4.14 "No Exit").

Cavil's "evil" is really the original human evil of the Old Testament: he strives for knowledge of the "forbidden," which would make him Godlike. Like Satan, he does not want to acknowledge the superiority of a god who made him, but instead wants to be responsible for his own happiness (Russell 1984, 201). He cannot comprehend why his creators would have made him so imperfect and strives for a more posthuman, mechanical existence. In this way, the series comments once again on posthuman thought. For Cavil, eternal life is not enough; he wants to experience the universe in a way that cannot be perceived by humans. Again, Cavil's issue is not with God whom he does not acknowledge, but with his creators. His response is that of a rebellious and frustrated child and is clearly emotional. Cavil represents negative feelings, a lack of faith, and a liability to violence and aggression. He is thus clearly a counterpoint to the female Cylons. Once again, the definition of good and evil stems from the series' moral message of hybridization. Like Felix Gaeta, Cavil is a "racial purist" who sees Hera's existence as dangerous and wants to be a "pure" machine. Ironically, because of his incredibly emotional reactions, Cavil is a really bad machine. The emotions he displays are typically "masculine" ones: aggression, anger, jealousy.[3]

Like Clarice, Cavil is first introduced to us as a priest, consulting a jailed Galen Tyrol who is afraid that he might be a Cylon—correctly so, as it turns out later (2.19 "Lay Down Your Burdens—Part I"). At first, we are unaware of his Cylon nature, but the advice he gives Tyrol already indicates that he is not as religious as we would expect a priest to be. Cavil is in fact an atheist, which puts him in strong contrast to the female Cylons. In his opinion, "there is no God. Supernatural divinities are the primitive's answer for why the sun goes down at night" (2.20 "Lay Down Your Burdens—Part II"). Cavil sees religion as a delusion (3.01 "Occupation")—he is a true enlightenment philosopher in that regard. Faith in the divine is irrational to him, while reason is the ultimate authority.

Yet significantly, even Cavil is not Satan in person. *The Plan* illustrates this by confronting an "evil" Cavil with another One model who has changed his opinion about humanity and the destructive Cylon plan. The movie begins and ends with a discussion between the two Ones, who are just about to be thrown out of the Galactica air-lock following the events of 2.20 "Lay Down Your Burdens—Part II." Cavil 1 had orchestrated acts of Cylon manipulation on Galactica for the past two years, while Cavil 2 had joined the human resistance movement back on Caprica. Cavil 2 tries to explain to Cavil 1 that the genocide was "a grievous error" that had made the Cylons "even more irredeemable in the eyes of our parents." Cavil 1 does not acknowledge this, mostly because he understands what this acknowledgement would mean: everything would have been for nothing.

Neither Cavil is a believer—for Cavil 2 redemption is associated with the Final Five, their parent-creators whom they had, in his opinion, wronged. But he has begun to see humanity in a different light while in the resistance; he learned something about them that Cavil 1 never experienced. We can see that the One model is not incapable of change—but as a group, they become "fallen" because they refuse to acknowledge the error of their ways. Significantly, God has nothing to do with any of this. Evil is purely "human" (by extension Cylon) and derives from negative human qualities. He acts as a serpent or devil by trying to convince the other Cylons of his message. He is only successful with the male Cylons (the Dorals and Simons), who are mostly portrayed as insignificant and complacent. The only notable exception is a Simon in *The Plan*, who resists Cavil's orders to blow up the ship where his wife and her child live by committing suicide. It is noteworthy that this happens outside of the regular series' narrative. Other than that, the Dorals and Simons are of little consequence for the progress of the story.

While Cavil's function in the narrative is diabolical, he is not constructed as God's great adversary. Following the *BSG*-logic, God knows and orchestrates everything, so Cavil must have some sort of function. In a way, he fulfills a role similar to the Deluge in the Old Testament story of Noah. In order for humans and Cylons to become allies and reach the Promised Land together, most of humanity first had to be wiped out, mirroring the story of Noah's arch. Like Cain, he is an evil doer—evil is once again defined as an action. His "evilness" is also constructed through misogyny, which the series frequently condemns by associating such attitudes with negative characters. We have already seen that Cavil exploits and subordinates Boomer and tries to do the same to his mother-creator Ellen. He frequently attacks the female Cylons for their "irrational" faith and refuses to acknowledge the sentience of the raiders and the (feminized) Centurions. Cavil is corrupted by evil to such an extent that he becomes irredeemable, although the discussion between the two Cavils in *The Plan* shows that neither did he start out that way nor was this result inevitable.

We can find some illuminating parallels between Cavil and the popular early modern literary figure of Faustus who makes a pact with the devil. Like Cavil, Faustus is not evil, but seduced by evil. Whereas comparable medieval legends usually ended on a happy note with the character's repentance and divine forgiveness, the early modern Faustus was taken over by his sinfulness and was not able or allowed to return to God. The legend was especially popular in Protestant countries such as Germany or England, since it focused both on the struggle of the individual and the danger of knowledge. Like Cavil, Faustus wants access to knowledge and is prepared to make a pact with the devil in order to achieve this (Russell 1990, 58–64). Both Faustus and Cavil end up paying for this original sin.

Overall, this construction of evil is closer to Jewish than to Christian tradition, since only the latter knows personified evil. The deterministic universe of *BSG* with its lack of free will (made rather apparent through the angels) also excludes the existence of a fallen rebel against God's authority. Lucifer was able to rebel because he had free will—in *BSG* there is no such thing. Of course the issue of free will has a rather complicated history and the theologies of Luther and Calvin show some similarities to the Jewish position of divine omnipotence without abandoning the devil altogether. For the reformers, the devil was an instrument of God in a similar manner as man could be an instrument of the devil (Russell 1990, 38). However, maintaining both the benevolence and the omnipotence of God without turning the devil into a powerful independent agent was always theologically problematic: Either everything is from God (including evil and thus the devil), or evil is irreconcilable with God, making the devil independent. In *BSG*, God both rewards and punishes through his angels, while supernatural beings independent from God do not exist.

Consequently even Cavil, who is the most obvious example for evil in *BSG*, is not a diabolical adversary without the potential for redemption. He lacks faith in anything except science, so unlike Faustus he does not turn to the Devil instead of God. He is not the Devil himself, as he is neither more powerful than the other Cylons nor in any way supernatural. His "God" is science in the traditional sci-fi manner, although this is not constructed as a good thing in the series. He, like the other evils we have come across so far, is secular evil. Cavil is fallen to such an extent that he needs to be destroyed in the series finale and is not allowed to enter paradise. He is jealous, manipulative, murderous, callous, exploitative, and controlling. These are character traits that add up to "evil" actions in the series, especially when combined with atheism. We have also seen that the "forbidden fruit" is generally technology which both Clarice and Cavil want to use in order to become God-like. Cavil the patriarch prohibited the female Cylons from searching for the Final Five, while it is God who prohibits apotheosis through technology. The latter is "evil," while the revolt against patriarchy is justified. Of course Clarice resembles Cavil in her misuse of technology, but not concerning her attitude to religion. Indeed, religion is more feminized on *Caprica*, where men are secularized to an even greater extent, as we shall see presently.

Fathers, Daughters and the Tauron Way

Caprica's only possible equivalent to *BSG'S* Cavil is Clarice, though I have already stated that I would rather link her to Baltar. Overall, evil is more difficult to define in the prequel series. On the other hand, men are dissociated from religion to an even greater extent on *Caprica*. The next chapter will look at the remnants of this connection by discussing religious zealotry and its relationship to terrorism, while this section will deal specifically with the "leading men" of *Caprica*, namely Daniel Graystone and the Adama brothers. Like the rest of this chapter's protagonists, these men have to position themselves morally entirely without God's guidance. Their relationship to technology, however, is more ambivalent. Two topics strike me as relevant in that regard. First, the mafia-like Tauron crime syndicate or Ha'la'tha is an obvious starting point to discuss the series' understanding of moral rights and wrongs, as well as the construction of traditional gender norms. Second, because *Caprica* is constructed as a "family drama," the series assigns much time and space to the relationship between the two dead daughters (Zoe and Tamara) and their fathers (Daniel and Joseph)—always an exciting area of research when it comes to gender. We will start with the latter.

We have already discussed Daniel Graystone's somewhat patriarchal tendencies towards his daughter, but I would like to explore this character in more detail. Daniel Graystone is the classical rational sci-fi scientist who is interested in technological advance and tries to find technological solutions for all of his problems—including emotional ones. He thus strongly objectifies machinery as he sees technology of any kind only as a tool. When he tries to convince the board of his company to switch their focus from the holobands to the robots, he effectively proposes the creation of a slave race: "this Cylon will become a tireless worker, who won't need to be paid. It won't retire or get sick, it won't have rights or objections, or complaints" (1.05 "There Is Another Sky"). To prove his point, he asks the robot unit U87 that is currently inhabited by Zoe-A to rip off her arm. This kind of attitude is of course unacceptable within the narrative, because we know that Cylons are sentient beings—and the impersonal U87 is actually the Zoe Graystone Avatar whom her father has just asked to mutilate herself. Daniel needs to be educated—and his daughter will teach him not only that machines cannot be treated like slaves, but also that he has to stop trying to control her. Once he understands this and starts to work with instead of against his daughter, Daniel can become a hero. Zoe-A is the one who has to rescue her father after he has lost his way.

Meanwhile, Tamara Adama has to do the same for her father. Like Daniel, Joseph Adama has lost his daughter (as well as his wife) in the terrorist attack and struggles to deal with this loss. In their desperation, both Daniel and Joseph turn to technology: First, Daniel tries to get Zoe back and drags Joseph along by creating the second self-conscious avatar, a copy of Tamara Adama. Joseph originally rejects Daniel's idea of re-creating his daughter in cyberspace, because he perceives the entire process as unnatural. He initially seems uncomfortable with this kind of advanced technology (1.01 "Pilot"). However, after learning that Tamara-A is still "alive" in the virtual world, he decides to find her and buys a holoband in order to access v-world.

Unlike Daniel Graystone, Joseph Adama is not accustomed to technology. In other ways, however, these two characters are indeed similar, especially concerning their protective, yet patriarchal, fatherly roles. They create Tamara and then leave her alone in a dark room. Both Daniel and Joseph are unaware that she is still there—frankly, they never consider that she might be. Zoe-A and Lacy later find Tamara and show her a door that connects them to "shared" virtual space. Although scared, Tamara then decides to "find my own way home" (1.03 "Reigns of a Waterfall"). The men created her and left, not even thinking about what may become of her—after all, she is just man-made technology and should only exist how and when they want her to exist. It is not her father who rescues her from isolation, but two women, and she is then strong enough to make her own way. When Zoe-A meets Tamara-A again, she has become strong and feared in the virtual world, both of which she accomplished without the help of others.

Although Tamara feels abandoned, her father does not need to rescue her—in fact, it is the other way around, as Wetmore also noted (Wetmore 2012, 181). Joseph neglects his "real" life in order to chase his dead daughter in the virtual world. As the only remaining member of the Adama family, his son Willie suffers from his father's obsession. Effectively, Joseph has abandoned both of his children at a vital stage of their "new" life after the paradigm changing terrorist attack. In v-world, Joseph becomes addicted to a drug that heightens his alertness. When Tamara finds out about this (from a female informant), she kills him in the game, which effectively means that he cannot return to look for her. She tells him, "You're wasting your life" (1.09 "End of Line"). When it comes to their daughters, Joseph and Daniel are remarkably similar: they feel that they need to rescue their daughters, when they are actually the ones in need of rescuing. Without their daughters, Daniel and Joseph are not only lost, but morally ambiguous: they both get involved with the Tauron crime syndicate, the Ha'la'tha. Daniel uses extortion to get his company back, while Joseph returns to the Tauron ways he had previously abandoned: They return to male-dominated circles.

The Ha'la'tha is presented as a crime syndicate reminiscent of the mafia. Through the visual depiction of the Tauron men involved in it, this association is reinforced (they often wear hats and are dressed either in suits or in leather). The role of women within this structure is stereotypically "Italian": mothers and daughters are often housewives, who nevertheless hold high authority within this sphere and whose "submission" to a seemingly patriarchal system is increasingly styled as deceiving as the series progresses. Joseph Adama's Tauron assistant Eve who later becomes his wife turns out to be his guide in v-world and is not unfamiliar with guns. His mother in law saves Joseph from an assassin by fearlessly stabbing the attacker from behind. It turns out that Tauron women can even hold authority in the crime syndicate, as evidenced by the daughter of the crime syndicate's leader (called the Gautrau). After successfully conspiring with the Adamas to have her father killed, she becomes the new Guatrau. Besides these obvious examples of female power, the Ha'la'tha is a strongly masculine organization that is dominated by men. The stereotypical presentation of masculinity through this crime syndicate is only partially eroded by the character Sam Adama.

Joseph Adama's brother Sam is a hit man with strong family values who nevertheless strikes us as a comparatively moral person. Sam's traditional masculinity is portrayed through his body, personality, and language. He is a tall, muscular man with various tattoos; his appearance demands respect and sometimes fear. It would be easy to interpret him as a stereotyped picture of the traditional masculine—where it not for the fact that he is married to a man. His masculinity is rendered subversive through his open homosexuality that is not even an issue for the Mafioso Tauron leadership. In this narrative, Sam Adama can be both normatively masculine and homosexual. Through this plot device, *Caprica* tried to do what *BSG* had previously done with the issue of heterosexual gender: they introduced a world in which homosexuality was socially acceptable to such an extent that it did not even need to be commented upon.

Concerning the character of Sam Adama, two aspects should be noted. Firstly, as stated, the character reconciles masculinity with homosexuality, challenging the stereotype that homosexual men are feminine and that "real men" cannot be homosexual (Connell 2000, 65). Second, Sam Adama could be seen as a sort of "updated" hegemonic masculinity. Because he is openly gay, he seems "progressive" to the viewer, a challenge to the social order. However, since it is not considered "progressive" to be gay in the narrative itself, he is really nothing of the sort. He is easily angered, uses violence consistently and without much remorse, and walks in patriarchal and male-dominated circles. Meanwhile his husband stays at home and is not involved in any of his business. Sam Adama is in fact thoroughly traditional. He also becomes a role-model for Willie Adama (who, we have seen, is neglected by his father) and teaches him how to be a "real" Tauron man. Through this character, the series shows how normative gender is socially constructed.[4] The social construction of masculinity in our society requires the oppression of homosexuality (Kauffmann 1996, 159). Yet since masculinity is not constructed as inherently heterosexual in Caprica, Sam challenges our society's concept of masculinity more than *Caprica*'s.

The relationship between the Tauron men and religion is never openly addressed. Their faith is mostly directed towards their own structures, both family and business. Tauron traditions and customs are important to them, and the series spends some time portraying Tauron rites of passage. Other than that, however, not much can be said about their religiosity. Their relationship to technology is more accessible to the viewer and, for the most part, seems rather odd. Joseph Adama is amusingly uneasy with technology, and traditional Taurons share this distance to advanced technology. The Ha'la'tha might trade Cylon Centurions for financial profits, but this trade is seen along the lines of traditional weapons trades. Sam Adama uses a Cylon to rid himself of an enemy, just like he would otherwise use more "traditional" guns. When Daniel asks Sam to join him in v-world in search for Tamara and Zoe, he initially refuses, until Eve convinces him to go. Amongst the Taurons, there is no particular interest in advanced technologies, and their encounters with the virtual world are both awkward and rare. Besides Daniel, none of the series' leading men connects with technology on more than a functional level—and Daniel is a patriarch whom his chosen daughter needs to rescue from his control issues. Moreover, all of them are dissociated from religion.

The men of *BSG* and *Caprica* certainly illustrate that morals are possible without religion. The series present us with quite a few unreligious heroes—none of whom are particularly involved with advanced technology, from which they usually distance themselves. It is quite noticeable, how frequently women mediate religion and morality for these men. Bill Adama is introduced to the spiritual realm by Laura, while Zoe-A needs to educate her father about the moral approach to technology. At the same time, men are more prone to extremist positions. Unchecked by religion, their idealistic nature can easily get the best of them and lead them down dangerous paths. Men like Lee Adama and Karl Agathon, who remain moral without much outside influence, are rare. Technological men without religion, on the other hand, are always morally dubious or even "bad," as exemplified by Cavil and Gaeta, and to a certain extent also Daniel. This means that the stereotypical connection between the male and technological spheres is breeched in both series, especially where morality is concerned. Male reason (and thus science) no longer guarantees morality; in fact, it oftentimes prohibits moral behavior. Having established that, we now need to turn to the male believers.

7

Violence and Crisis: Religious Men

Scholarship has postulated that religion has been "feminized" in the West since the 19th century, especially in Northern America and England (Sohn-Kronthaler 2009). The association of women with the irrational likely provided a basis for this tendency (McLeod 1988, 134; Connell 2000, 185). The question remains where this leaves men. Is masculinity even compatible with religion? On the other hand, technology is frequently seen as the domain of men and is one of the areas where women are still frequently excluded. We have established that the connection between men and advanced technology is breeched in the series, while women are linked to scientific progress. In this section, we will investigate this tendency further by analyzing how religious conviction affects men and their relationship to the traditionally masculine technological sphere. We will begin with an investigation into the connection between terrorism and gender and then look at the case studies of Leoben, Galen Tyrol, and Sam Anders as examples of how masculinity is constructed when coupled with religion. These men are interesting for the purposes of this study because they can be connected to both technology and religion. They will put my theory to the ultimate test as they will show us whether religion and technology are really coded female in *BSG*.

Religious Terrorism and Gender

Born in a post–9/11 world, in a country that had just declared a "war on terror," *BSG* has tackled issues of terrorism and torture from the very beginning. However different *Caprica* was from its predecessor, this connection remained intact. Both series begin with a terrorist act that would have far reaching consequences—in *BSG* the Cylons nuke the 12 colonies while *Caprica*'s protagonist Zoe Graystone is killed in a suicide bombing. Yet both series make it difficult for the viewer to assess the (im)morality of terrorism because central protagonists are frequently placed in this context. In *BSG*, the beginning of season three (including the Webisodes *The Resistance*) is a testament to this complicated depiction. In this story plot, the humans commit acts of terrorism against their Cylon oppressors, killing not only Cylons but also humans in the attacks. Finally, they even resort to suicide bombings. Although former president Laura Roslin is not connected to the attacks, she tells president Baltar that "desperate people take desperate measures" (3.02 "Precipice"). *Caprica* goes even further by putting two key protagonists with the terrorist organization STO (Zoe and Lacy). Has terrorism become justified?

As Erika Johnson-Lewis remarked in her discussion of *BSG* terrorism's relation to the Bush administration's War on Terror, "it helps if terrorists are not actually people" (Johnson-Lewis 2008, 30). By making them people—and sympathetic ones at that—the series try to illustrate that in the eyes of terrorists, their actions are justified. Nevertheless, terrorism itself is never seen as morally legitimate and truly moral characters need to be disturbed by this kind of violence. If they are not, they are damaged, as is the case with Saul Tigh. Tigh becomes the leader of the violent anti–Cylon resistance on New Caprica. As such, he is tortured by the Cylons, culminating in the removal of one of his eyes. He also feels forced to kill his wife Ellen after learning that she had supplied the Cylons with crucial information. The tragedy here is, of course, that Tigh is later revealed to be one of the Final Five—as are his wife Ellen and two of the most prominent resistance members, Galen Tyrol and Samuel Anders. In the long run, this plot twist serves to remind us how senseless terrorism is by blurring the boundaries between "us" and "them." The terrorist protagonist is not necessarily evil, but desperate and misguided. Lacy is not fond of the STO's strategy, although she does admit to the cause, Laura Roslin silently tolerates the attacks while drawing a line at suicide bombings, and both Tyrol and Anders think that Tigh is going too far with the latter.

Meanwhile Clarice's interest in terrorism is connected to her own lust for power. Clarice is nevertheless not a fraud who uses religion as a cover—she is a true believer. The series contrasts her with STO cell-leader Barnabas. While Clarice plans to change not only the monotheist religion but also the world as such, Barnabas is all about the reality of terrorism. His fanaticism is clearly visible in his self-chastisement in episode six ("Know Thy Enemy"), where he wraps a thorny chain tightly around his arm. He tells Clarice, "The leaders like action, not crazy plans that make you into a bouncer in some home-made heaven" (1.09 "End of Line"). Barnabas acts religious, but it is not about the purpose as much as the violence. Religion is a means to a sado-masochistic end for him. His masculine rationality also leads Barnabas to conclude that "apotheosis is a fraud" (1.11 "Retribution"). Barnabas of course has no chance against religious zealotry, and is really only a minor nuisance for Clarice who finally kills him, ridding herself of this problem of purposeless violence.

Quite frequently, male religiosity is coupled with acts of violent terrorism on *Caprica*, which sees a lot more male than female bombers, in particular when it comes to suicide missions. In addition, we are not allowed to get to know these men (or boys). Female terrorists—in particular Clarice, Lacy, and Zoe—are introduced as major protagonists with whom we get quite acquainted, while male terrorists remain superficial and minor characters. *BSG* had previously also tended towards male terrorism with the Webisodes *The Resistance*, which focused on male terrorists and finally culminated in a male suicide bomber in the beginning of season three (3.01 "Occupation"). Both series conclude that killing innocent people is wrong while allowing for scenarios in which such actions might seem justified to certain people. In a nutshell, *BSG* and *Caprica* are saying that terrorists are people—and as such have rights the Bush administration was unwilling to grant them. However, the violent and more "senseless" aspects of terrorism are strongly associated with male characters, while the more in-depth discussion of terrorism is conducted through women.

Since the series was embedded discursively into issues of the Bush era, especially concerning terrorism, torture and war, the question of gendered terrorism should be analyzed in the same context. First of all, we should note that the female suicide bomber and the female terrorist usually take second stage in our contemporary understanding of terrorism, although she is historically a rather active protagonist. To take two examples from Germany: the left-wing *Rote Armee Fraktion* (RAF) that conducted kidnappings and acts of terrorism in the 1970s was populated by prominent female members, in particular Gudrun Ensslin and Ulrike Meinhof, the latter of whom lend her name to the organizations unofficial designation *Baader-Meinhof-Gruppe*. More recently another woman, Beate Zschäpe, has been on trial for acts committed in the name of right-wing terror organization *Nationalsozialistischer Untergrund* (NSU). Several such examples can be found not only in the West, but in religiously motivated Middle Eastern terrorism as well. The assumption that terrorism is male is thus not supported by facts.

However, male and female terrorists are not interpreted in the same manner in Western discourse, which we need to be aware of when analyzing their depiction in *Caprica*. Claudia Brunner has analyzed how recent monographs on terrorism and suicide bombings deal with gender and came to the conclusion that certain Western stereotypes about Arab society (as well as antiquated Western stereotypes of gender) greatly influence this discussion (Brunner 2007, 958–963). She found that female suicide bombers were usually constructed as deceived and naïve victims of oppressive patriarchal structures. Quite frequently, the female terrorists' sanity is put into question and she is depicted as highly irrational. While men are either accorded the position of tactical strategists or (if they conduct suicide missions themselves,) are portrayed as religious or nationalist fanatics, women are rendered as personally motivated terrorists, who either seek revenge or an escape from patriarchal structures. In other words: men have political reasons for terrorism while women have private ones. Although Muslim women in particular are constructed as unable of political agency, they share this focus on the private life of female terrorists with their Western counterparts (such as the RAF).

Beginning with *BSG*'s *The Resistance*, this discursive pattern is already breached through a male character who becomes a suicide bomber for purely personal reasons, although he had previously already been linked to the terrorist organization as such. Yet the act of suicide for the cause is, for him, purely personal, as his wife was previously killed in a counterterrorist raid initiated by the Cylons. It is not political or religious fanaticism that motivate this male suicide bomber, but a personal tragedy. On *Caprica*, male terrorists and suicide bombers remain highly inaccessible. Zoe Graystone's boyfriend is presented as religiously motivated, but shortsighted. His act is not tactical—the strategists in this plot are Zoe and Clarice whose plans have now been obstructed by one single act of senseless male violence. Barnabas, though certainly more tactical, is not presented as the best strategist either. His plans are shortsighted and he cannot appreciate Clarice's more elaborate plans.

If we compare these men's attacks to Clarice's carefully thought-out mass suicide bombings (with the eventual ascent of the martyred bombers to virtual heaven), we are immediately struck by the men's rash behavior. The same is true for Lacy, though she is originally constructed as the typical teenager who finds her way to the terrorist organization through peer-pressure. This first impression is deceiving, and she turns out to be a convinced monotheist who is not afraid to use violence for her goals. She is nevertheless more responsible and careful about its use than either the men or Clarice. Overall, the women are the ones with the strategy, the ones that are truly committed to religious and political goals, while the men more often than not simply enjoy the power and violence of terrorism.

The comparison with Muslim terrorism has usually served as an entry-point for contextualizing *BSG*'s terrorism, both because it seemed to provide the logical discursive framework for a post– 9/11 America and because the series depicted religious—not secular—terrorism. But such a comparison has its limits, especially where the issue of patriarchal structures is concerned. While we have seen that Western discourse constructs female suicide bombers as trapped in (and possibly revolting against) patriarchal societies, the women of *Caprica* are not confined by such structures. This means that one rather typical explanatory element for female terrorism cannot be employed, namely the revolt against patriarchy that, in a way, justifies female involvement in these violent organizations in the Western mind.

On *Caprica*, the issue of justifications remains open and is never fully resolved. While the illegitimacy of terrorism is rather clear where Barnabas and Zoe's suicide bomber boyfriend are concerned, the women are another matter. Clarice's terrorism is not portrayed as justified, but her religious issues are not without merit. Zoe is a convinced terrorist, but is never actually seen committing an act of terrorism. Lacy is a terrorist who is nevertheless constructed in a positive light and is seen revolting against established terrorist structures without giving up on the cause. The overall tenor is that of ambivalence, and an engagement with Western discourse about terrorism and its gender is an inherent part of this ambivalence.

Concerning the limits of the "Muslim terrorist model," we should also note the difference between terrorism from the outside and terrorism from the inside. The latter variety was analyzed by Brunner and Krieger regarding the 2005 London bombings that were conducted by British Muslims. In this case, terrorism was constructed as male, irrational and backwards, the bombers' driving force found in hate and anger (Brunner and Krieger 2008, 194–197). The terrorists of *Caprica* are also enemies from within, but the male suicide bombers are not depicted as driven by hate and anger, but by genuine belief in their cause. Zoe's boyfriend who blows up the train in the series opening is indeed constructed as irrational insofar as he is contrasted with rational Zoe, but we know too little about this man to conclude on his motives and emotional state confidently.

Neither is terrorism on Caprica depicted as "backwards," it simply advocates a different belief system but does not want to return to a more "traditional" way of life. Both religions essentially advocate Western values and belief systems, and both are equally technologically advanced. The series is thus less interested in maintaining an image of a rational, modern, and moral "self" in contrast to the irrational, backwards "other" represented by the terrorists, but describes a conflict of belief and world views that results in a violent confrontation. *Caprica* does not re-enact the "real world" discourse of Muslim terrorism in the West, but instead offers a balanced account of internal conflicts rather than outside dangers.

We should not disregard the fact that the monotheist religion of *BSG* and *Caprica* is decidedly not Islamic. This is one of the reasons why I feel uneasy with several scholars' assertion that the Cylons or monotheist terrorists represent Muslim terrorists and that the series reproduces corresponding discourses.[1] We have seen that this was in many ways not the case. Certainly, 9/11 and the war on terror was a major "inspiration" for the prominence of terrorism in both series, but I propose that they actually discuss something quite different by using it: the fragmentation of Western identity and, more to the point, the internal ideological conflicts arising from Muslim terrorism that are particularly pronounced in the United States.

Returning to the issue at hand, we can summarize that *Caprica* subverts the traditional image of the religious terrorist, especially by putting an emphasis on female protagonists. Male terrorism and suicide bombings are usually depicted as irrational and shortsighted, in addition to being unnecessarily violent: the series proposes that religious men are violent and irrational. Female terrorists are strategists who pursue a certain goal with their actions: they are rational, technological, and more calculating when it comes to using violence. Senseless terrorism, on the other hand, is coupled with the religious zealotry of men.

Leoben: Torture and Violence

Ambivalence is also the motto concerning the subject of torture and abuse. Torture was (and is) a highly controversial topic in the U.S. public. *BSG* takes the position that torture is always "wrong," based on the asymmetry of power that guides the situation (Rodin 2010, 822). And yet the series frequently puts protagonists that are generally coded "good" in the position of torturer. Torture is nevertheless never positive—again, it serves to illustrate that nobody is purely "good" or "evil." The series discusses torture most prominently through the Cylon character Leoben, who is the only male humanoid model fully committed to his religion. Leoben also has a religious function in the narrative that connects him to Starbuck. Leoben's obsession with Kara's destiny is both religious and violent. As such, we need to explore this relationship in detail in order to assess this Cylon's connections to the religious and technological spheres.

Leoben and Kara first meet on Galactica, where he is identified as a Cylon and Starbuck is asked to question him about the presence of Cylons in the fleet (1.08 "Flesh and Bone"). Because the Cylons are not considered human, Starbuck feels no reservations whatsoever to torture him—after all, he is just a machine. The episode questions humanity's "goodness" by having a heroic character such as Starbuck act "evil." Yet Leoben is not innocent. He lies about having placed a nuclear weapon in the fleet and plays with Kara by referring to her "special destiny" and revealing his knowledge of her childhood. As the Cylon philosopher-theologian, Leoben repeatedly speaks of God's plan and humanity's sins against their creator which legitimizes the Cylons' actions. The fact that Leoben lies in the face of torture and continues to play mind games reinforces the criticism that testimony gathered form torture is notoriously unreliable (Rodin 2010, 825). "Flesh and Bone" ends with Roslin putting an end to the interrogation and ordering Leoben's execution. Having developed a highly complicated relationship with her prisoner, Kara later prays to the gods for Leoben's soul, though she is unsure if he even has one.

In the beginning of season three, the roles are reversed. Now Starbuck is the prisoner and Leoben the torturer. The torture he has in store for her is of a special kind: he confines her in a domestic environment where he wants them to play husband and wife. Kara refuses to submit to his continued requests to profess her love for him and instead kills him repeatedly (after which he of course resurrects and returns). Johnson-Lewis established that the body in pain is a recurrent theme in *BSG* (Johnson-Lewis 2008, 34–37), which is certainly the case for the relationship between Kara and Leoben that is based on a destructive cycle of violence. His violence against her is not just physical but also psychological. When all else fails, he brings a child "home" and claims that the girl is their daughter (explaining that her ovaries had been harvested while she was at the Cylon reproduction facility in season two). He forces Kara to care for the girl until she develops strong feelings for her, leading to a heartbreaking scene when Kara has to find out that she is not the mother after all.

There are several ways to read Leoben's violence. We could interpret it as a result of desperation, maybe resulting from masculinity crisis, a reaction to the feminist structures that surround him (e.g.,

MacInnes 2008; Whitehead 2002, 47–63)—structures that are so natural in this fictional world that he cannot even express who or what his enemy is. After all, Leoben is part of a society in which he does not have much say. When with the other Cylons, Leoben frequently disappears into the background, in particular when paired with female Cylons. The second interpretation focuses more strongly on the reality of Kara's childhood that was laced with pain caused by her abusive mother. Her mother claims that she was trying to prepare Kara for her destiny, so Leoben might try to recreate these memories on purpose. His violence is in any case an attempt to control Kara, a woman with whom he is obsessed and whom he also claims to be emotionally connected to. Kara Thrace, however, is not a woman who is easily controlled.

Leoben's controlling nature is connected to his belief: he is convinced that Starbuck has a role to play in God's plan and that he is charged with preparing her for this role. His engagement with religion is unique among the Cylons. Leoben is the Cylon theologian-philosopher who relates Cylon religion to the viewer (and the human characters) from the very beginning. While Six repeatedly speaks of God's plan, she is a believer who feels no need to explain her faith, while Leoben always makes it a point to "rationalize" Cylon religion. Listening to Leoben, we find that everything seems logical and stringent. We first meet him in *Miniseries*, although we are initially unaware of his Cylon nature. In talking to Bill Adama, we begin to notice that he is taking an unusual position. He tells Adama that the Cylons might be "God's retribution for our many sins" and that he might have given the Cylons souls. For the first time, we are introduced to the Cylons' position towards humans—but we are also made aware of the foundations of their faith. Assuming that God created humans and infused them with souls, Leoben explains that it is completely feasible that God would ensoul other creatures as well.

Leoben then reappears in 1.08 "Flesh and Bone," where the series uses his presence once again to relate Cylon faith to the humans and the viewer. When he posits "God loved you and you repaid his divine love with anger, corruption, evil," he is not saying anything particularly untrue, he is listing human vices that the viewer would agree exist. That makes his conclusion—that God could turn his back on humans and ensoul Cylons—all the more feasible. Starbuck tries to break his faith with torture and counter-arguments that mostly circle around the fact that he is a machine and machines cannot have souls.

For Leoben, his most important task is always to convince Kara of her own destiny. The series never explains how he knows so much about her. He repeatedly states that he "saw" her destiny, which implies that he has visions. This would make him the only male Cylon to have divinely inspired visions comparable to those of Laura Roslin or Caprica Six. Leoben is also initially the only Cylon who believes in the prophetic voice of the hybrids (3.06 "Torn"). Leoben's religious role is reinforced through his appearance in Kara's dreams. When she consults an oracle about these dreams, the oracle confirms that Leoben knows her better than she does, that he "sees patterns." Before Kara dies, she talks to an angel that takes the form of Leoben—another sign of his "chosen" status, because God's angels only appear in the form of chosen people (3.17 "Maelstrom").

Leoben is "reunited" with Kara in the beginning of the fourth season, after her resurrection. While Kara is on a mission to find Earth with a skeleton crew and a frater, she finds Leoben in a Cylon raider. When Leoben sees Kara, he immediately knows that something changed, that there is a "difference between the way that you were on New Caprica and now," and he attributes this change to God who has removed her doubt (4.05 "The Road Less Travelled"). Leoben tells Kara to let go of her past, because she is something different now; he calls her an angel who will "lead our people home." Leoben also reveals that he knows about Kara's paintings and helps her complete them.

It is certainly troubling that their relationship starts to become rather intimate despite his actions against her on New Caprica, as Helo correctly points out. We should nevertheless remember that Kara had also tortured him in season one—can we really interpret this as a one-sided abusive relationship? Leoben insists that he only ever wanted Kara to understand her destiny. Whether we agree with Leoben's actions morally is not the point; the relevance for our topic lies in his own belief system. In this episode, he repeats something to Anders he had already brought up in "Flesh and Bones": "What is the most basic article of faith? That this is not all that we are." For Leoben, no other explanation is needed, because he is a true believer.

7. Violence and Crisis: Religious Men

Leoben has an exceptionally strong faith. Not only does he believe in God, but he especially believes in Kara's destiny and his role as her guide. Yet he, too, is disillusioned by the reality of Earth I. When he sees her body in the viper, he backs away. Like everyone else, he is thrown into the ultimate crisis of faith (4.11 "Sometimes a Great Notion"). After that, he does not play a major role anymore. He has led Kara this far, now she has to walk the rest of the way alone. In the end, Leoben is the only male Cylon to enter paradise, Earth II (not counting the Final Five, which I will discuss separately). All of the male Cylons must be destroyed—with the exception of the religious one. After all, he has done his part to fulfill God's plan.

The example of Leoben (and in a way also that of Baltar which will be analyzed in the last chapter) seems to contradict my general thesis of an inherent connection between femininity, religion, and technology in the series. However, if we take a closer look at this highly ambivalent character, a different picture emerges. We have talked about Leoben's wish to be loved and to live in a normative family unit and his inability to attain either. This puts him in direct opposition to all of the female Cylons who are able to achieve both (or, like D'Anna, decide not to take either). Like them, Leoben wants to be more human and he believes in God and in Kara's destiny. Yet he always seems unpredictable, sometimes almost insane. He is a highly unstable character. This is a stark contrast to the female Cylons, who are, for the most part, the picture of stability.

The violence Leoben expresses towards Starbuck reinforces this confused and instable portrayal, which we could read as a remnant of patriarchal power indicating masculinity in crisis. Leoben longs to be a "new man," but is unable to escape these remnants. Studies have shown that religious men tend towards a more feminine gender orientation while traditional masculinity is seen as incompatible with spirituality—at least this seems to be the case for white masculinity (Thompson and Remmes 2002, 521–522). This is essentially Leoben's "problem": His religious orientation feminizes him, so he is trying to re-assert his masculinity through violence in a classic act of overcompensation. This is why his entire relationship to Kara (and thus to religion) is marked by violence. Maybe we should turn this argument around a little—after all, Leoben is not a real-life person, but a fictional character. The writers felt that they needed to make the only religious male Cylon violent, controlling, and abusive. While this could also describe the initial depiction of Six, they then decided to take her into a different direction while Leoben (and Cavil!) remained stuck with these violent traits. Cavil could simply be the atheistic villain, but Leoben shared the female Cylons' religion and was thus on their side.

I find it significant that Leoben stops being important for the story once he loses his violent tendencies that had previously defined him and his religious attitude: he is effectively neutered. Nothing distinguishes him from the female Cylons now, besides the fact that they are stronger than him psychologically and generally more important for the narrative. I suggest that Leoben illustrates not only our society's ambivalent attitude towards traditional masculinities and patriarchal structures, but also towards strong women. Leoben desires to both control and be loved by Kara, he wants to fit into Cylon society and yet struggles to find a place in it. This struggle is always present within him. It seems that Leoben's maleness inhibits the well-rounded portrayal of a religious machine, while the connection between the female Cylons and religion seems to work. Two other religious machines are equally problematic, namely Samuel Anders, and Galen Tyrol.

The Traditional Man

Galen Tyrol is a significant case study for our topic because he is connected to both technology and religion and can consequently be a potential challenge for my thesis. As one of the Final Five, he also goes through his very own identity crisis, and it is interesting to see that the three men of the "Final Four" (excepting the resurrected Ellen) can deal with this crisis much more constructively than Tory, the only other woman. But first things first: Tyrol is originally introduced to us as Galactica's deck chief. As such, he is in charge of the vipers and ensures that they are in working order when the pilots need them. He is portrayed as a mechanic, engaged in the traditionally male task of handling and taking care of vehicles. Yet we have already seen that the Galactica is not a high-tech ship. When Lee Adama first lands on the Galactica, he shows a somewhat arrogant surprise that he had to land his viper

7. Violence and Crisis: Religious Men

manually, to which Tyrol immediately responds that everything is "hands-on here" (*Miniseries*). Like Bill Adama, Galen Tyrol does not handle advanced technology, but antiquated machinery. The kind of nostalgia for the past (and in particular for outmoded masculinities) that we have already seen in Adama, also applies to Tyrol.

Of course this nostalgia is not one for a patriarchal system—Tyrol is not a macho. In fact, he is originally in a (somewhat, but not really) secret relationship with Boomer Sharon, a superior officer whom he respectfully addresses as "Sir." He takes on a responsible, fatherly role for his crew (again reminiscent of Bill Adama), and acts as a protector for Boomer. Galen Tyrol is a "man's man" in many ways. On New Caprica, he becomes a rather traditional husband and father as well as the head of the trade union, and supports the anti–Cylon resistance and its terrorist attacks. He is protective of the ones he loves and has a strong moral compass, though we will later see that he also tends to lose his temper.

Tyrol clearly opposes suicide bombings (3.01 "Occupation"). As already stated, truly moral characters are always appalled by suicide bombings, so Tyrol joins the ranks of Laura Roslin and Samuel Anders, and consequently also illustrates how far gone Saul Tigh is in advocating them. Although Tyrol originally joined "the Circle" after the events on New Caprica in order to punish collaborators, he also realizes that Gaeta should not be convicted because he had supplied the resistance with information and had thus also acted heroically. In a wonderful scene at the end of the episode, Tyrol, the sympathetic and heroic moralist, is offered various seats in the cafeteria, but chooses to sit with Gaeta, who is shunned by everyone even after his role has become public (3.05 "Collaborators").

In a similar way, he joins Helo in saving Athena Sharon from rape in season two (2.12 "Resurrection Ship—Part II"). As stated, the Pegasus is a negative mirror for the Galactica, which also includes Cain's crew. Their distorted idea of right and wrong becomes more than obvious with the attempted rape of Galactica's Cylon prisoner Athena. When Tyrol and Helo discover what the Pegasus Cylon investigator Lieutenant Thorne is about to do, they both rush to save her. Although Tyrol has no personal connection to Athena Sharon and his relationship with Boomer Sharon ended badly, he immediately rushes to protect her from this kind of violence. He is a protector and a man of high moral values.

Galen Tyrol is also religious. When he is afraid of being a Cylon in season two (long before we know that he is a member of the Final Five), he asks to see a priest. He is confronted with Cavil, in retrospect making this a Cylon-Cylon conversation. He tells Cavil that he asked to see a priest because (like Starbuck) he never believed in psychotherapy: "My father was a priest.... I pray to the gods every night. I don't think they listen to me" (2.19 "Lay Down Your Burdens—Part I"). Not only was his father a priest, but his mother was an oracle. Tyrol is thus religious in much the same way as Kara, because he was raised that way. However, he is much more ambivalent about his religious heritage than Starbuck. We find out later that he resented his parent's religiosity because he found it restricting. He rebelled against it and initially does not display much faith. His relationship to religion starts to change in season three when he discovers the Temple of Five, foreshadowing the revelation of his Cylon identity at the end of the season (3.11 "The Eye of Jupiter"). The temple is connected to his own Cylon past that he cannot remember, but seems to sense. The experience returns him to his religious roots to a certain extent. As his relationship to religion changes, so does his relationship to technology: discovering his mechanical nature is coupled with discovering his spiritual side.

Galen Tyrol is a Cylon. As such, he is a technological being "made, not born." Yet he is not just any Cylon—he is one of the mythical ones, the Final Five, thousands of years old. Although he is connected to technology because he is both a Cylon and a deck chief, he is never visually connected to advanced technologies. Anders later informs us that all of the Final Five were researchers and that Galen Tyrol had been working on the resurrection technology. He tells Tyrol, "Your work was amazing. But it was Ellen who made the intuitive leap that brought the system back online" (4.15 "No Exit"). However brilliant Tyrol's work might have been, it still needed a woman to actually work. This once again puts women at the forefront of technological development. As R. Connell observed, in our society both science and technology are culturally marked as male spheres—according to this ideology, men thus guarantee progress. This connection, according to Connell and others, also ensures male domination in our world, as well as the domination of certain masculinities over others (Connell 2000, 185–186). But in *BSG* women, not men, guarantee progress—Ellen, not Tyrol, is the architect of resurrection. In addition, Tyrol never truly returns to advanced technology. He tries to save the Galactica from breaking apart by infusing it with Cylon tech (4.15 "No Exit")—but once again, the goal is to maintain antiquated technology: this is what he cares about. Overall, the examples of Tyrol and Bill Adama would suggest that there is not just one kind of technology. There is the advanced kind of technology mostly associated with the Cylons (and Baltar) that is clearly feminized, while the more "antiquated" type of technology is thoroughly masculinized and, in fact, expresses a certain longing for past constructions of masculinity.

While Tyrol is clearly one of the most likeable characters in the show, there is an issue that clouds his otherwise moral portrayal: not unlike Leoben, he has a violent side. Considering the deep embeddedness of violence in the traditional construction of masculinity (Whitehead 2002, 35–38), this is not surprising. Bill Adama and Helo also have violent streaks (as do many of the series' women), but they never use this violence against physically weaker characters or without appropriate cause. Leoben's violence against Kara, though troubling, is at least met with resistance and counter-attacks. Tyrol's violence is far more problematic, especially since it often lacks purpose or is a disproportionate reaction. In several instances, he exhibits unrestrained rage. After Boomer's identity is revealed and Helo has returned to Galactica with another copy of Sharon, Tyrol provokes a fist fight with Helo (2.09 "Flight of the Phoenix"). Of course there is more to this scene. Tyrol had to find out that Boomer was a Cylon sleeper agent and that he had been in love with and protected a Cylon. In addition, Helo has developed a romantic relationship with the "other" Sharon. The same thing happens again in season four when he beats up Hotdog after finding out that he had been sleeping with his wife and is actually his son's father (4.12 "A Disquiet Follows My Soul"). Again, there is more to this, namely an identity crisis after finding out that he is not who he thought he was, which naturally has him reevaluating his life.

However, fighting over a girl is a rather traditional masculine trait, as is this violent response to personal issues. Yet these two instances at least have a certain amount of purpose behind them and we can relate to his reaction. In another instance, Tyrol's violence is utterly senseless and incomprehensible. When he is afraid of being a Cylon in season two (after learning about Boomer's true identity), he beats his future wife Cally bloody in what we are to assume was a dream-like state (2.19 "Lay Down Your Burdens—Part I"). When he apologizes to her, she claims that an apology is unnecessary because he was not himself and reveals her feelings for him (2.20 "Lay Down Your Burdens—Part II"). Excusing male violence against a woman by suggesting that he was not himself seems troubling, especially if it is the injured woman who proposes it.

Of course Tyrol shows remorse and is disgusted by his own actions—but this neither excuses nor explains the incident. Yes, he struggles with his own identity and his loss of control, but should he really be rewarded for these actions by getting to marry his victim? Tyrol never loses his violent streak and continues to act violently and out of proportion when it comes to women. In the series finale, he ruthlessly kills Tory. The impulse is once again explainable, as she had previously murdered his wife. However, he is never brought to account for this murder. It is constructed as an action of unrestrained rage, which nobody even tries to stop. The scene does not stand by itself but is instead a culmination of several acts of violence committed by this highly moral male.

Once again, a religious character who is constructed as an altogether masculine man exhibits violent tendencies that are difficult to explain away. Leoben at least seems to have his violent outbursts under control, whereas Tyrol is frequently blindsided by them. In his violent outbursts, he seems to be a different person, making him appear almost schizophrenic. It is unclear what exactly is upsetting him. Again, there is usually a certain amount of purpose behind his action (with the exception of the attack on Cally), but why the extreme reaction? As noted by several scholars, violence can be a way of re-asserting masculinity in a postfeminist world that has "deprived" men of traditional markers of their gender identity (Quiney 2007; Brabon 2007). We can read the appearance of these violent males in the series as a reaction to the loss of exclusively male space in the military or mechanical (Tyrol) and the scientific or technological spheres (Leoben) and possibly even to the strong dominance of women in the religious sphere.

The series displays some angst in that regard, which is also re-enforced by the already mentioned disappearance or death of several female characters before and during the series finale.

Compared to Leoben, Tyrol's religious side of course remains vague. Only when finding the Temple of Five in the middle of the third season does he ever show true commitment to a religious world-view. His function in the religious narrative is likewise narrow, restricted to his identity as one of the Final Five. Although I find Tyrol to be an interesting challenge to my theory, in the end I would suggest that he confirms it. He is a traditional man who works with traditional technology and is never quite swept up into the religious sphere. In addition, the series outfits this character with violent outbursts that rip into the stability the character is supposed to embody. Masculinity destabilizes the religious machine. Having established this, I will now turn to the next challenger. With Samuel Anders, the series went in a completely different direction in dealing with the (dis)connections between technology, religion and gender.

The (Non)Normative Male Body

The complicated relationship between masculinity and the religious or technological spheres is brought to the point by the character of Samuel T. Anders and the gradual erosion of his originally normative body. Samuel T. Anders is introduced in the season two episode "Resistance" (2.04) as one of the leading resistance fighters on Caprica. Starbuck and Helo join them, and Kara in particular develops a close relationship with Anders. Anders' masculinity is especially established through his normative body. Several scholars have alerted us to the fact that the portrayal of male bodies often escapes closer scholarly attention, in particular as far as normative bodies are concerned (Hutter 2007, 5–7; Whitehead 2002, 181–183). The normative male body is strongly associated with heterosexuality and thus with hegemonic masculinity (McKay et al. 2005, 271). In fact, this is why its depiction was ignored for so long: it represented the established norm. Any other body was interpreted on the basis of its difference to the normative male body—which of course shifted form throughout the decades.

Regardless of these shifts, there was always one type of body (and one type of masculinity) that was constructed as a norm that everyone should aspire to.

Sam is a former professional athlete competing in the series' popular game "pyramid." The game itself is, as everything else in the series, described as genderless, so the teams consist of both women and men. The series once again breaks the rules of our own society, where sports tend to highlight the differences between the genders and, according to some scholars, assert male dominance over women and non-normative men (Messner 2005, 314, 318). In the area of sport, the normative masculine body is allowed to occupy "natural" space that, as we have seen, is otherwise constructed as feminine. Since the 19th century (especially connected to Romanticism), sport has been constructed as a natural and moral activity outside of the industrialized cities that would create "manly men" with desirable male attributes such as leadership or teamwork, and muscular bodies (Magdalinski 2009, 16–17). The "male" elements of competition, physical strength, and strategy tamed nature into a controllable masculine space. While traditional masculinity is destabilized by the elimination of gender boundaries in sports, Anders is nevertheless portrayed as a traditional male: a tall, athletic, and strong man who enjoys competition. Initially, *BSG* thus constructs Anders in a similar way as Tyrol, as a conventionally masculine man without the macho aspects.

While Anders seems to be a perfect example for this portrayal, his heteronormativity is gradually eroded in the course of the story. First, Anders later marries Starbuck, the masculinized woman. We know that Kara is unfaithful—so does Anders, who learns to live with this fact (3.11 "The Eye of Jupiter"). When Anders is revealed to be sickly in the finale of season two while his wife Kara desperately tries to find medication for him, this subverts the depiction of his stereotypical "tight male body as defensive armor against the outside world" (Eynikel 2007, 66) for the first, but not the last time (2.20 "Lay Down Your Burdens—Part II"). When it comes to his relationship with Kara, Anders positions himself between the traditionally masculine and feminine spheres. His body codes him thoroughly masculine, while his lenient (and sometimes submissive?) attitude towards his wife implies passivity traditionally ascribed to femininity (McKay et al. 2005, 280).

7. Violence and Crisis: Religious Men

When he realizes his true identity, this does not change his loyalties towards Starbuck, which also makes him a supporter of her post-resurrection cause. In this he resembles Lee, who is not religious either but has faith in Kara. While this revelation certainly impacts him greatly, another event is much more important in discussing Anders' relationship to the technological and religious. During the Gaeta and Zarek mutiny, Anders is shot in the head. The bullet releases his blocked Cylon memories (4.15 "No Exit). Anders now becomes a source of knowledge for characters and the viewer. Throughout the episode, the scene alternates quite skillfully between the conversation between Cavil and the resurrected Ellen, and the one Anders has with the rest of the Final Five. Both provide vital background information, but do so in a rather different manner. While Anders is the somewhat chaotic, almost frantic voice on the Galactica, Ellen is the calm and contained voice on the Cylon baseship. In essence, the scene is gendered backwards, as chaotic speech is usually associated with femininity (Jowett 2010, 71), while Ellen fulfills the function of the classically male voice of reason.

Sam's injuries are extremely severe, yet he refuses surgery because he is afraid to lose these memories. As his wife, Kara makes a different decision. Before he goes into surgery, he urges Galen, Tory, and Saul to stay with the human fleet. The surgery goes wrong and Anders ends up brain dead. The Cylons proceed to place him in amniotic fluid and hook him up to the datanet (on Galactica)—Anders effectively becomes a hybrid (4.18 "Islanded in a Stream of Stars"). Anders' transformation into a hybrid is intriguing from a gender perspective. The hybrids are in theory introduced as genderless, though the fact that they are embodied effectively voids this idea because we can clearly distinguish hybrid actors from actresses, the latter of which are more common. We also discovered that men are not usually portrayed in the amniotic fluid (for example during the process of resurrection), while women frequently are. The naked body in the tub filled with white fluid is constructed as feminine space or, in the case of the hybrids, a gender-free zone. The hybrids are genderless Cyborgs who represent the "other" that cannot be integrated into society. By becoming a hybrid, Anders' formerly normative body erodes and is effectively "queered."

The "queered" male body has appeared in popular television for some time now. Increasingly conscious of the gender politics of staging bodies, some significant shifts occurred in the past two decades. In the "feminine" space of television in particular, the male body was discovered as an object of desire for both female and non-heterosexual male viewership and staged accordingly (MacInnes 2008, 314; Hutter 2007, 1–4). Naked and vulnerable male bodies became more common. In discussing the vampire Angel in the TV-Series *Buffy the Vampire Slayer* and its spin-off *Angel* (The WB 1999–2004), Allison McCracken has illustrated that the show queered a seemingly normative male body by turning him into the subject of female "erotic and sadistic fantasies" (Schipper 2007, 117). They did so by positioning his body in a "permeable" state—by torturing him and showing him in pain. Angel did not remain the only "queered" male whose body was staged as permeable and in pain. The male body in pain is also at the center of other television shows in the fantasy genre, for example *The Vampire Diaries* (The CW, since 2009) or *Teen Wolf* (MTV, since 2011). Yet these "fantastic" bodies do not remain broken since part of their appeal is their ability to heal quickly. These narratives thus break the normative male body only to re-establish it. Effectively, masculinity must do penance in order to survive.

This is not Anders' fait. His body is never allowed to return to its normative state. Instead, his masculinity is voided forever as soon as he becomes a hybrid (see also Lorna Jowett's discussion of hybrid-Anders: Jowett 2010, 71–72). For my argument, the most significant aspect of this shift is that he becomes God's medium at this point. While he had already held an extraordinary position in the series' mythology as one of the Final Five, he had not previously been a mouthpiece of God. He is only able to access God by becoming a hybrid, surrendering his masculinity to technology. His body is now disabled, non-normative, and androgynous. In Judaism (and effectively also in Islam), gender has been understood as something that distinguishes humans from God, something that marks us as incomplete (Schumacher 2008, 25). Following this logic, the hybrids are closer to God precisely because they are genderless.

Anders loses his normatively masculine body in the process of hybridization—a body that is now only partially functional. His movement is restricted to the resurrection tub; he effectively becomes "disabled," thus taking on the position of the non-normative body. Only when he becomes a hybrid is the link between technology and religion achieved, at least to a certain extent. Anders now acknowledges the one true God and his angels, and becomes his medium. The idea that disabled or physically "different" bodies can be mediators of the divine is in fact quite common in non-Western traditions (Isherwood and Stuart 1998, 90–91). In *BSG*, it seems that the normative male body is unequipped to serve the Divine or, at least, acknowledge its existence, while the non-normative body can. Yet the depiction of Anders as a hybrid always seems somewhat awkward, even uncomfortable, just as the relationship between masculinity and advanced technology as well as religion is altogether uncomfortable in the series. Moreover, this connection is not allowed to last.

Anders' last act in the series is to pilot the Galactica and the rest of the fleets' ships into the sun at the humans' request. They want to rid themselves of all of their technology, and Anders is the executing vessel. The normative male body is completely destroyed in one final act of heroism that is in itself no longer a free choice. His story illustrates the gradual erosion of the normative male body: at first, it is subverted from within until it is destroyed from the outside through a bullet that renders him disabled and androgynous. Anders' body is not put through trials only to be restored; his body is constantly under attack until it is finally destroyed. On *BSG*, the male body cannot be "queered" or rendered non-normative without serious consequences. Like the Centurions (and unlike Hera and the humanoid Cylons), hybrid Anders is a visual marker of difference. Like the Centurions, he cannot enter paradise.

I would suggest that the depiction of Anders' body is subversive, while the final destruction of this subversive body re-establishes masculine normativity as the series' goal. The question whether the destruction of a penetrated male body re-establishes or destroys established gender norms was posed by Judith Halberstam (Halberstam 2007) and further addressed by Alison Peirse (Peirse 2009). I would summarize that there is no definite answer to this question, as this depends strongly on the overall story and especially its conclusion. We need to assess who destroys the male body, how it is destroyed, and to what end. In Anders' case, his death is put in service of the more traditional males instead of women such as Starbuck or Roslin, who also die for the same goal, namely the men's entry into paradise. We can thus once again find a rather negative attitude towards non-normative gender in the series.

The religious man is one of two things: either a violent extremist or a Cylon. In the case of Leoben, we could argue that he is both. Leoben is unstable, erratic, always searching for something that seems unattainable, desperately wanting to be loved. In certain scenes, he borders on insanity. Leoben has a religious function in the narrative (guiding Starbuck) that is nevertheless defined by a more significant woman. He is a religious machine that is never as well-rounded as his female counterparts. Samuel and Tyrol's religious function is minor to non-existent—their connection is more to the mythological than to the overtly religious. They are introduced as rather conventional males, but then take completely different paths. Tyrol always remains a mechanic at heart, a nostalgic for past technologies. Anders embraces advanced technology, but is stripped of his normative masculinity in the process. Human men, on the other hand, are only overtly religious if they are terrorists—religious humans never function as heroes for the narrative. It is also striking how frequently religious men are associated with disproportional acts of violence which I suggested results from this uneasy connection between masculinity and religion. Of course there is one significant exception from this rule, everyone's favorite crazy scientist, Dr. Gaius Baltar—who really deserves his own chapter.

8

The Ambiguity of Dr. Baltar

In the original series, Baltar was a classical villain: a human who willingly plots with the Cylons to have humanity destroyed or subjugated. He lures the quorum into a trap and commands a Cylon baseship—he is clearly evil. The new Baltar, on the other hand, is an unknowing participant in the genocide and is physically placed with the human fleet instead of with the Cylons. He is a deceiver of questionable morals whose only concern is his own wellbeing. He is a narcissist and a coward, an atheist and a charming genius. And yet the series' God chooses him of all people to be his agent and Hera's guardian. He sends Gaius an angel who will finally turn him into a heroic character. Initially, the Cylons choose Baltar to be seduced because they need access to the colonies' defense mainframe. Baltar is an easy target for Caprica Six because he is a womanizer and is susceptible to flattery. Yet his complicity in the genocide also makes him an ideal target for God's angel, who carries the message of Cylon-human reconciliation. Baltar will help both humans and Cylons in his need for self-preservation and can consequently be a mediator. At the end of *Miniseries*, Baltar tells Messenger-Six: "I am not on anybody's side." This makes him a perfect instrument of God, who is not on anybody's side either.

I suggest that Baltar's case illustrates the fall of rationalized enlightenment thought. Although many scholars have postulated that religion would eventually disappear or at least become insignificant as reason and science advance, the recent decades have suggested that this has not been the case. Specifically, some scholars have unmasked the entire theory of secularization as an invention of Western intellectuals that is far-removed from the everyday experience of "ordinary people" (Berger 1999). As the genre of reason and science, science fiction has long been a defender of the secularization paradigm. Since *BSG* tried to challenge classical conventions of the genre, it is not surprising that they also challenged this idea. Moore felt that it was more realistic to include religion in the story instead of creating yet another sci-fi world that presumed its insignificance. This is one of the reasons why Baltar seems awkward, somewhat displaced in the narrative: he is the rational scientist of traditional sci-fi. Baltar finally has to accept religion, just as Western scholars have to accept the "re-enchantment of the West" (Partridge 2004–2005). Since *BSG* is a religious narrative, Baltar can only become a hero after he has abandoned his rationalized enlightenment doctrines and embraced the "irrational." On the following pages, I offer an in-depth analysis of Baltar's journey towards heroism, suggesting that the microcosm of Baltar reflects the macrocosm of *BSG*'s more general message: that the triumph of rationalized science over religion is a myth.

Atheist in Crisis

If Baltar cannot be described as evil, he can certainly not be called heroic either. In order to become a hero, he needs to renounce rationalized science and especially atheism and become religious. He has to break the "shackles" of Western intellectualism and faith in science and embrace the seemingly irrational and unexplainable spiritual world. This is a painful and bumpy process. We should note that historically, the break between religion and reason was never complete. The two spheres had complemented each other until the 18th century, when philosophers such as the Frenchman Denis Diderot (1713–1784) decided to rid science of metaphysics. In doing so, Diderot became the first public and self-designated atheist (Hyman 2007, 30). Atheism was thus clearly linked to the rise of science. Yet although radical enlightenment philosophers thought that religion would eventually be replaced by reason, more moderate thinkers simply sought an "enlightened" religion that recognized God but discarded "superstitions" (Kelleter 2002, 190–214). Deists, for example, believed that God had created the universe but then retreated from it completely. 19th century Europe in fact saw an upsurge of nostalgic religion, especially within Romanticism, while the United States was simultaneously confronted with several "Great Awakenings" that propelled religion unto the Center Stage of politics and society.

The secularization theory that emerged from radical enlightenment thought was originally not anti-religious either. Among the major proponents of the theory that religion was in inevitable decline in Western civilization were scholars like Max Weber (1864–1920) who actually looked favorably on religion, as well as several theologians (Berger 2001, 444). The idea of secularization was mostly propagated in intellectual circles of both Europe and the United States, while religion remained important for the largest parts of the population.[1] Baltar embodies the extreme position of an intellectual who strongly believes in science and reason and fails to acknowledge the very real presence of religion in the world he lives in.

In Baltar's world, it is not only religion as a player in society and politics that needs acknowledgement, but also the actual presence of the divine. In the beginning, Baltar is convinced that "there is no God" and states that he believes "in a world I can and do understand. A rational universe, explained through rational means" (1.01 "33"). God is dealing with a complete atheist, someone who does not believe in God's existence (as opposed to an agnostic who believes that we are unable to know whether God exists or not). Baltar is a strong believer, but his faith is in science, not God. Baltar needs tangible proof for God's existence—and even when he gets proof, he tries to find scientific explanations in order to save his scientific belief system.

God offers proof by throwing Baltar into dangerous situations and pulling him out as soon as he is acknowledged. In "33" (1.01), a doctor Emereck who claims to have information about a human traitor complicit in the Cylon attacks is a potential threat to Baltar. God reacts by making his ship, the Olympic Carrier, disappear during the next jump. When Baltar refuses to acknowledge God's involvement, the Olympic Carrier returns. Messenger-Six suggests that "it's God's punishment for your lack of faith," leading Baltar to demand "a more logical and useful explanation, please!" Yet the situation becomes increasingly threatening—and Baltar increasingly nervous. When the president has to decide whether or not to destroy this ship as a possible Cylon ploy, Baltar is at the end of his rope and offers to repent for his sins. Shortly after, Roslin gives the order to destroy the Olympic Carrier. Messenger-Six proposes that this was not actually Roslin's decision, but God's, who is testing Baltar's reserve through his angel.

The angel has several tools at her disposal to convince Baltar of God's existence and his active role in the universe. One of these tools are the so-called "projections"—virtual environments only visible to certain people. While Baltar occupies one such projection with Messenger-Six in the beginning of the episode "Six Degrees of Separation" (1.07), we discover more about his initial belief system. He begins to mock Messenger-Six's faith excessively, ending in a monologue that expresses his feelings towards religion. He tells Messenger-Six that her beliefs are "superstitious dribble" and "metaphysical nonsense" which a rational being could never accept. Essentially, Baltar believes that religion is for stupid people. Baltar is the embodiment of the enlightenment philosopher who elevates reason and science above irrationality and superstition. His intolerance of religious worldviews mirrors similar attitudes held by many early enlightenment philosophers, who even proposed to censure conservative religious writings (Munck 2000, 7). Such an attitude is of course ironic, considering that we usually associate enlightenment thinking with values such as freedom and equality. Baltar illustrates the kind of arrogance that can go along with a "scientific belief system." In the series, these values have to be questioned and eventually shot down as they inhibit posthumanity and Cylon-human reconciliation. Through Baltar, the series questions our reliance on reason and challenges the intellectualism of a secular worldview. As a scientist, Baltar is brilliant and charming, but also callous and cowardly. As a believer, he becomes a hero who is selfless and brave.

How can such a change be accomplished? Effectively, Baltar needs to convert, to switch from one belief system to another. God and his angel begin their project by threatening Baltar. They continuously put him in a position of such personal danger that—for reasons of self-preservation and lack of other options—he accepts God (temporarily).

8. The Ambiguity of Dr. Baltar

This course of events is repeated several times. The events of "33" are replicated in the already mentioned episode "Six Degrees of Separation" (1.07), where Baltar angers the angel enough with his arrogant anti-religious speech to chase her away. As soon as Messenger-Six (and thus God) has left, things start to fall apart for Baltar. (Fake) evidence for his involvement in the initial Cylon attack is discovered and Baltar is imprisoned as a traitor. Desperate, Baltar speaks to God for the first time and acknowledges him as the one true God, asking him to "deliver me from this evil" (whatever he imagines that to be). In this moment, Messenger-Six returns and Baltar is freed shortly after. The messenger continues to play with Baltar's sanity, leading him towards irrational belief. Yet for the most part, it is still his will for self-preservation and his narcissism that (sometimes) makes him believe. It is a long way from his uncanny and arrogant acknowledgement "I am an instrument of God" (1.10 "The Hand of God") to his actual commitment to this God and the acknowledgement of God's angels in the season finale.

When we discussed God's angels in the third chapter, we saw that Messenger-Six sometimes resorts to violence when dealing with Baltar. If he cannot not be enticed by her sexuality or convinced by God's actions, he needs to be forced. Twice, she viciously screams at him when he wants to abandon working on the Cylon detector, and she even attacks him physically at times (1.03 "Bastille Day," 1.06 "Litmus," 1.12 "Kobol's Last Gleaming, Part I"). He has to learn to listen to the angel by any means possible. For the convinced atheist Baltar this includes threatening his person in various ways. However, the angel can really only try to persuade Baltar. Since he is a narcissist and an atheist, he needs guidance, but his actions are technically his own. Of course there are serious constraints to his agency, as everyone seems to have an opinion about what he should do and who he should be. In order to survive, Baltar has to do many things he would not ordinarily consider.

J. Robert Loftis described Baltar as a "tyrant," defining "tyrant" as "a powerful person who gets what he wants, and who wants a lot" (Loftis 2008, 31). I find this image to be a bit misleading—Baltar might want a lot, but neither does he always (or even sometimes) get it, nor is he actually powerful. In fact, I would argue that he is initially quite the opposite: completely powerless. First of all, Gaius Baltar does not do anything willingly. For the most part, his decisions are not his own, he is forced into positions he never wanted. In the first season, the president appoints him as her advisor because of his intelligence and knowledge of Colonial defenses, Adama charges him with constructing a Cylon detector, and Messenger-Six and others push him into politics.

Baltar is completely bored by his scientific work on the Cylon detector that is not exactly challenging, and has no political ambitions whatsoever. When he is elected to the Quorum of Twelve on behalf of Caprica, not only does he find the notion of himself as a politician ridiculous, but he also proposes that "politics is the only thing more boring than blood samples" (1.11 "Colonial Day"). Moments later, the narrative is forwarded to a Quorum meeting at which we find Baltar sound asleep. He never wanted to get involved in politics. The people of Caprica elected him and only shortly afterwards Roslin asks him to be her vice-president, mainly because she needs his popularity to counter the growing influence of former terrorist and idealist Tom Zarek. As we will see, this is a recurring pattern in Baltar's life—others put him in positions he never wanted in the first place, and then complain about the results.

The interactions between Messenger-Six and Baltar serve not only to amuse the viewer (mission accomplished!), but also to inform them of God's nature and the Cylon religion. Through these dialogues we learn that God is not "the Cylon God," but the only God, and that he, apparently does not take sides (e.g., 1.10 "The Hand of God"). Since God and Messenger-Six frequently act against Cylon interests, Baltar starts to find this explanation more logical than the idea that Messenger-Six is a Cylon plot. At the end of the first season, his previously firm atheism has come under serious attack. Going back to the meta-level of Western intellectual enlightenment, we can liken this process to the realization that religion did not disappear as quickly as the philosophers had thought. This does not mean that belief in science and reason was immediately abandoned, but their theories needed to be questioned and, possibly, altered. In Baltar's case, his scientific belief system simply failed to produce explanations for several events, and his rational mind leads him to conclude that something unscientific might be transpiring. The events prepared him for God's real plan for him: the protection of Hera, who would join the fleet soon.

8. The Ambiguity of Dr. Baltar

The Politician

In the second season of *BSG*, Baltar's story arch centers on his growing political influence and eventual election as president as well as his role as a protector and advocate for Hera. Messenger-Six clarifies for Baltar that the child means salvation, that she is a gift from God. That bad men can be turned into good men (or at least slightly less bad men) through the innocence of a child has been a staple of Hollywood story production ever since women stopped being innocent and were thus no longer able to fulfill this function (Aronson and Kimmel 2001, 44–45). When it comes to Hera, Baltar is indeed frequently more sympathetic than many of our more heroic characters. In 2.18 "Downloaded," for example, Hera's right to exist is put into question by people such as Laura Roslin and Bill Adama. While everyone else believes she should be terminated, Baltar is outraged at the thought of killing a baby and is the only one in the room to acknowledge her as an innocent, sentient being.

For most of the characters, Hera is a "thing," a machine. In this particular discussion, Baltar seems to be the only one (besides her parents) to recognize that she is also a baby. It is in this second season that Baltar increasingly becomes a mediator as someone who appreciates and understands both sides. At this point we should remember why God chooses Baltar in the first place: God needs a mediator between Cylons and humans who can understand both worlds without belonging to either. In the second season, the series does not focus on Baltar's beliefs as much as this mediating position. He repeatedly proposes moral behavior towards Cylons. This is fascinating considering that Baltar is generally not a very moral character. However, when it comes to acknowledging machine sentience, he is a pioneer. This pioneering role is certainly connected to his scientific more than his religious side. Scientifically, it seems plausible to him that Cylons might be sentient.

His empathy for Cylons extends beyond the hybrid child Hera, as we discover during the Pegasus story arc. He develops a strong connection to the Six-Copy Gina, the abused Cylon prisoner on Pegasus. As a consequence, he tells Messenger-Six that he has lost interest in the projections that had frequently framed his meetings with the angel and showed his old house on Caprica (2.11 "Resurrection Ship—Part I"). Baltar has grown. He feels protective both of Gina and of Hera, and he feels that he has to fight for their rights when nobody else will. He even begins to stand up to God's messenger, who disapproves of his close relationship with Gina. For the first time, he realizes that the angel has no real power, that he can make his own decisions (and will not be punished by God if they are morally right). Although the protection of Hera is in God's interest and is certainly propagated by Messenger-Six, Gina's protection is not. When Baltar stands up for Hera and Gina, he does so because he believes it to be right, and not simply because God asks him to.

Lorna Jowett has pointed out that Baltar, like many sci-fi scientists, is a rather isolated character (Jowett 2008, 65–67). He has no friends we know of, only occasional allies like Tom Zarek—but never actual friends. His genius singles him out as different, peculiar, and even creepy. Though, and Jowett also mentions this, he is brilliant and charming in front of the camera, he is nevertheless unapproachable in real life. This is really the only reason Baltar can be a mediator between Cylon and human—he does not belong to either group. This becomes even more pronounced in the third season, when he is openly abandoned by everyone but God and his angel. Baltar is an outsider, which is certainly necessary in order for him to be impartial. Despite all that, Baltar is elected president by the end of the season, a course of events God's angel pushes to a much stronger extent than his role as a Cylon protector.

Baltar's political career, as stated above, is largely brought about by outside forces, of which Messenger-Six is only one factor. Everything begins with his election to the Quorum brought about by the voters of Caprica and Roslin's subsequent decision to appoint him as her vice-president. Since Roslin does not hold Baltar in high regard and actually begins to suspect his involvement in the initial attack very early on (she is our political messiah, after all), it is not difficult for Tom Zarek and Messenger-Six to convince him to aspire to presidency (2.17 "The Captain's Hand"). Messenger-Six tells Baltar that he has been "chosen to lead these people by almighty God" and that everything would work out if he just had faith. Messenger-Six indicates that God wants him to be president, while Zarek clearly has his own motifs in supporting

8. The Ambiguity of Dr. Baltar

(or pushing) Baltar's presidency. Zarek wrongly believes that he can control Baltar and shape his politics for his own goals. Although Baltar might have developed a commitment to help certain individuals, he is still motivated primarily by his wish for self-preservation: he knows that Roslin suspects him and does not trust him.

Baltar begins his campaign for the presidency by taking a stand against Roslin's unpopular decision to criminalize abortion. As Heather Hendershot points out, *BSG* is certainly unique in its treatment of the value and danger of pregnancies, especially when it comes to the topic of abortion. Unlike many other television series, "the control of women's bodies by others is portrayed as the worst crime imaginable" (Hendershot 2009, 226). The violation of the female body is repeatedly treated as the highest evil, as exemplified by the serially raped Gina as well as the "farm" created by Cylons to experiment on humans and their reproductive ability. The criminalization of abortion by the generally heroic, yet ethically complex President Laura Roslin is, in any case, presented as a grave error in judgment and, as it turns out, politics. Of course Baltar does not object to her decision on moral grounds, but does so strategically. Yet another strategic decision would have much bigger consequences: Messenger-Six and Zarek convince Baltar that he should advocate the settlement of humanity on a recently discovered planet in order to win the election. With this issue, he can make a stand against Roslin, who wants to keep looking for Earth (2.20 "Lay Down Your Burdens").

Season Two ends with Baltar's election to presidency, the settlement of the planet New Caprica, and eventually the arrival of the Cylons on humanity's new home. President Baltar surrenders and becomes the political puppet who legitimizes the Cylon occupation. Season three's Baltar is much darker than he had previously been—the years as president under Cylon occupation and the feeling of being hated as well as being powerless left a mark. In many ways, there is much wisdom and morality in his depiction at the beginning of the season. As a viewer, we develop a previously unfamiliar understanding for Baltar's actions— what would have happened to the humans, had Baltar not surrendered? This war could never have been won.

At the same time, the humans become increasingly unsympathetic with their use of violence and terrorism as a means of political expression. No matter how much we might sympathize with their motives, the means are not portrayed as justified. In 3.02 "Precipice," Baltar visits Laura Roslyn in prison in an attempt to convince her to speak out against the bombings. Roslyn refuses, but it is clear that she does not condone suicide bombings as such. Baltar is portrayed as sincere in his belief that suicide bombings are wrong—a position that is shared by the much more heroic Laura Roslyn. Though he might appear to be motivated by self-interest (after all, one of the attacks was directed at his life), he is obviously shocked by the mere fact that humans would kill each other and his concern and grief for the thirty-something victims of the last attack does not seem to be fake. When Roslyn mentions that the Cylons had tortured humans, Baltar is quickly outraged and repeats twice "Nobody's been tortured!" in a manner that clearly shows that he needs to convince himself more than anyone else. Nothing he says seems dishonest, though there is certainly a considerable amount of self-deception going on.

Let's not forget that in the very same episode, Baltar initially refuses to sign the assassination order for Laura Roslyn, Tom Zarek, and others until the Cylons force him to do so by putting a gun to his head. The essence of the Baltar character was always his humanity. He is just as flawed as most of us, very unlike a hero (Rogers 2008). In addition, God's angel Messenger-Six convinces him to finally sign the order against his own wishes. Baltar protests that he simply cannot do it, but Messenger-Six stresses that he has to do it in order to survive.

As president, Baltar has been put in an impossible situation. One could find blame with him for deciding in favor of human settlement on Caprica (a decision he only made in order to win the election), but in the end he was elected by the people because THEY wanted to settle there. After his presidency is a complete fiasco, everyone seems to forget that they elected him or supported his political career. Baltar is turned into the scapegoat—the Cylon collaborator who betrayed his own people. His is demonized and described as evil, because the people need someone to blame. While Baltar's egotism and arrogance are as strong as ever, he is not the villain he is made out to be. First of all, he was elected and did not seize power undemocratically. Neither was the idea to become president his own. Most importantly, he does not appear callous or anti-human, and is clearly shown as a conflicted, even broken man with a conscience.

All of these events work towards Baltar's eventual conversion. We find that he has morals that certainly originate in his scientific beliefs but are supported by divine intervention. His political career builds on his narcissism, but eventually disillusions him and discredits his position with humans and, as we shall see, Cylons alike. The failure on New Caprica will make him a stronger mediator and deprive him of any sympathies he might have had in the fleet or with the Cylons, which makes him more open to acknowledging Messenger-Six as an angel of God. Essentially, the angel cleverly maneuvers Baltar in a situation where everything is taken from him in order to open his mind for divine influence. Baltar's naïve optimism about his own abilities is broken when he is confronted with the harsh reality. Things only got worse for him before they got better.

The Traitor

Although I have stated before that I feel somewhat uncomfortable with Loftis' idea of Baltar as a "tyrant," there is certainly value in the idea of Baltar as a tyrannized soul—a soul that cannot help but become a traitor. In season three, Baltar's main role is that of a man who is hated, tortured, and seen as a traitor by both humans and Cylons. Significantly, this reinforces and even strengthens his in-between status that made God choose him as a mediator in the first place. In season three, Baltar is first placed with the Cylons, then with the humans, is tortured in both scenarios and finally has to face trial on charges of treason. He contemplates suicide more than once and struggles with his own identity. The former atheist is broken and shattered into pieces, giving Messenger-Six the opportunity to re-assemble his faith according to God's will.

After the successful rebellion on New Caprica, both humans and Cylons leave the planet and this failed experiment of coexistence behind. Baltar joins the Cylons because he would clearly not be safe with the humans. Yet the Cylons are unsure whether he should be allowed to stay. With three models in favor of his presence and three against, the final decision has to be made by the Sixes (3.05 "Collaborators"). God's angel charges him with learning as much as possible about the Cylons while he is on board. We also learn that he has the gift of Cylon projection, though the series never clearly explains, why. Baltar's initial response is to ask whether he is a Cylon, which would explain the ability to project (3.06 "Torn"). Since, as we know, he is not a Cylon, the projection seems to have a spiritual dimension, though there is not much clarity on this issue. In any case, the projections re-affirm Baltar's role as a mediator and chosen of God. Without being a Cylon, Baltar can do something that other humans cannot.

Finally, the Cylons decide that Baltar is a traitor because he withheld significant information from them. Of course once again, Baltar is blamed for something he did not exactly do. While he did withhold some information, the Cylons' conclusion that he is working with the humans in order to find an ultimate weapon against them is simply not correct. For the first (but not the last) time in this season, Baltar is tortured. The torture is administered by female Cylons, notably D'Anna with Caprica Six standing by. Messenger-Six protects Baltar by helping him to escape into the projections and telling him that the pain he is feeling is only physical—"neural impulses sent to the brain" and that he himself could decide how to interpret them. "Separate your mind from your body. Keep your mind in that room. Use your intellect against her. Reason, logic, analysis" (3.07 "A Measure of Salvation"). This notion is both rather posthuman and rather Gnostic as it is based on mind-body dualism. Messenger-Six then instructs Gaius to examine D'Anna's faith, which is when we get another glimpse at Baltar's true feelings concerning God. While he had clearly espoused an atheist position that elevated science and reason above all else while discrediting belief in the divine as "superstitious dribble," he now proposes that "if God exists, our knowledge of him is imperfect." Baltar has effectively become an agnostic.

Baltar no longer denies God's existence as such, but refutes the idea that anyone can truly know him, let alone speak for him. He is still a scientist who acknowledges that myths are man-made stories that can, at the very best, approach the divine, but never truly know or understand it. Baltar wants to help D'Anna to "reconcile her faith with fact" in order to "find a way to a more rational universe." It seems that

8. The Ambiguity of Dr. Baltar

Baltar has accepted that faith in God is not in itself "incorrect," but the absolutes proposed by religious systems are, in his opinion, irrational and cannot be reconciled with science. With the help of Messenger-Six (and a considerable amount of misunderstanding), Baltar convinces D'Anna to stop torturing him. While he can hardly be described as a true believer, he is at least open to faith and finds solace in this faith (especially in his "guardian angel"). Making a detour to our meta-level, we find that science and reason have accepted the power of religion as well as the possibility that spirituality might be reconcilable with science. To "reconcile faith with fact" does not mean abandoning faith, but finding a middle ground.

Besides his position as a mediator, season three also plays with the idea that Baltar might be a Cylon. More precisely, the series plays with the notion of Baltar believing or rather wishing he were a Cylon. Then he would "stop being a traitor to one set of people and be a hero to another. And have a place to belong" (3.10 "The Passage"). In the middle of the season, Baltar moves from the Cylon baseship back to the Galactica (not entirely by choice) and is imprisoned as a traitor. In his cell, Baltar tries to hang himself and has a vision of waking up in a resurrection tub, indicating that he might be a Cylon. Of course he is only dreaming. He clearly feels relief during the dream because this would mean that he was not a traitor, and we learn that it bothers Baltar to be seen as one. We also find that his narcissism is alive and well as he adds, "I always knew I was different, special. Maybe a little gifted" (3.13 "Taking a Break from All Your Worries"). As if being chosen by God was not enough. Baltar probably finds his role as God's chosen elusive, since he knows neither if God really exists, nor what his role is. Being a Cylon sure would explain a lot.

The humans also torture him, especially because they want him to finally admit to his involvement in the initial Cylon attack, which he still refuses to do. He is put under with a military drug that creates the illusion of imminent death. Under torture, he partially confesses to this crime, though he refuses to see himself as an active participant since, as he puts it, "conspiracy requires intent. I never intended" (3.17 "A Measure of Salvation"). And in fact, he is right. Unlike the Baltar of the original *BSG*, he never actively conspired to commit genocide. That was indeed not his crime. However, in his assertion that he is not actually responsible for his actions because he did not consciously commit genocide, he is once again deceiving himself. Baltar did commit various crimes: allowing someone access to the defense mainframe and lying about this (and so many other things), deceiving various people, etc. Under torture, he finally admits that he has made mistakes and that he is flawed. In the final analysis, however, he understands himself as a player, in the fourth season even refers to himself as "the flood" (4.09 "The Hub").

Under torture, Baltar also reveals the more spiritual aspects of his relationship to Six, that he was "guided between the light and the dark," wondering if Messenger-Six was "an angel or a demon." This is the second rare mention of demons in the series which, as we discussed in an earlier chapter, are altogether rather rare. Again, I would propose that the appearance of a demon (of course only in rhetoric and not in actuality) is inconsistent with the rest of the narrative. Be that as it may, Baltar admits once again that he wants to be one of the Final Five. In this instance, he appropriates religious language—something that would have seemed impossible in the first season. He now understands the world in categories of good and evil, but he is unsure which part he is supposed to play. His confusion and insecurity reflect Western society's feelings in a postmodern world, where it has become unclear who the enemy is and how good and evil are defined. The question of who or what Baltar is, and what role he plays becomes a microcosm of these anxieties that are also reflected in his crisis of belief. How his scientific and his religious sides relate, and whether they can be reconciled is an issue of wide-ranging importance. The atheist intellectual has been broken and is now unsure of his position in the world.

Post-presidency Baltar clearly understands his own flawed nature much better than pre-presidency Baltar. He admits to his own mistakes and sins, though only gradually. Although he still tries to justify his actions so he is able to live with himself, he is ultimately unsuccessful, as evidenced by his suicide attempt. Only being a Cylon would rid him of any responsibility and clear his conscience. Of course this is why the narrative cannot allow him to be one of the Final Five—that would have been too easy. The conflict between Baltar the scientist and Baltar the believer is even more pronounced in the fourth and last season, with his scientific self continuously forced into the background.

8. The Ambiguity of Dr. Baltar

From Cult Leader to Hero

In season four, Baltar becomes the leader of a human monotheist cult. Once again, he does not seek this position out. Instead, people visit him in his prison asking him to bless them and their children and explaining that they believe in him—a notion that Baltar himself finds completely ridiculous (3.19 "Crossroads—Part I"). He eventually goes along with it because he has nowhere else to go, but he never really believes himself to be a chosen leader or healer. In depicting the "cult of Baltar," *BSG* obviously builds on familiar pictures of historical and contemporary cults from the Branch Davidians to the People's Temple. However, by stylizing the scientist Baltar of all people as their leader, the series suggests that cults are not simply built on a megalomaniac leader, but also respond to the needs of certain people. As Philip Zimbardo pointed out, in order to understand cults one has to understand what kind of needs they fulfill for the group of people who participate in them, specifically what kind of needs "traditional society" is unable to fulfill for them (Zimbardo 2007, 25).

Zimbardo further explains that cults are "diagnostic of where and how society is failing its citizens" (Zimbardo 2007, 26). In the case of *BSG*'s society, the leadership has obviously neglected a certain portion of the population and has failed to make them feel safe. Very likely, these people lost someone close to them either in the initial Cylon attack or as a consequence of the occupation and rebellion on New Caprica. Unlike other citizens, they have not felt comforted by society's "traditional" support systems, including the established polytheistic religion and of course political and military leadership. They have experienced a major trauma (possibly more than one) and have chosen to contextualize this trauma through a cult that offers a grand narrative that includes salvation (Kuncewicz 2007, 56). They turn to someone who is rejected by and excluded from traditional society and has a different view of both politics and religion. In this particular case, the people construct their own messiah figure in order to fulfill their own needs for clarity and safety.

However, we should not assume that the "cult of Baltar" portrays the reality of cult life. In many ways, the depiction is a farce, an over-the-top presentation of well-known stereotypes of religious cults. The "cult of Baltar" includes mostly women who gather around him in oriental-style dwellings, build shrines for him, and encourage him to spread the monotheist faith through fleet-wide broadcasts. Baltar finds the role he is put in ridiculous, which clearly distinguishes him from historical and contemporary cult leaders. He calls himself "king of fools" and concludes that it is better to be hated by everyone "than to be loved by this lot" (4.01 "He That Believeth in Me").

Influenced by Messenger-Six, he makes the best of the situation and starts spreading the monotheist message. This is where Baltar makes an original contribution to his cult, which had not previously been acquainted with monotheism. Since Baltar actually talks to an angel, God obviously does use him to spread his message. Messenger-Six also makes sure that Baltar is seen as a hero by his flock by hilariously picking him up after he is beaten down by marines (4.04 "Escape Velocity"). However, since the "cult of Baltar" always remains somewhat creepy, this plot device does not act as a justification for cults as such. The fact that Baltar's prayers actually lead to a miraculous recovery of a sick child might reinforce Baltar's status as God's chosen, but it never legitimizes the cult itself. While leading the cult, Baltar goes back and forth between religion and atheism, which Baltar-actor James Callis found increasingly problematic to play. The writing staff explained to him that this was just typical of cult leaders, and referred specifically to People's Temple founder Jim Jones (Gosling 2009, 137). The point for Gaius is that he always feels uncomfortable with this cult of his, and leaves them the first chance he gets. Again (unlike Jim Jones), he has been pushed into a role he does not want to play. When he decides to return to his cult, they have already moved on and found a new leader, which reinforces the series' depiction of the cult as essentially self-made and Baltar as a man whose power depends on others.

In season four, Baltar also meets his angelic alter-ego for the first time (4.02 "Six of One"). His wonderfully annoyed reaction to Messenger-Baltar's appearance ("Who the frack are you?") reinforces his confusion and feelings of insanity. Of course at this point, Baltar has either fallen from grace as far as most humans are concerned, or been accepted as a religious figure, so he has no reservations anymore about talking to the (otherwise invisible) angel in public, as ridiculous as it may look. At the end of the season he publically announces that

8. The Ambiguity of Dr. Baltar

he talks to angels, saying: "Angels take the guise of those who are nearest and dearest to you. Those who can understand your doubts and your trials. And steer you back on the road to salvation. I believe in these angels because I see them" (4.18 "Islanded in a Stream of Stars"). At the end of the series we can consequently see Baltar embracing the religious sphere and accepting his own role in God's plan. In a final step, Baltar has to become a selfless hero.

This process is completed in the series finale, when Baltar volunteers for Hera's rescue mission (4.20 "Daybreak—Part II"). Significantly, Messenger-Six does not force this decision on him. For the first time, he makes a heroic decision by himself. The Baltar we met in *Miniseries* never would have put himself in danger for somebody else. This decision shows Caprica Six that Baltar really has changed and that she can finally be proud of him. Baltar then delivers the final speech explaining that he talks to angels and that "God is not on any one side," reminding us of the end of the *Miniseries*, where Baltar had declared his impartiality as well.

In the course of the narrative, Baltar is transformed from villain to hero largely through religion. The lack of clear boundaries between good and evil in the series is characteristic of postmodern stories. The nature of evil can of course be discussed in a variety of ways and has been tackled by many disciplines, most notably theology, philosophy, and ethics. Most popular culture provides a moral message that implies a certain understanding of what is good and what is evil—what is right and what is wrong. On contemporary TV, a growing number of television programs complicate the boundaries between good and evil, leaving the audience with an ambivalent feeling about morality. *BSG* and *Caprica* surely qualify for this, and Baltar is the most significant case study in this regard. We have already seen that some moral problems remain rather open, for example the issue of God's complicity in genocide. The characters on the show are likewise not perfect heroes who are unable to err or are completely without sin, regardless of their gender. Kara commits adultery, Laura suggests and implicitly commits murder, and Caprica Six is an agent of genocide. Since our heroines are flawed and can commit "evil" acts, our villains are likewise not completely evil, but have their positive sides that make them relatable to a certain extent.

Although Baltar's narrative seems erratic and even inconsistent,

I argue that he, more than any other character on the show, relates Western society's ambivalence regarding the interconnections between religion and science. The series first establishes him as the archetype of the traditional sci-fi scientist who assumes a clear contrast between the two spheres. The narrative then proceeds to poke holes in this contrast and to blur the borders between them. It tests Baltar's assumptions and proposes questions he cannot answer with science alone. It then deprives him of any position within society, in order to make him more susceptible to a non-scientific worldview. Finally, the series forces him to reconcile the two positions and even abandon some of his former scientific principles in favor of faith. He has to recognize that science alone does not explain the world. Whether one agrees with this assessment or not is a different issue; the gist of his story shows clear parallels to the way Western intellectuals have had to adapt to a reality where religion has held its ground despite the triumph of science.

In Baltar, we have an ambiguous and rather unique figure that navigates between religion and science—and is male. I would propose that there is one big difference between him and the female saviors: Baltar has to renounce technology in order to embrace his new self—something that the female Cylons are not (and cannot) be asked to do. After arriving in "paradise" (our Earth), Baltar plans to become a farmer—as we found out, he was raised on a farm and thus knows all about cultivation. He had previously despised this heritage, so it is clearly difficult for him to return to farming and leave his other "rational" self behind. While Matthew Jones stated that in the end "Baltar is reconciled with normative masculinity through his embracing of the military and manual labor" (Jones 2010, 176), I would argue that by embracing religion, he also embraces the feminine as constructed by the series. While some aspects of his masculinity are clearly non-normative, his rationality and association with science presented him with typically masculine traits at the outset of the journey. Normative masculinity is associated with reason, which Baltar has to leave behind in order to become a hero. Religion thus feminizes him in a way that necessitates a break from science and technology. More importantly, Baltar is an unstable and erratic character—something he has in common with Leoben and Tyrol. Even Baltar then, cannot safely reconcile science and religion. Only women can.

Conclusion

This book set out to explore how religion and technology are gendered in two connected early 21st century science fiction series. I suggest that various stereotypes are reinterpreted in the series in a way that impacts the genre of science fiction in general and that these reinterpretations are strongly connected to the return of religion in postmodern narratives. To start with the most basic, let us consider the gender of good and evil. In the Christian religious tradition, both good and evil are predominantly male—God, angels, Devil, and demons are coded male (Janowski 2006, 25). In the universe of *BSG*, the picture is more ambiguous. Both men and women can be both "good" and "evil." In *Caprica*, the roles are even completely reversed as savior (Zoe-A) and villain (Clarice) are both female. Evil as such does not originate with the supernatural on the shows, but is a purely human quality. Demons or fallen angels do not populate the series, while human evil is often (but not always) related to a lack of faith in the divine. The central issue is not with the gender of evil per se, but with the connection or disconnection between evil, religion, and technology. Concerning these (dis)connections, the following interesting trends emerge.

Men are still portrayed in accordance with enlightenment logic, in that their morality is derived from rationality. This is completely in keeping with humanist thought and, consequently, traditional science fiction. Yet men also strongly leave the scientific or technological sphere because they are no longer the guardians of technological advance.

Instead, women now fulfill this role, all the while remaining religious—and thus, in keeping with enlightenment logic, irrational. "Good" men are generally neither comfortable with advanced technology, nor with religion. If men are associated with technology (like Gaeta or Cavil, but also Baltar and even Daniel Graystone) their morals are seen as instable, their actions as too emotional, and they are connected to the abuse of power. If men embrace religion (like Baltar), they have to renounce technology.

On the other hand, as soon as women are associated with religion, they are usually good. The exception is Clarice Willow, who nevertheless does not have to renounce technology in order to be religious. She continues preaching to the Cylons, connecting the technological to the religious. Clarice always remains a mediator who can be both. Men who try to reconcile the technological with the religious (notably the Cylon Leoben) display almost psychotic behavior, suggesting that this connection is an uneasy one that creates instable masculinity. As a conclusion, we find that women can navigate between religion and technology, while men cannot. They have to decide for one or the other.

Through God and religion, the out-of-control machine is tamed and returned to nature. Traditionally, artificial creations have been interpreted as blasphemy with the out-of-control machine acting as a punishment for this act against God or nature (Schumacher 2008, 97). In contrast, the *Battlestarverse* portrays the artificial being as willed and created by God. As such, the story can find a "happy ending" that neither includes erasing the machine nor ends in the destruction of mankind through this ill-conceived creation. Not coincidentally, this machine was not the product of a male "mad scientist" who objectifies the machine right from the beginning, but of the religious woman with respect for her creation.

According to some, science fiction is a genre in crisis. As technology advances at an increasing speed, it has become almost impossible to construct a believable future. In addition, criticism from cyberpunk and the general trend of postmodernity have destabilized the core of sci-fi's humanist worldview. The issue is now one of eroding boundaries, of navigating between extremes and reconciling opposing opinions. Far from being answered, the question what makes us human has become even more complicated. Although despised by many fans and critics of the shows, religion actually offers a solution for many of these problems. Religion furthers the reconciliation between (wo)man and machine and mediates between female stereotypes and female empowerment. In literature, film, and TV, women who venture into technology have frequently exhibited destructive behavior, while religious women are presented either as nutcases or as passive victims. Religion makes the technological woman more plausible or less threatening, while technology makes the religious woman saner—and more powerful. Sci-fi's commitment to rational masculinity is nevertheless not completely dismissed in *BSG* and *Caprica*, though it does strike us as somewhat outdated and old-fashioned when compared to the innovative and risk-taking female heroes (and even villains).

It is not just the mere fact that religious leaders are female or that technology is associated with women—what really makes the difference is the confluence of all three elements. This in turn alters the three aspects. Technology is no longer rational, because it is no longer masculine. It has become thoroughly "irrational," because it is feminine and religious. Since religion triumphs over science, the irrational becomes rational. Thus the technophobe or technophile ending of the series: it is posthuman, because the boundaries between human and machine have completely eroded and Cyborgs are revealed as our ancestors. Yet it is also utterly humanist because it preserves the integrity of the human body with the devolution of the Cylons to humanoid form and, in the end, discards dangerous or invasive technology and opts for a "simple" life in the country. Postmodernity sends its regards.

Sci-fi is fascinated by religion, and many TV-Series, movies, and literature have told stories that have been described as religious in content. However, *BSG* and *Caprica* differ from these stories in two important regards. Firstly, most other sci-fi narratives limit their religious deliberations to the metaphysical, thus promoting an ideology that is anti-body. The body is seen as hampering for the mind, when the evolution of humans is imagined to lead to an immaterial presence or eternal life in cyberspace. *BSG* and *Caprica*, on the other hand, are strongly pro-body. Immaterial virtual existence is seen as incomplete in *Caprica*, when Zoe-A needs to find her way back to the "real" world in a "real" flesh-and-bone body. The Cylons' mind-body dualism is also revealed as flawed when the Self as immortal data is revealed as morally questionable. These narratives cling to the physical body, where other sci-fi narratives hope to finally discard it. I suggest that this message is strongly linked to the centrality of women who, as we have seen, are traditionally associated with nature-body instead of science-mind.

Second, the narratives employ Judeo-Christian elements in a way untypical for sci-fi—a genre that is usually more interested in non-European religious systems. Eastern religions, voodoo, or Egyptian and Norse gods and myths feature more strongly in other sci-fi narratives. If Judeo-Christian concepts such as "angel" are discussed, they are seen as culture-specific examples of universal phenomena that have different names in various earth and alien cultures. *BSG* and *Caprica* tap directly and rather openly into Judeo-Christian imagery: they overtly employ the exodus-theme (surely leftover from the original Mormon story), explicitly use messiah concepts that can be linked to the Judeo-Christian tradition, depict angels in the Jewish sense and do not offer alternative names or concepts for these beings while at the same time engaging Christian ideas of heaven or paradise. *BSG* and *Caprica* live in a Judeo-Christian universe interspersed with Greek and posthuman ideas.

Certainly criticism of *BSG*'s ending is not unfounded, as it presents us with a lot of problems. As we have seen, far too many women die after leading the men to "paradise" (and after having been thoroughly feminized), while we witness with horror the imperialist message of Caucasians invading the African continent and deciding to bring the "primitive people" speech and everything else that is culturally relevant (personally, I found this part of the ending more shocking than the death or disappearance of the narrative's leading women). Yet I believe that something else about the ending is incredibly important, the aspect that has most frequently been criticized by fans and even scholars, namely the triumph of religion over science. I have already hinted at this: the women of the narrative would have been completely discredited if a scientific explanation would have been offered instead of a religious one. Then once again, masculine science would have proven the easily confused irrational womenfolk wrong.

Science fiction is about rationality, it is deeply infused with enlightenment thinking that states that emotion cannot be a source of knowledge—only reason can provide insights. Thus according to enlightenment thinking (and most of science fiction) women need to learn to "talk rationally" if they want men to take them seriously (Seidler 1994, 23, 28). By stating that emotion (and religion!) can be "rational"—and consequently a source of knowledge, *BSG* and *Caprica* force their men to acknowledge irrational-religious women (which they are of course not happy about initially). Men are forced to listen because these women hold actual power not just over politics or military assets, but most importantly over technology. Who can ignore the religious woman who creates artificial life, or the physically and intellectually superior God-fearing female Cyborg? Women who appropriate technology become powerful and their voices are heard—and essentially, that is what Donna Haraway was talking about.

For science fiction to acknowledge not only biological women but also qualities and character traits traditionally understood as "feminine" (such as irrational religion) and to question enlightenment ideology and the humanist worldview seems essentially important in order for the genre to remain viable in a postmodern world. This includes the occasional religious interpretation of the world, the courage to dethrone science as modern man's God, and the willingness to masculinize women and to feminize men. Not to say that *BSG* and *Caprica* are perfect contemporary narratives—rather, they illustrate Western society's crisis of identity and the ambiguity of postmodern life. Whether we want science to rule or religion, it seems women are most likely to navigate both worlds.

Episode Guide

Battlestar Galactica

[Sci-Fi, Ronald D. Moore, 2003–2009]

Miniseries W: Ronald D. Moore, D: Michael Rymer, Dec. 8–9, 2003 (2 Parts)]

1.01. "33" [W: Ronald D. Moore, D: Michael Rymer, Oct. 18, 2004]

1.03 "Bastille Day" [W: Toni Graphia, D: Allan Kroeker, Nov. 1, 2004]

1.05 "You Can't Go Home Again" [W: Carla Robinson, D: Sergio Mimica-Gezzan, Nov. 15, 2004]

1.06 "Litmus" [W: Jeff Vlaming, D: Rod Hardy, Nov. 22, 2004]

1.07 "Six Degrees of Separation" [W: Robert Young, D: Michael Angeli, Nov. 29, 2004]

1.08 "Flesh and Bone" [W: Toni Graphia, D: Brad Turner, Dec. 6, 2004]

1.09 "Tigh Me Up, Tigh Me Down" [W: Jeff Vlaming, D: Edward James Olmos, Dec. 13, 2004]

1.10 "The Hand of God" [W: Bradley Thompson & David Weddle, D: Jeff Woolnough, Jan. 3, 2005]

1.11 "Colonial Day" [W: Carla Robinson, D: Jonas Pate, Jan. 10, 2005]

1.12 "Kobol's Last Gleaming—Part I" [Story: David Eick, Teleplay: Ronald D. Moore, D: Michael Rymer, Jan. 17, 2005]

1.13 "Kobol's Last Gleaming—Part II" [Story: David Eick, Teleplay: Ronald D. Moore, D: Michael Rymer, Jan. 24, 2005]

2.03 "Fragged" [W: Dawn Prestwich & Nicole Yorkin, D: Sergio Mimica-Gezzan, July 29, 2005]

2.04 "Resistance" [W: Tonia Graphia, D: Allan Kroeker, Aug. 5, 2005]

2.05 "The Farm" [W: Carla Robinson, D: Rod Hardy, Aug. 12, 2005]

2.06 "Home—Part I" [W: David Eick, D: Sergio Mimica-Gezzan, Aug. 19, 2005]

2.07 "Home—Part II" [W: David Eick & Ronald D. Moore, D: Jeff Woolnough, Aug. 26, 2005]

2.09 "Flight of the Phoenix" [W: David Weddle & Bradley Thompson, D: Michael Nankin, Sept. 16, 2005]

2.10 "Pegasus" [W: Anne Cofell Saunders, D: Michael Rymer, Sept. 23, 2005]
2.11 "Resurrection Ship—Part I" [Story: Anne Cofell Saunders, Teleplay: Michael Rymer, D: Michael Rymer, Jan. 6, 2006]
2.12 "Resurrection Ship—Part II" [W: Michael Rymer & Ronald D. Moore, D: Michael Rymer, Jan. 13, 2006]
2.17 "The Captain's Hand" [W: Jeff Vlaming, D: Sergio Mimica-Gezzan, Feb. 17, 2006]
2.18 "Downloaded" [W: Bradley Thompson & David Weddle, D: Jeff Woolnough, Feb. 24, 2006]
2.19 "Lay Down Your Burdens—Part I" [W: Ronald D. Moore, D: Michael Rymer, Mar. 3, 2006]
2.20 "Lay Down Your Burdens—Part II" [W: Anne Cofell Saunders & Mark Verheiden, D: Michael Rymer, Mar. 10, 2006]
The Resistance Webisodes [W: Bradley Thompson & David Weddle, D: Wayne Rose, Sept. 5, 2006—Oct. 5, 2006]
3.01 "Occupation" [W: Ronald D. Moore, D: Sergio Mimica-Gezzan, Oct. 6, 2006]
3.02 "Precipice" [W: Ronald D. Moore, D: Sergio Mimica-Gezzan, Oct. 6, 2006]
3.03 "Exodus—Part I" [W: Bradley Thompson & David Weddle, D: Félix Enríquez Alcalá, Oct. 20, 2006]
3.04 "Exodus—Part II" [W: Bradley Thompson & David Weddle, D: Félix Enríquez Alcalá, Oct. 10, 2006]
3.05 "Collaborators" [W: Mark Verheiden, D: Michael Rymer, Oct. 28, 2006]
3.06 "Torn" [W: Anne Cofell Saunders; D: Jean de Segoznac, Nov. 3, 2006]
3.07 "A Measure of Salvation" [W: Michael Angelic, D: Bill Eagles, Nov. 10, 2006]
3.08 "Hero" [W: David Eick, D: Michael Rymer, Nov. 17, 2006]
3.10 "The Passage" [W: Jane Espenson, D: Michael Nankin, Dec. 8, 2006]
3.11 "The Eye of Jupiter" [W: Mark Verheiden, D: Michael Rymer, Dec. 15, 2006]
3.12 "Rapture" [W: Bradley Thompson & David Weddle, D: Michael Rymer, Jan. 21, 2007]
3.13 "Taking a Break from All Your Worries" [W: Michael Taylor, D: Edward James Olmos, Jan. 28, 2007]
3.14 "The Woman King" [W: Michael Angeli, D: Michael Rymer, Feb. 11, 2007]
3.17 "Maelstrom" [W: Bradley Thompson & David Weddle, D: Michael Nankin, Mar. 11, 2007]
3.19 "Crossroads—Part I" [W: Michael Taylor, D: Michael Rymer, Mar. 18, 2007]
3.20 "Crossroads—Part II" [W: Mark Verheiden, D: Michael Rymer, Mar. 25, 2007]
Razor Flashback Webisodes [W: Michael Taylor, D: Wayne Rose & Félix Enríquez Alcalá, Oct. 5—Nov. 16, 2007]
"Razor" [W: Michael Taylor, D: Félix Enríquez Alcalá, Nov. 24, 2007]
4.01 "He That Believeth in Me" [W: Bradley Thompson & David Weddle, D: Michael Rymer, Apr. 4, 2008]
4.02 "Six of One" [W: Michael Angeli, D. Anthony Hemingway, Apr. 11, 2008]

4.03 "The Ties That Bind" [W: W: Michael Taylor, D: Michael Nankin, Apr. 18, 2008]
4.04 "Escape Velocity" [W: Jane Espenson, D: Edward James Olmos, Apr. 25, 2008]
4.05 "The Road Less Travelled" [W: Mark Verheiden, D: Michael Rymer, May 2, 2008]
4.06 "Faith" [W: Seamus Kevin Fahey, D: Michael Nankin, May 9, 2008]
4.07 "Guess What's Coming to Dinner?" [W: Michael Angeli, D: Wayne Rose, May 16, 2008]
4.08 "Sine Qua Non" [W: Michael Taylor, D: Rod Hardy, May 27, 2008]
4.09 "The Hub" [W: Jane Espenson, D: Paul Edwards, June 6, 2008]
4.10 "Revelations" [W: Bradley Thompson & David Weddle, D: Michael Rymer, June 13, 2008]
The Face of the Enemy Webisodes [W: Jane Espenson & Seamus Kevin Fahey, D: Wayne Rose, Dec. 12, 2008- Jan. 12, 2009]
4.11 "Sometimes a Great Notion" [W: Bradley Thompson & David Weddle, D: Michael Nankin, Jan. 16, 2009]
4.12 "A Disquiet Follows My Soul" [W & D: Ronald D. Moore, Jan. 23, 2009]
4.13 "The Oath" [W: Mark Verheiden, D: John Dahl, Jan. 30, 2009]
4.14 "Blood on the Scales" [W: Wayne Rose, D: Michael Angeli, Feb. 6, 2009]
4.15 "No Exit" [W: Ryan Mottesheard, D: Gwyneth Horder-Payton, Feb. 13, 2009]
4.16 "Deadlock" [W: Jane Espenson, D: Robert Young, Feb. 20, 2009]
4.17 "Someone to Watch Over Me" [W: Bradley Thompson & David Weddle, D: Michael Nankin, Feb. 27, 2009]
4.18 "Islanded in a Stream of Stars" [W: Michael Taylor, D: Edward James Olmos, Mar. 6, 2009]
4.20 "Daybreak—Part II" [W: Ronald D. Moore, D: Michael Rymer, Mar. 20, 2009]
"The Plan" [W: Jane Espenson, D: Edward James Olmos, Jan. 10, 2010]
Behind the scenes featurette "Production," *Battlestar Galactica: The Complete Series on DVD*, Bonus Disc.

Caprica

[SyFy, Remi Aubuchon & Ronald D. Moore, 2009–2010]
1.01 "Pilot" [W: Remi Aubuchon & Ronald D. Moore, D: Jeffrey Reiner, Jan. 22, 2010]
1.02 "Rebirth" [W: Mark Verheiden, D: Jonas Pate, Jan. 29, 2010]
1.03 "Reins of a Waterfall" [W: Michael Angeli, D: Ronald D. Moore, Feb. 5, 2010]
1.05 "There Is Another Sky" [W: Kath Lingenfelter, D: Michael Nankin, Feb. 26, 2010]
1.06 "Know Thy Enemy" [Story: Patrick Massett & John Zinman & Matthew B. Roberts, Teleplay: Patrick Massett & John Zinman, D: Michael Nankin, Mar. 5, 2010]
1.07 "The Imperfections of Memory" [W: Matthew B. Roberts, D: Wayne Rose, Mar. 12, 2010]
1.09 "End of Line" [W: Michael Taylor, D: Roxann Dawson, Mar. 26, 2010]
1.10 "Unvanquished" [W: Ryan Mottesheard, D: Eric Stoltz, Oct. 5, 2010]

1.11 "Retribution" [W: Patrick Massett & John Zinman, D: Jonas Pate, Oct. 12, 2010]
1.12 "Things We Lock Away" [W: Drew Z. Greenberg, D: Tim Hunter, Oct. 19, 2010]
1.14 "Blowback" [W: Kevin Murphy, D: Omar Madha, Nov. 2, 2010]
1.15 "The Dirteaters" [W: Matthew B. Roberts, D: John Dahl, Nov. 9, 2010]
1.16 "The Heavens Will Rise" [W: Michael Taylor, D: Michael Nankin, Nov. 16, 2010]
1.17 "Here Be Dragons" [W: Patrick Massett & John Zinman, D: Michael Nankin, Nov. 23, 2010]
1.18 "Apotheosis" [W: Kevin Murphy & Jane Espenson, D: Jonas Pate, Nov. 30, 2010]

Other Series

Angel [The WB, Joss Whedon & David Greenwalt, 1999–2004]
Babylon 5 [PTEN and TNT, J. Michael Straczynski, 1993–1998]
Battlestar Galactica [ABC, Glen A. Larson, 1978–1979]
Battlestar Galactica: Blood and Chrome [SyFy, Michael Taylor & David Eick, 2012]
Buffy the Vampire Slayer [The WB and UPN, Joss Whedon, 1997–2003]
Lost [ABC, Jeffrey Lieber, J.J. Abrams & Damon Lindelof, 2004–2010]
Star Trek [NBC, Gene Rodenberry, 1966–1969]
Star Trek: The Next Generation [Gene Rodenberry, 1987–1994]
06.23 *Rightful Heir* [Teleplay: Ronald D. Moore, Story: James E. Brooks, D: Winrich Kolbe, May 17, 1993]
Star Trek: Deep Space Nine [Rick Berman & Michael Piller, 1993–1999]
1.01–1.02 Emissary [Teleplay: Michael Piller, Story: Rick Berman & Michael Piller, D: David Carson, Jan. 3, 1993]
Star Trek: Voyager [UPN, Rick Berman, Michael Piller & Jeri Taylor, 1995–2001]
Stargate SG-1 [Showtime and Sci-Fi Channel, Brad Wright & Jonathan Glassner, 1997–2007]
Supernatural [The WB and The CW, Erik Kripke, since 2004]
Teen Wolf (MTV, Jeff Davis, since 2011)
The Vampire Diaries (The CW, Kevin Williamson & Julie Plec, since 2009)

Movies

Alien (Ridley Scott, 1979)
Eve of Destruction (Duncan Gibbins, 1991)
The Last Temptation of Christ (Martin Scorsese 1988)
The Matrix (Andy & Larry Wachowski 1999)
Metropolis (Fritz Lang, 1927)
Species (Roger Donaldon 1995)
Star Trek: Generations (David Carson, 1994)
Star Wars (George Lucas, 1977)
Superman: The Movie (Richard Donner, 1978)
Terminator (James Cameron 1984)
Terminator 3—Rise of the Machines (Johnatan Mostov 2003)

Chapter Notes

Introduction

1. The prominence of "energy beings" in sci-fi TV is discussed by Gardella 2007, 228–230, while a more in-depth analysis of *Babylon 5*'s intriguing metaphysics is offered by Johnson-Smith 2005, 190–193.

2. See especially the following essay collections: Kaveney and Stoy 2010; Porter et al. 2008; Eberl 2008a; and Steiff and Tamplin 2008. Several articles have also appeared in collections discussing sci-fi television, e.g., George 2008, and Pank and Caro 2009.

3. I should note that I only discovered Wetmore's book after I had already finished the manuscript, which makes it all the more interesting to compare how we chose to tackle the subject. Sometimes we offer similar interpretations, sometimes we come to quite different conclusions. I read and incorporated Wetmore's analysis retrospectively where it seemed fitting.

Chapter 1

1. Seven of Nine is often discussed in Cyborg scholarship, e.g., zur Nieden 2001, 113–119, and Graham 2002, 151–152.

2. Since I recently attended a conference where several scholars expressed their unease with the term "postmodern," I feel compelled to say a few words on the issue. First, as a historian I share this discomfort. I generally reject the idea that we can explain any phenomenon by "post-ing" something that has gone before it. However, for the moment we do not possess a better word for describing the very real developments the term is referring to. It may very well be true that we cling too much to our idea of the modern in order to describe the present, which in itself could be an indicator of our conflicted ("postmodern") relationship to its legacy. Be that as it may, until someone proposes a better terminology, we are probably stuck with it.

3. *The Journal of Evolution & Technology* offers insights into contemporary posthuman ideology. See http://jetpress.org/.

4. See Carter 2007, 99–100, and Figueroa-Sarriera 1995, 132–134. A recent critical analysis of this posthuman search for immortality and invulnerability was given by Coeckelbergh 2011.

5. To give an example, this was the opinion expressed by the poster Zoompton on battlestarforum.com (mistakes in spelling are original): "I will bump my

vote down to a good since this series used a "god" to explain its story rather than science. I suppose i [sic] should have also rated the final episode a good for the same reason." http://www.battlestarforum.com/showthread.php?t=3165. Last checked February 22, 2013.

6. Ronald D. Moore has given many interviews to this effect—scholars frequently quote Moore's article that explained his concept of "naturalistic science fiction" in this context (Moore 2003).

7. This pioneering role of *DS9* was also noted by Linford 1999, 84–85, though he focused more strongly on the series' respect for religion. The article was written and published while *DS9* was still on the air, so Linford could not know which direction the series would finally take.

8. The story of Jews in America is of course a very long and complex one. Like other immigrants, they arrived in waves of both Sephardi and Ashkenazi migration. An overview can be found in Blau 1976, 21–72.

Chapter 2

1. Biblical (and extra-Biblical) references to the Davidic line are rather diverse. A thorough analysis is provided by Pomykala 1995, who also questions the premise that belief in a Davidic messiah was far spread in Early Judaism – an assumption that is usually seen as the precondition for the concept's usage in Christian and Rabbinic thought.

2. Sjö connected a variety of ideas from other scholars and conflated them to construct her theory, namely Conrad Oswalt, Sherrie Innes, Maria LaPlace, and Jane Via. I have followed Sjö's summaries and interpretations of these ideas.

Chapter 3

1. Behind the scenes featurette "Production," *Battlestar Galactica: The Complete Series*, Bonus Disc.

2. For the importance of the free will motif in *Supernatural*'s depiction of angels see Wimmler and Kienzl 2011, 181–183.

3. Of course we could immediately counter this argument with the Hindu Vedas, as discussed by Tworuschka 2003, 602–606.

4. Paradoxically, the oral Torah was written down in what is today known as the Talmud – writings that were then effectively canonized. Jacob Neusner has suggested that the process of canonizing the oral Torah was in many ways a reaction to the triumph of Christianity (most pronounced through the Christianization of the Roman Empire). Christians argued that the Jews misinterpreted the Torah – with the Talmud, Jews canonized their own understanding of the Torah as opposed to the Christians' (Neusner 1990, 25–30).

5. In fact, the oracles probably answered "easy" and "everyday" questions in a rather uncomplicated yes or no manner. Scholars even believe that they may have answered in a simple manner altogether, while the idea of "riddles" is associated with historical literature concerning the oracles (Gehrke 2003, 78, and Wiesehöfer 2010, 342–344, 348). The role of oracles in the Near East is discussed in Blenkinsopp 1998, 47–51.

Chapter 4

1. The image of the Cyborg and its use in scholarship and science fiction is discussed, among others, by Graham 2002, 208; Springer 1999, 41; Featherstone, Burrows 1995, 4; Holland 1995; Mitchell 2006, 111, 114; Jowett 2010, 78; Lupton 1995, 101; and Chipman 2010.

2. The idea that we could become both immortal and invulnerable through enhanced technology was recently contested by Mark Coeckelbergh, who pointed out how many dangers the enhanced human could expect in a non-

material virtual space (Coeckelbergh 2011).

Chapter 5

1. A rather important catalyst for this development was the destruction of the Temple by the Babylonians in 586 BCE which removed God's previous dwelling place (the Temple) from the picture. This – and the deportation of the Israeli elite to the cosmopolitan capital – led to major changes in Jewish thinking. Scholars today refer to this period as Judaism's true hour of birth. I also want to point out that the matter of "distance" between humans and Gods as suggested by Vorgrimler is not uncontested. Wright, for example, proposes that this distance became smaller during this exact time because humans could now expect to join God in heaven after death (Wright 2000, 201).

2. Walker even seems to copy that line from *BSG*: "Perhaps God implants souls in humans and computers" (Walker 2011). Considering that Walker makes references to both *Star Trek* and *Babylon 5*, it is not unreasonable to assume that he watched *BSG*.

3. See, e.g., "Apotheosis (episode)," available at: http://en.battlestarwiki.org/wiki/Apotheosis_%28episode%29. Last checked February 26, 2013.

Chapter 6

1. The German term "Schwärmerei" has no clear equivalent in the English language. Late enlightenment philosophers used it to refer to things previously called "superstitions" and generally meant to describe sentimental enthusiasm for irrational things. German enlightenment thinkers in particular "allowed" a certain amount of *Schwärmerei* to enter reasonable, enlightened thinking (see Conrad 2008, 8–10).

2. This is visible in many areas. Paul Greenhalgh, for example, has found a clear connection between modernity and idealistic reduction and postmodernity and complexity/ destabilization in the visual arts (see Greenhalgh 2005).

3. Interestingly, anger has typically been associated with reason rather than emotion in philosophy (Newmark 2010, 51).

4. There is of course a wealth of literature on this subject. I would especially like to refer the reader to Connell 2000 and Butler 2006.

Chapter 7

1. This notion can be felt in all of the essay collections published on *BSG* so far as a sort of permanent undercurrent. Emily McAvan stated that Islam is represented a bit more thoroughly in *BSG* than in other postmodern narratives (which altogether hardly deal with it) and has once again connected this representation to Cylon terrorism and monotheism (McAvan 2012, 138). Again, I understand the idea behind it, but it seems to be unsustainable from both the religious and the terrorist discursive perspective. I see neither Islam nor Muslim terrorists in the narrative. Kevin Wetmore seems to agree with me —for him, the Cylons are "monotheistic mystics" rather than (Christian or Muslim) fundamentalists (Wetmore 2012, 38), though he still links STO terrorism to "Islamic extremism" on p. 177.

Chapter 8

1. Today, most scholars assert that the historical development has proven the secularization theory wrong. The only region of the world where the theory still has some merit is Western and Central Europe, though this depends on our definition of the concept. In explaining why the theory has proven so persistent despite empirical evidence to the contrary, Peter Berger famously noted

that intellectuals tended to mingle with one another internationally, which creates the misleading impression that the world is indeed secularized. The problem with this conclusion, as Berger further noted, is that Western educated intellectuals do not reflect the religious atmosphere of their respective countries. Berger discusses this (and the curiosity of European exceptionalism) in various publications, one of which is Berger 2001, 445–446.

Bibliography

Anders, Jake. 2013. "Violent Monotheists, Violent Corporations, and the Body: *Caprica*'s Theological Vision." In *Imaginatio et Ratio: A Journal of Theology and the Arts* 2 (1): 7–17.

"Apotheosis (episode)." available at http://en.battlestarwiki.org/wiki/Apotheosis_%28episode%29. Last checked February 26, 2013.

Aronson, Amy, and Michael Kimmel. 2001. "The Saviors and the Saved: Masculine Redemption in Contemporary Films." In *Masculinity: Bodies, Movies, Culture*. Edited by Peter Lehman, 43–50. New York: Routledge.

Augustijn, C. 2003. *Humanismus*. Göttingen: Vandenhoeck & Ruprecht.

Balsamo, Anne. 1999. "Reading Cyborgs Writing Feminism." In *Cybersexualities: A Reader on Feminist Theory, Cyborgs, and Cyberspace*. Edited by Jenny Wolmark, 145–56. Edinburgh: Edinburgh University Press.

Baynes, Leslie. 2012. *The Heavenly Book Motif in Judeo-Christian Apocalypses, 200 B.C.E.-200 C.E.* Leiden: Brill.

Benford, Gregory, and Elisabeth Malartre. 2008. *Beyond Human: Living with Robots and Cyborgs*. New York: Tom Doherty Associates.

Berger, Peter L. 1999. *The Desecularization of the World: Resurgent Religion and World Politics*. Grand Rapids: W.B. Eerdmans.

———. 2001. "Reflections on the Sociology of Religion Today." *Sociology of Religion* 62 (4): 443–54.

Bertens, Johannes W. 1995. *The Idea of the Postmodern: A History*. London: Routledge.

Bieberstein, Sabine. 2005. "Es kommt auf die Perspektive an! "Böse" Frauen in der Bibel." In *"Böse" Frauen*. Edited by Anneliese Hecht, 8–13. Stuttgart: Verl. Kath. Bibelwerk; KlensVerl.

Blau, Joseph L. 1976. *Judaism in America: From Curiosity to Third Faith*. Chicago: Universiof Chicago Press.

Blenkinsopp, Joseph. 1998. *Geschichte der Prophetie in Israel: Von den Anfängen bis zum hellenistischen Zeitalter*. Stuttgart: Kohlhammer.

Boustan, Ra'anan, S., and Annette Y. Reed. 2009. "Introduction: 'In Heaven as It Is on Earth.'" In *Heavenly Realms and Earthly Realities in Late Antique Religions*. Edited by Ra'anan S. Boustan and Annette Y. Reed, 1–15. Cambridge: Cambridge University Press.

Brabon, Benjamin. 2007. "The Spectral Phallus: Re-Membering the Postfeminist Man." In *Postfeminist Gothic: Critical Interventions in Contemporary Culture. Edited by Benjamin Brabon and Stéphanie Genz, 56–67. New York: Palgrave Macmillan.

Bremmer, Jan N. 1983. *The Early Greek Concept of the Soul*. Princeton: Princeton University Press.

Broderick, Damien. 2009. *Unleashing the Strange: Twenty-first Century Science Fiction Literature*. The Borgo Press.

Brunner, Claudia. 2007. "Occidentalism Meets the Female Suicide Bomber: A Critical Reflection on Recent Terrorism Debates; A review essay." *Signs* 32 (4): 957–71.

Brunner, Claudia, and Helmut Krieger. 2008. "Der Ort des Anderen in Europas Mitte: Zur okzidentalistischen Repositionierung des Orientalismusdispositivs am Beispiel englischsprachiger medialer Diskursfragmente über die Selbstmordanschläge von London im Juli 2005." In *Gewalt und Präzision: Krieg und Sicherheit in Zeiten des War on Terror*. Edited by Wolfgang Sützl and Doris Wallnöfer, 187–209. Wien: Turia & Kant.

Burrows, Karen K. 2010. "The Luxury of Being Simply Human: Unwritten and Rewritten Queer Histories in Battlestar Galactica." In *Battlestar Galactica: Investigating Flesh, Spirit and Steel*. Edited by Roz Kaveney and Jennifer Stoy, 199–218. London: I.B. Tauris.

Butler, Anthea D., and Diane H. Winston. 2009. "'A Vagina Ain't a Halo:' Gender and Religion in Saving Grace and Battlestar Galactica." In *Small Screen, Big Picture: Television and Lived Religion*. Edited by Diane H. Winston, 259–86. Waco: Baylor University Press.

Butler, Judith. 2006. *Gender Trouble: Feminism and the Subversion of Identity*. New York: Routledge.

Bynum, Caroline W. 1995. *The Resurrection of the Body in Western Christianity, 200–1336*. New York: Columbia University Press.

Campbell, Heidi, and Mark Walker. 2005. "Religion and Transhumanism: Introducing a Conversation." *Journal of Evolution & Technology* 14 (2): i–xiv.

Cancik, Hubert, and Hildegard Cancik-Lindemaier. 2011. *Europa, Antike, Humanismus: Humanistische Versuche und Vorarbeiten*. Bielefeld: Transcript.

Carter, Matt. 2007. *Minds and Computers: An Introduction to the Philosophy of Artificial Intelligence*. Edinburgh: Edinburgh University Press.

Chipman, Jay S. 2010. "So Where Do I Go from Here? Ghost in the Shell and Imagining Cyborg Mythology for the New Millennium." In *Millennial Mythmaking: Essays on the Power of Science Fiction and Fantasy Literature, Films and Games*. Edited by John R. Perlich and David Whitt, 167–91. Jefferson: McFarland.

Clark, Andy. 2004. *Natural-Born Cyborgs: Minds, Technologies, and the Future of Human Intelligence*. Oxford: Oxford University Press.

Coeckelbergh, Mark. 2011. "Vulnerable Cyborgs: Learning to Live with our Dragons." *Journal of Evolution & Technology* 22 (1): 1–9.

Cohn, Norman. 2001. *Cosmos, Chaos, and the World to Come: The Ancient Roots of Apocalyptic Faith*. New Haven: Yale University Press.

Cohn-Sherbok, Dan. 1997. *The Jewish Messiah*. Edinburgh: T. & T. Clark.

Collins, Adela Y. 2007. "The Messiah as Son of God in the Synoptic Gospels." In *The Messiah in early Judaism and Christianity*. Edited by Magnus Zetterholm, 21–32. Minneapolis: Fortress Press.

Collins, John J. 1995. *The Scepter and the Star: The Messiahs of the Dead Sea Scrolls and other Ancient Literature*. New York: Doubleday.

Condra, Ed. 2002. *Salvation for the Righteous Revealed: Jesus amid Covenantal and Messianic Expectations in Second Temple Judaism*. Leiden: Brill.

Conly, Sarah. 2008. "Is Starbuck a Woman?" In *Battlestar Galactica and Philosophy: Knowledge Here Begins Out There*. Edited by Jason T. Eberl, 230–40. Chichester: John Wiley & Sons.

Connell, Robert W. 2000. *Der gemachte Mann: Konstruktion und Krise von Männlichkeiten*. Opladen: Leske und Budrich.

Conrad, Anne. 2008. *Rationalismus und Schwärmerei: Studien zur Religiosität und Sinndeutung in der Spätaufklärung*. Hamburg: DOBU Verlag.

Corea, Gena, and Paula Bradish. 1988. *Muttermaschine: Reproduktionstechnologien – von der künstlichen Befruchtung zur künstlichen Gebärmutter*. Frankfurt am Main: Fischer-Taschenbuch-Verl.

Dallmayr, Fred. 1997. "The Politics of Nonidentity: Adorno, Postmodernism and Edward Said." *Political Theory* 25 (1): 33–56.

Dieckmann, Bernhard. 1991. *Judas als Sündenbock: Eine verhängnisvolle Geschichte von Angst und Vergeltung*. München: Kösel.

Doane, Mary A. 1999. "Technophilia: Technology, Representation, and the Feminine." In *Cybersexualities: A Reader on Feminist Theory, Cyborgs, and Cyberspace*. Edited by Jenny Wolmark, 20–33. Edinburgh: Edinburgh University Press.

Döge, Peter. 2001. "Technik, Männlichkeit und Politik: Zum verborgenen Geschlecht staatlicher Forschungs- und Technologiepolitik." In *Männlichkeit und soziale Ordnung: Neuere Beiträge zur Geschlechterforschung*. Edited by Peter Döge and Michael Meuser, 123–39. Opladen: Leske und Budrich.

Dunn, George A. 2008. "Being Boomer: Identity, Alienation, and Evil." In *Battlestar Galactica and Philosophy: Knowledge Here Begins Out There*. Edited by Jason T. Eberl, 127–40. Chichester: John Wiley & Sons.

Eberl, Jason T., ed. 2008a. *Battlestar Galactica and Philosophy: Knowledge Here Begins Out There*. Chichester: John Wiley & Sons.

———. 2008b. "'I am an Instrument of God:' Religious Belief, Atheism, and Meaning." In *Battlestar Galactica and Philosophy: Knowledge Here Begins Out There*. Edited by Jason T. Eberl, 155–68. Chichester: John Wiley & Sons.

Ernst, Michael. 2007. "Angels in Orthodox Religious Practice and Art." In *Angels: The Concept of Celestial Beings: Origins, Development and Reception*. Edited by Friedrich V. Reiterer, Tobias Nicklas, and Karin Schöpflin, 671–93. Berlin: Walter de Gruyter.

Eynikel, Erik. 2007. "The Angel in Samson's Birth Narrative Judg 13." In *Angels: The Concept of Celestial Beings: Origins, Development and Reception*. Edited by Friedrich V. Reiterer, Tobias Nicklas, and Karin Schöpflin, 109–23. Berlin: Walter de Gruyter.

Featherstone, Mike, and Roger Burrows. 1995. "Cultures of Technological Embodiment: An Introduction." In *Cyberspace/Cyberbodies/Cyberpunk: Cultures of Technological Embodiment*. Edited by Mike Featherstone and Roger Burrows, 1–19. London: Sage.

Figueroa-Sarriera, Heidi J. 1995. "Children of the Mind with Disposable Bodies: Metaphors of Self in a Text of Artificial Intelligence and Robotics." In *The Cyborg Handbook*. Edited by Chris H. Gray, 127–35. New York: Routledge.

Forbes, Bruce D., and Jeffrey H. Mahan, eds. 2005. *Religion and Popular Culture in America*. Rev. ed. Berkeley: University of California Press.

Freedman, Carl. 1987. "Science Fiction and Critical Theory." *Science Fiction Studies* 14 (2): 180–200.

Gardella, Peter. 2007. *American Angels: Useful Spirits in the Material World*. Lawrence: University Press of Kansas.

Gehrke, Hans-Joachim. 2003. *Geschichte des Hellenismus*. München: Oldenbourg.

George, Susan A. 2008. "Fraking Machines: Desire, Gender, and the (Post)Human Condition in Battlestar Galactica." In *The Essential Science Fiction Television Reader*. Edited by J. P. Telotte, 159–75. Lexington: University Press of Kentucky.

Geraci, Robert M. 2010. *Apocalyptic AI: Visions of Heaven in Robotics, Artificial Intelligence, and Virtual Reality*. New York: Oxford University Press.

Gosling, Sharon. 2009. *Battlestar Galactica: The Official Companion Season Four*. London: Titan Books.

Gözen, Jiré E. 2012. *Cyberpunk Science Fiction: Literarische Fiktionen und Medientheorie*. Bielefeld: Transcript.

Graham, Elaine L. 2002. *Representations of the Post/human: Monsters, Aliens, and Others in Popular Culture*. New Brunswick: Rutgers University Press.

Greenhalgh, Paul. 2005. *The Modern Ideal: The Rise and Collapse of Idealism in the Visual Arts from the Enlightenment to Postmodernism*. London: V&A Publications.

Gregory, Chris. 2000. *Star Trek: Parallel Narratives*. New York: St. Martin's Press.

Griffin, David R. 1989. *God and Religion in the Postmodern World: Essays in Postmodern Theology*. Albany: State University of New York Press.

Gumpert, Matthew. 2008. "Hybridity's End." In *Cylons in America: Critical Studies in Battlestar Galactica*. Edited by Tiffany Potter and C. W. Marshall, 143–55. New York: Continuum.

Halberstam, Judith. 1998. *Female Masculinity*. Durham: Duke University Press.

_____. 2007. "Neo-Splatter: Bride of Chucky and the Horror of Heteronormativity." In *Postfeminist Gothic: Critical Interventions in Contemporary Culture*. Edited by Benjamin Brabon and Stéphanie Genz, 30–42. New York: Palgrave Macmillan.

Halberstam, Judith, and Ira Livingston. 1995. "Introduction." In *Posthuman Bodies*. Edited by Judith Halberstam and Ira Livingston, 1–19. Bloomington: Indiana University Press.

Hannah, Darrell D. 2007. "Guardian Angels and Angelic National Patrons in Second Temple Judaism and Early Christianity." In *Angels: The Concept of Celestial Beings: Origins, Development and Reception*. Edited by Friedrich V. Reiterer, Tobias Nicklas, and Karin Schöpflin, 413–35. Berlin: Walter de Gruyter.

Haraway, Donna J. 2004. "A Manifesto for Cyborgs: Science, Technology, and Socialist Feminism in the 1980s." In *The Haraway Reader*. Edited by Donna J. Haraway, 7–45. New York: Routledge.

Häring, Hermann. 2003. "Das Böse in der christlichen Tradition." In *Das Böse in den Weltreligionen*. Edited by Johannes Laube, 63–130. Darmstadt: Wissenschaftliche Buchgesellschaft.

Heinricy, Shana. 2008. "I, Cyborg." In *Battlestar Galactica and Philosophy: Mission Accomplished or Mission Frakked Up?* Edited by Josef Steiff and Tristan D. Tamplin, 95–102. Chicago: Open Court.

Heller, Birgit. 2003. "Götter/ Göttinnen." In *Handbuch Religionswissenschaft: Religionen und ihre zentralen Themen*. Edited by Johann Figl. Lizenzausg., 530–44. Darmstadt: Wiss. Buchges.

Hendershot, Heather. 2009. "'You Know How It Is with Nuns...:' Religion and Television's Sacred/ Secular Fetuses." In *Small Screen, Big Picture: Television and Lived Religion*. Edited by Diane H. Winston. Waco: Baylor University Press.

Herbrechter, Stefan. 2009. *Posthumanismus: Eine kritische Einführung*. Darmstadt: Wiss. Buchges.

Higate, Paul, and John Hopton. 2005. "War, Militarism, and Masculinities." In *Handbook of Studies on Men & Masculinities*. Edited by Michael S.

Kimmel, Jeff Hearn, and Raewyn Connell, 432–47. Thousand Oaks: Sage.

Holderegger, Adrian, ed. 2011. *Humanismus: Sein kritisches Potential für Gegenwart und Zukunft*. Basel: Schwabe.

Holderegger, Adrian, Siegfried Weichlein, and Simone Zurbuchen. 2011. "Einleitung: Hat der Humanismus eine Zukunft?" In *Humanismus: Sein kritisches Potential für Gegenwart und Zukunft*. Edited by Adrian Holderegger, 11–26. Basel: Schwabe.

Holland, Samantha. 1995. "Descartes Goes to Hollywood: Mind, Body and Gender in Contemporary Cyborg Cinema." In *Cyberspace/Cyberbodies/Cyberpunk: Cultures of Technological Embodiment*. Edited by Mike Featherstone and Roger Burrows, 157–74. London: Sage.

Hollinger, Veronica. 2003. "Feminist Theory and Science Fiction." In *The Cambridge Companion to Science Fiction*. Edited by Edward James and Farah Mendlesohn, 125–48. Cambridge: Cambridge University Press.

Horsley, Richard A. 2009. *Revolt of the Scribes: The Origins of Apocalyptic Literature*. Minneapolis: Fortress Press.

Hultgren, Arland J. 1997. "Matthew's Infancy Narrative and the Nativity of an Emerging Community." *Horizons in Biblical Theology* 19 (1): 91–108.

Hurst, Matthias. 2000. *Im Spannungsfeld der Aufklärung: Von Schillers Geisterseher zur TV-Serie The X-Files: Rationalismus und Irrationalismus in Literatur, Film und Fernsehen 1789–1999*. Heidelberg: Universitätsverlag C. Winter.

Hurwitz, Siegmund. 1992. *Lilith, the First Eve: Historical and Psychological Aspects of the Dark Feminine*. Einsiedeln: Daimon Verlag.

Hutchings, Kimberly. 2008. "Making Sense of Masculinity and War." *Men and Masculinities* 10: 389–404.

Hutter, Manfred. 2007. "Demons and Benevolent Spirits in the Ancient Near East: A Phenomenological Overview." In *Angels: The Concept of Celestial Beings: Origins, Development and Reception*. Edited by Friedrich V. Reiterer, Tobias Nicklas, and Karin Schöpflin, 21–34. Berlin: Walter de Gruyter.

Huyssen, Andreas. 1987. *After the Great Divide: Modernism, Mass Culture, and Postmodernism*. Bloomington: Indiana University Press.

Hyman, Gavin. 2007. "Atheism in Modern History." In *The Cambridge Companion to Atheism*. Edited by Michael Martin, 27–46. Cambridge: Cambridge University Press.

"In the Name of God(s): Monotheism and Polytheism in Battlestar." 2008. In *Finding Battlestar Galactica: An Unauthorized Guide*. Edited by Lynnette R. Porter, David Lavery, and Hillary Robson, 103–06. Naperville: Sourcebooks.

Isherwood, Lisa, and Elizabeth Stuart. 1998. *Introducing Body Theology*. Sheffield: Sheffield Academic Press.

Janowski, J. C. 2006. "Das Gewirr des Bösen – böses Gewirr: Semantische, strukturelle und symbolische Aspekte ‚des Bösen' in Zuspitzung auf Genderkonfigurationen." In *Hat das Böse ein Geschlecht? Theologische und religionswissenschaftliche Verhältnisbestimmungen*. Edited by Helga Kuhlmann, 12–30. Stuttgart: Kohlhammer.

Jensen, Anne. 2003. *Gottes selbstbewusste Töchter: Frauenemanzipation im frühen Christentum?* Münster: Lit Verlag.

Jezler, Peter, and Hans-Dietrich Altendorf. 1994. *Himmel, Hölle, Fegefeuer: Das Jenseits im Mittelalter*. Zürich: Gesellschaft für das Schweizerische Landesmuseum; Verlag Neue Zürcher Zeitung.

Johnson, David K. 2008. "'A Story that is Told Again, and Again, and Again:' Recurrence, Providence, and Freedom." In *Battlestar Galactica and Philosophy: Knowledge Here Begins Out There*. Edited by Jason T. Eberl, 181–91. Chichester: John Wiley & Sons.

Johnson-Lewis, Erika. 2008. "Torture, Terrorism, and Other Aspects of Human Nature." In *Cylons in America: Critical Studies in Battlestar Galactica*. Edited by Tiffany Potter and C. W. Marshall, 27–39. New York: Continuum.

Johnson-Smith, Jan. 2005. *American Science Fiction TV: Star Trek, Stargate and Beyond*. London: I. B. Tauris.

Jones, Matthew. 2010. "Butch Girls, Brittle Boys and Sexy, Sexless Cylons: Some Gender Problems in Battlestar Galactica." In *Battlestar Galactica: Investigating Flesh, Spirit and Steel*. Edited by Roz Kaveney and Jennifer Stoy, 154–84. London: I.B. Tauris.

Jordanova, L. J. 1989. *Sexual Visions: Images of Gender in Science and Medicine Between the Eighteenth and Twentieth Centuries*. Madison: University of Wisconsin Press.

Jowett, Lorna. 2008. "Mad, Bad, and Dangerous to Know? Negotiating Stereotypes of Science." In *Cylons in America: Critical Studies in Battlestar Galactica*. Edited by Tiffany Potter and C. W. Marshall, 64–75. New York: Continuum.

_____. 2010. "Frak Me: Reproduction, Gender, Sexuality." In *Battlestar Galactica: Investigating Flesh, Spirit and Steel*. Edited by Roz Kaveney and Jennifer Stoy, 59–80. London: I.B. Tauris.

Jung, Leo. 1974. *Fallen Angels in Jewish, Christian, and Mohammedan Literature*. New York: Ktav Publishing House.

Kauffmann, Michael. 1996. "Die Konstruktion von Männlichkeit und die Triade männlicher Gewalt." In *Kritische Männerforschung: Neue Ansätze in der Geschlechtertheorie*. Edited by BauSteineMänner, 138–71. Hamburg: Argument-Verl.

Kaveney, Roz. 2010. "The Military Organism: Rank, Family and Obedience in Battlestar Galactica." In *Battlestar Galactica: Investigating Flesh, Spirit and Steel*. Edited by Roz Kaveney and Jennifer Stoy, 110–28. London: I.B. Tauris.

Kaveney, Roz, and Jennifer Stoy, eds. 2010. *Battlestar Galactica: Investigating Flesh, Spirit and Steel*. London: I.B. Tauris.

Kee, Howard C. 1997. *The Cambridge Companion to the Bible*. Cambridge: Cambridge University Press.

Kelleter, Frank. 2002. *Amerikanische Aufklärung: Sprachen der Rationalität im Zeitalter der Revolution*. Paderborn: Schöningh.

Kelly, Henry A. 2006. *Satan: A Biography*. Cambridge: Cambridge University Press.

Kienzl, Lisa. 2014. "Digital Participatory Culture: Transnationality, Fandom & Diversity: Religion and Gender in German-written Fan Fiction and Fan Forums." *Heidelberg Journal of Religions on the Internet* 6: 66–89. http://dx.doi.org/10.11588/rel.2014.0.17360.

King, Karen L. 2003. *What is Gnosticism?* Cambridge: Belknap Press of Harvard University Press.

Kirkland, Ewan. 2008. "Starbuck and the Gender Dynamics of Battlestar Galactica." In *Finding Battlestar Galactica: An Unauthorized Guide*. Edited by Lynnette R. Porter, David Lavery, and Hillary Robson, 131–44. Naperville: Sourcebooks.

Kozlovic, Anton K. 2002. "Superman as Christ-Figure: The American Pop Culture Movie Messiah." *Journal of Religoin and Film* 6 (1).

Kraemer, Ross S., William Cassidy, and Susan L. Schwartz. 2001. *Religions of Star Trek*. Boulder: Westview Press.

Krochmalnik, Daniel. 2003. "Das Böse in der jüdischen Tradition." In *Das Böse in den Weltreligionen*. Edited by Johannes Laube, 13–62. Darmstadt: Wissenschaftliche Buchgesellschaft.

Krueger, Oliver. 2005. "Gnosis in Cyberspace? Body, Mind and Progress in Posthumanism." *Journal of Evolution & Technology* 14: 77–89.

Kukkonen, Taneli. 2008. "God against the Gods: Faith and the Exodus of the

Twelve Colonies." In *Battlestar Galactica and Philosophy: Knowledge Here Begins Out There*. Edited by Jason T. Eberl, 169–80. Chichester: John Wiley & Sons.

Kuncewicz, Dariusz. 2007. "Rewriting Narratives of Traumatic Experiences in a Cult Environment." In *The Phenomenon of Cults from a Scientific Perspective*. Edited by Piotr T. Nowakowski, 55–61. Cracow: Dom Wydawniczy Rafael.

Läpple, Alfred. 1993. *Engel & Teufel: Wiederkehr der Totgesagten. Eine Orientierung*. Augsburg: Pattloch.

Linford, Peter. 1999. "Deeds of Power: Respect for Religion in Star Trek: Deep Space Nine." In *Star Trek and Sacred Ground: Explorations of Star Trek, Religion, and American Culture*. Edited by Jennifer E. Porter and Darcee L. McLaren, 77–100. Albany: State University of New York Press.

Livingston, Sara. 2008. "The Razor's Edge: Galactica, Pegasus, and Lakoff." In *Battlestar Galactica and Philosophy: Mission Accomplished or Mission Frakked Up?* Edited by Josef Steiff and Tristan D. Tamplin, 143–53. Chicago: Open Court.

Loftis, J. R. 2008. "'What a Strange Little Man:' Baltar the Tyrant?" In *Battlestar Galactica and Philosophy: Knowledge Here Begins Out There*. Edited by Jason T. Eberl, 29–39. Chichester: John Wiley & Sons.

Lupton, Deborah. 1995. "The Embodied Computer/ User." In *Cyberspace/Cyberbodies/Cyberpunk: Cultures of Technological Embodiment*. Edited by Mike Featherstone and Roger Burrows, 97–112. London: Sage.

Lynch, Gordon, ed. 2007. *Between Sacred and Profane: Researching Religion and Popular Culture*. London: I.B. Tauris.

_____. 2008. *Understanding Theology and Popular Culture*. Malden: Blackwell.

Maass, Michael. 2007. *Das antike Delphi*. München: Beck.

MacInnes, John. 2008. "The Crisis of Masculinity and the Politics of Identity." In *The Masculinities Reader*. Edited by Stephen M. Whitehead and Frank J. Barrett, 311–29. Cambridge: Polity Press.

Magdalinski, Tara. 2009. *Sport, Technology and the Body: The Nature of Performance*. London: Routledge.

Mann, Nicholas. 1996. "The Origins of Humanism." In *The Cambridge Companion to Renaissance Humanism*. Edited by Jill Kraye, 1–19. Cambridge: Cambridge University Press.

Maxwell, Marilyn. 2000. *Male Rage, Female Fury: Gender and Violence in Contemporary American Fiction*. Lanham: University Press of America.

McAvan, Emily. 2012. *The Postmodern Sacred: Popular Culture Spirituality in the Science Fiction, Fantasy and Urban Fantasy Genres*. Jefferson: McFarland.

McKay, Jim, Janine Mikosza, and Brett Hutchins. 2005. "'Gentlemen, the Lunchbox Has Landed:' Representations of Masculinities and Men's Bodies in the Popular Media." In *Handbook of Studies on Men & Masculinities*. Edited by Michael S. Kimmel, Jeff Hearn, and Raewyn Connell, 270–88. Thousand Oaks: Sage.

McLeod, Hugh. 1988. "Weibliche Frömmigkeit – männlicher Unglaube? Religion und Kirchen im bürgerlichen 19. Jahrhundert." In *Bürgerinnen und Bürger: Geschlechterverhältnisse im 19. Jahrhundert; 12 Beiträge*. Edited by Ute Frevert, 134–55. Göttingen: Vandenhoeck u. Ruprecht.

Mendelsohn, Farah. 2003. "Religion and Science Fiction." In *The Cambridge Companion to Science Fiction*. Edited by Edward James and Farah Mendlesohn, 264–75. Cambridge: Cambridge University Press.

Menon, Elizabeth K. 2006. *Evil by Design: The Creation and Marketing of the Femme Fatale*. Urbana: University of Illinois Press.

Merrick, Helen. 2003. "Gender in Science Fiction." In *The Cambridge Companion to Science Fiction*. Edited by Edward James and Farah Mendlesohn, 241–52. Cambridge: Cambridge University Press.

Messner, Michael A. 2005. "Still a Man's World? Studying Masculinities and Sport." In *Handbook of Studies on Men & Masculinities*. Edited by Michael S. Kimmel, Jeff Hearn, and Raewyn Connell, 313–25. Thousand Oaks: Sage.

Milsky, Daniel. 2008. "The Narrative Disruptions of Model Eight." In *Battlestar Galactica and Philosophy: Mission Accomplished or Mission Frakked Up?* Edited by Josef Steiff and Tristan D. Tamplin, 3–15. Chicago: Open Court.

Mitchell, Kaye. 2006. "Bodies That Matter: Science Fiction, Technoculture, and the Gendered Body." *Science Fiction Studies* 33 (1): 109–28.

Moore, Ronald D. 2003. "Battlestar Galactica: Naturalistic Science Fiction or Taking the Opera out of Space Opera." http://web.archive.org/web/20070208103915/http://www.galactica2003.net/articles/concept.shtml. Last checked February 4, 2013.

Mulligan, Rikk. 2008. "The Cain Mutiny: Reflecting the Faces of Military Leadership in a Time of Fear." In *Cylons in America: Critical Studies in Battlestar Galactica*. Edited by Tiffany Potter and C. W. Marshall, 52–63. New York: Continuum.

Müllner, Ilse. 2005. "Isebel, Atalja, die Macht und das Böse." In *"Böse" Frauen*. Edited by Anneliese Hecht, 29–40. Stuttgart, Düsseldorf: Verl. Kath. Bibelwerk; KlensVerl.

Munck, Thomas. 2000. *The Enlightenment: A Comparative Social History, 1721–1794*. London, New York: Oxford University Press.

Murphy, Nancy. 2002. "The Resurrection Body and Personal Identity: Possibilities and Limits of Eschatological Knowledge." In *Resurrection: Theological and Scientific Assessments*. Edited by Ted Peters, Robert J. Russell, and Michael Welker, 202–18. Grand Rapids: W.B. Eerdmans.

Neusner, Jacob. 1990. *Scriptures of the Oral Torah: Sanctification and Salvation in the Sacred Books of Judaism*. Atlanta: Scholars Press.

Newmark, Catherine. 2010. "Vernünftige Gefühle? Männliche Rationalität und Emotionalität von der frühneuzeitlichen Moralphilosophie bis zum bürgerlichen Zeitalter." In *Die Präsenz der Gefühle – Männlichkeit und Emotion in der Moderne*. Edited by Manuel Borutta, 41–55. Bielefeld: Transcript.

Novakovic, Lidija. 1997. "Jesus as the Davidic Messiah in Matthew." *Horizons in Biblical Theology* 19 (1): 148–91.

Olyan, Saul M. 1993. *A Thousand Thousands Served Him: Exegesis and the Naming of Angels in Ancient Judaism*. Tübingen: Mohr Siebeck.

Pank, Dylan, and John Caro. 2009. "'Heaven't you heard? They look like us now!' Realism and Metaphor in the New Battlestar Galactica." In *Channeling the Future: Essays on Science Fiction and Fantasy Television*. Edited by Lincoln Geraghty, 199–215. Lanham: Scarecrow.

Partridge, Christopher H. 2004–2005. *The Re-Enchantment of the West: Alternative Spiritualities, Sacralization, Popular Culture, and Occulture*. 2 vols. London: T & T Clark International.

Peirse, Alison. 2009. "Destroying the Male Body in British Horror Cinema." In *Mysterious Skin: Male Bodies in Contemporary Cinema*. Edited by Santiago Fouz-Hernández, 159–73. London: I. B. Tauris.

Peters, Ted. 2002. "Introduction: What is to Come." In *Resurrection: Theological and Scientific Assessments*. Edited by Ted Peters, Robert J. Russell, and Michael Welker, viii–xv. Grand Rapids: W.B. Eerdmans.

Piepke, Joachim G. 2000. "Die Engel –

Gottes traditionelle Boten: Zur christlichen Engellehre in Tradition und Gegenwart." In *Engel im Aufwind: Gottes Boten auf der Spur*. Edited by Hermann Kochanek, 47–70. Mödling bei Wien: Verl. St. Gabriel.

Pomykala, Kenneth. 1995. *The Davidic Dynasty Tradition in Early Judaism: Its History and Significance for Messianism*. Atlanta: Scholars Press.

Porter, Jennifer E., and Darcee L. McLaren. 1999. "Introduction: Star Trek, Religion, and American Culture." In *Star Trek and Sacred Ground: Explorations of Star Trek, Religion, and American Culture*. Edited by Jennifer E. Porter and Darcee L. McLaren, 1–9. Albany: State University of New York Press.

Porter, Lynnette R., David Lavery, and Hillary Robson, eds. 2008. *Finding Battlestar Galactica: An Unauthorized Guide*. Naperville: Sourcebooks.

Potter, Tiffany, and C. W. Marshall, eds. 2008. *Cylons in America: Critical Studies in Battlestar Galactica*. New York: Continuum.

Quiney, Ruth. 2007. "'Mr. Xerox,' the Domestic Terrorist, and the Victim-Citizen: Masculine and National Anxiety in Fight Club and Anti-Terror Law." *Law and Literature* 19 (2): 327–54.

Rebiger, Bill. 2007. "Angels in Rabbinic Literature." In *Angels: The Concept of Celestial Beings: Origins, Development and Reception*. Edited by Friedrich V. Reiterer, Tobias Nicklas, and Karin Schöpflin, 629–44. Berlin: Walter de Gruyter.

Reckwitz, Andreas. 2010. "Umkämpfte Maskulinität: Zur Historischen Kultursoziologie männlicher Subjektformen und ihrer Affektivitäten vom Zeitalter der Empfindsamkeit bis zur Postmoderne." In *Die Präsenz der Gefühle – Männlichkeit und Emotion in der Moderne*. Edited by Manuel Borutta, 57–77. Bielefeld: Transcript.

Rennes, Magali. 2008. "Kiss Me, Now Die!" In *Battlestar Galactica and Philosophy: Mission Accomplished or Mission Frakked Up?* Edited by Josef Steiff and Tristan D. Tamplin, 63–76. Chicago: Open Court.

Robins, Kevin. 1995. "Cyberspace and the World We Live In." In *Cyberspace/Cyberbodies/Cyberpunk: Cultures of Technological Embodiment*. Edited by Mike Featherstone and Roger Burrows, 135–55. London: Sage.

Rodger, Lynlea. 1997. "The Infancy Stories of Matthew and Luke: an Examination of the Child as a Theological Metaphor." *Horizons in Biblical Theology* 19 (1): 58–81.

Rodin, David. 2010. "Torture and Terrorism." In *The Routledge Companion to Ethics*. Edited by John Skorupski, 820–31. London: Routledge.

Rogers, Adam. 2008. "Read an Extended Version of Wired's Interview with Ron Moore." http://www.wired.com/entertainment/hollywood/magazine/16-06/ff_moore_transcript?currentPage=all. Last checked February 25, 2013.

Rolufs, Heather. 2008. "Eve, Lilith, and the Cylon Connection." In *Battlestar Galactica and Philosophy: Mission Accomplished or Mission Frakked Up?* Edited by Josef Steiff and Tristan D. Tamplin, 349–58. Chicago: Open Court.

Rorie, Matt. May 11th, 2011. "Is Star Trek Anti-Religion Or Merely Ambiguous About It?" *Screened*, May 11, 2011. http://www.screened.com/news/is-star-trek-anti-religion-or-merely-ambiguous-about-it/2212/. Last checked April 7, 2013.

Rosenberg, Alfons. 1986. *Engel und Dämonen: Gestaltwandel eines Urbildes*. München: Kösel.

Rudolph, Kurt. 1990. *Die Gnosis: Wesen und Geschichte einer spätantiken Religion*. Göttingen: Vandenhoeck & Ruprecht.

Russell, Jeffrey B. 1984. *Lucifer. The Devil in the Middle Ages*. Ithaca: Cornell University Press.

_____. 1990. *Mephistopheles: The Devil*

in the Modern World. Ithaca: Cornell University Press.
———. 1999. *Geschichte des Himmels*. Wien: Böhlau.
Ryman, Geoff. 2010. "Adama and (Mitrochondrial) Eve: A Foundational Myth for White Folks." In *Battlestar Galactica: Investigating Flesh, Spirit and Steel*. Edited by Roz Kaveney and Jennifer Stoy, 37–58. London: I.B. Tauris.
Sacchi, Paolo. 1990. *Jewish Apocalyptic and its History*. Sheffield: Sheffield Academic Press.
Scarre, Geoffrey. 2010. "Evil." In *The Routledge Companion to Ethics*. Edited by John Skorupski, 584–95. London: Routledge.
Schäfer, Peter. 1975. *Rivalität zwischen Engeln und Menschen: Untersuchungen zur rabbinischen Engelvorstellung*. Berlin: Walter de Gruyter.
Schipper, Bernd U. 2007. "Angels or Demons? Divine Messengers in Ancient Egypt." In *Angels: The Concept of Celestial Beings: Origins, Development and Reception*. Edited by Friedrich V. Reiterer, Tobias Nicklas, and Karin Schöpflin, 1–19. Berlin: Walter de Gruyter.
Schumacher, Florian. 2008. *Das Ich und der andere Körper: Eine Kulturgeschichte des Monsters und des künstlichen Menschen*. Marburg: Tectum.
Seidler, Victor J. 1994. *Unreasonable Men: Masculinity and Social Theory*. London: Routledge.
———. 1996. "Vernunft, Moral und Männlichkeit." In *Kritische Männerforschung: Neue Ansätze in der Geschlechtertheorie*. Edited by BauSteineMänner, 111–37. Hamburg: Argument-Verl.
Shipman, Hal. 2008. "Some Cylons Are More Equal than Others." In *Battlestar Galactica and Philosophy: Mission Accomplished or Mission Frakked Up?* Edited by Josef Steiff and Tristan D. Tamplin, 155–62. Chicago: Open Court.
Sjö, Sofia. 2007. "Are Female Messiahs Changing the Myth? Women, Religion, and Power in Popular Culture and Society." In *Reconfigurations: Interdisciplinary Perspectives on Religion in a Post-Secular Society*. Edited by Stefanie Knauss and Alexander D. Ornella, 59–72. Wien: Lit-Verlag.
———. 2010. "Who's your Saviour? The Changing Messiahs of Contemporary Science Fiction Film and TV." 5th Global Conference Visions of Humanity in Cyberculture, Cyberspace and Science Fiction. http://www.inter-disciplinary.net/wp-content/uploads/2010/06/ssjopaper.pdf.
Sohn-Kronthaler, Michaela. 2009. "Zu Gehalt und Relevanz der These von der ‚Feminisierung der Religion' im 19. Jahrhundert: Beobachtungen an Fallbeispielen aus dem Bistum (Graz-) Seckau." In *... männlich und weiblich schuf er sie (Gen 1,27). Zur Brisanz der Geschlechterfrage in Religion und Gesellschaft*. Edited by Sigrid Eder, 44–59. Innsbruck: Tyrolia-Verl.
Springer, Claudia. 1999. "The Pleasure of the Interface." In *Cybersexualities: A Reader on Feminist Theory, Cyborgs, and Cyberspace*. Edited by Jenny Wolmark, 34–54. Edinburgh: Edinburgh University Press.
Squier, Susan M. 1995. "Reproducing the Posthuman Body: Ectogenetic Fetus, Surrogate Mother, Pregnant Man." In *Posthuman Bodies*. Edited by Judith Halberstam and Ira Livingston, 113–32. Bloomington: Indiana University Press.
Steiff, Josef, and Tristan D. Tamplin, eds. 2008. *Battlestar Galactica and Philosophy: Mission Accomplished or Mission Frakked Up?* Chicago: Open Court.
Steinrötter, Kolja. 2004. *Science and a Sense of Hope: Zum Verhältnis von Wissenschaft und Religion in der Fernsehserie ‚Star Trek: Deep Space Nine.'* Münster: Telos Verlag.
Storm, Jo. 2007. *Frak you! The Ultimate Unauthorized Guide to Battlestar Galactica*. Toronto: ECW Press.
Stoy, Jennifer. 2010. "Of Great Zeitgeist

and Bad Faith: An Introduction to Battlestar Galactica." In *Battlestar Galactica: Investigating Flesh, Spirit and Steel*. Edited by Roz Kaveney and Jennifer Stoy, 1–36. London: I.B. Tauris.

Strauss, Mark L. 1995. *The Davidic Messiah in Luke-Acts: The Promise and its Fulfillment in Lukan Christology*. Sheffield: Sheffield Academic Press.

Stucky, Mark D. 2005. "He is the One: The Matrix Trilogy's Postmodern Movie Messiah." *Journal of Religoin and Film* 9 (2).

Theissen, Gerd, and Annette Merz. 1996. *Der historische Jesus: Ein Lehrbuch*. Göttingen: Vandenhoeck & Ruprecht.

"This Razor's Edgy." 2008. In *Finding Battlestar Galactica: An Unauthorized Guide*. Edited by Lynnette R. Porter, David Lavery, and Hillary Robson, 257–62. Naperville: Sourcebooks.

Thompson, Edward H., Jr., and Kathryn R. Remmes. 2002. "Does Masculinity Thwart Being Religious? An Examination of Older Men's Religiousness." *Journal for the Scientific Study of Religion* 41 (3): 521–32.

Toffoletti, Kim. 2007. *Cyborgs and Barbie Dolls: Feminism, Popular Culture and the Posthuman Body*. London: I.B. Tauris.

Tuschling, R. M. M. 2007. *Angels and Orthodoxy: A Study in their Development in Syria and Palestine from the Qumran Texts to Ephrem the Syrian*. Tübingen: Mohr Siebeck.

Tworuschka, Udo. 2003. "Heilige Schriften." In *Handbuch Religionswissenschaft: Religionen und ihre zentralen Themen*. Edited by Johann Figl. Lizenzausg, 588–611. Darmstadt: Wiss. Buchges.

Vallant, Christoph. 2008. *Hybride, Klone und Chimären: Zur Transzendierung der Körper-, Art- und Gattungsgrenzen; ein Buch über den Menschen hinaus*. Würzburg: Königshausen & Neumann.

von Braun, Christina. 2010. "Heteronormativität in den drei Religionen des Buches." In *Frau – Gender – Queer: Gendertheoretische Ansätze in der Religionswissenschaft*. Edited by Susanne Lanwerd and Lárcia E. Moser, 23–36. Würzburg: Königshausen & Neumann.

Vorgrimler, Herbert. 2008. *Geschichte des Paradieses und des Himmels: Mit einem Exkurs über Utopie*. München: Fink.

Walker, Mark. 2011. "Personal Identity and Uploading." *Journal of Evolution & Technology* 22 (1): 37–52.

Watts Henderson, Suzanne. 2009. "Jesus' Messianic Self-Consciousness Revisited: Christology and Community in Context." *Journal for the Study of the Historical Jesus* 7: 168–97.

Westfahl, Gary. 2003. "Space Opera." In *The Cambridge Companion to Science Fiction*. Edited by Edward James and Farah Mendlesohn. Cambridge: Cambridge University Press.

Wetmore, Kevin J., JR. 2012. *The Theology of Battlestar Galactica: American Christianity in the 2004 – 2009 Television Series*. Jefferson: McFarland.

Whitehead, Stephen. 2002. *Men and Masculinities: Key Themes and New Directions*. Cambridge: Polity Press.

Wiesehöfer, Josef. 2010. "Die Geheimnisse der Pythia – Orakel und das Wissen der reisenden Weisen." In *Die griechische Welt: Erinnerungsorte der Antike*. Edited by Elke Stein-Hölkeskamp and Karl-Joachim Hölkeskamp, 336–52. München: C.H. Beck.

Willems, Brian. 2008. "When the Non-Human Knows its Own Death." In *Battlestar Galactica and Philosophy: Knowledge Here Begins Out There*. Edited by Jason T. Eberl, 87–98. Chichester: John Wiley & Sons.

Wimmler, Jutta. 2014. "Masters of Cyber-Religion: The Female Body as God's 'Interface' in the TV Series Caprica." *Journal of Religion, Media & Digital Culture* 3 (1). http://jrmdc.

com/wp-content/uploads/2014/05/Wimmler.pdf.

Wimmler, Jutta, and Lisa Kienzl. 2011. "'I am an Angel of the Lord:' An Inquiry into the Christian Nature of Supernatural's Heavenly Delegates." In *TV Goes to Hell: An Unofficial Road Map of Supernatural*. Edited by Stacey Abbott and David Lavery, 176–86. Toronto: ECW Press.

Winston, Diane H. 2009a. "Introduction." In *Small Screen, Big Picture: Television and Lived Religion*. Edited by Diane H. Winston, 1–14. Waco: Baylor University Press.

____, ed. 2009b. *Small Screen, Big Picture: Television and Lived Religion*. Waco: Baylor University Press.

Wolfe, Ivan. 2008. "Why Your Mormon Neighbor Knows More about This Show than You Do." In *Battlestar Galactica and Philosophy: Mission Accomplished or Mission Frakked Up?* Edited by Josef Steiff and Tristan D. Tamplin, 303–16. Chicago: Open Court.

"Women on Top." 2008. In *Finding Battlestar Galactica: An Unauthorized Guide*. Edited by Lynnette R. Porter, David Lavery, and Hillary Robson, 149–69. Naperville: Sourcebooks.

Wright, J. E. 2000. *The Early History of Heaven*. Oxford: Oxford University Press.

Zimbardo, Philip G. 2007. "What Messages Are Behind Today's Cults?" In *The Phenomenon of Cults from a Scientific Perspective*. Edited by Piotr T. Nowakowski, 25–30. Cracow: Dom Wydawniczy Rafael.

Zimmerman, Michael E. 2008. "The Singularity: A Crucial Phase in Divine Self-Actualization?" *Cosmos and History: The Journal of Natural and Social Philosophy* 4 (1–2): 347–70.

Zur Nieden, Andrea. 2001. "'Schönheit ist irrelevant?' Die Sexualisierung von Cyborgs in Star Trek." In *Data/Body/Sex/Maschine: Technoscience und Sciencefiction aus feministischer Sicht*. Edited by Karin Giselbrecht and Michaela Hafner, 96–123. Wien: Turia & Kant.

Index

Numbers in ***bold italics*** indicate pages with photographs.

abortion 44, 173, 175
Adama, Joseph 18, 81, 114, 139–143
Adama, Lee 46, 48, 50, 86, 94, 124, 126, 127, 129–134, 143, 156, 163
Adama, Sam 103, 139, 142–143
Adama, Tamara 19, 139, 140
Adama, William (commander) 16, 19, 29, 30, 32, 37, 38, 50, 53, 69, 103–107, ***124–127***, 128, 129, 143, 153, 157, 159, 172, 173
Adama, Willie 141–142
Agathon, Karl 40, 103, 107, 124, 127–129, 143, 154, 157, 159, 161
Agathon, Sharon 40–43, 69, 107–110, 127, 128, 157, 159; *see also* Valerii, Sharon
Alien (franchise) 34, 46, 47, 194
Anders, Samuel 145, 146, 147, 154, 156, 157, 158, ***161–165***, 166
Angels 2, 18, 30, 32, 41, 47, ***56–66***, 98–99, 101, 112, 119, 135, 138, 165, 185, 188; Messenger-Baltar 72, 97, 182; Messenger-Leoben 59, 65, 154; Messenger-Six 40, 43, 69, 70, 77, 167, ***169–183***; Messenger-Zoe 59, 65, 72, 81
apocalypse 14, 39, 42, 47, 50, 51, 68, 113
Apollo (character) *see* Adama, Lee
Apollo, arrow of 37, 53, 124–125
atheism 51, 63, 124, 136, 139, 156, 167–169, 171, 172, 177, 178, 180, 182

Athena (character) *see* Agathon, Sharon
Babylon 5 2, 195*intro.n*1, 197*ch*5*n*2
Baltar, cult of 70, 181–182
Baltar, Gaius 7, 29, 32, 37, 38, 43, 59–63, 65, 69, 70, 74, 75, 77, 86, 107–111, 121, 131, 132, 159, ***167–184***, 186
Barnabas 119–121, 147, 149–150
baseship 73, 75, 88, 109, 110, 163, 167, 179
basestar 109
Battlestar Galactica (original series) 16, 17, 20, 27, 28, 46, 70, 102, 134, 167, 179, 188
Battlestar Galactica (ship) 16, 21, 23, 36, 49, 51, 62, 102–103, 107–108, 126–129, 136, 156–157, 159, 163, 165
Battlestar Pegasus 19, 92, 102–105, 128, 157, 173
Biers, D'Anna 63–64, 71, 74, 76, 93, 94, 107, 155, 178–179
Boomer *see* Valerii, Sharon
Buffy the Vampire Slayer 46, 164
Bush era 3, 17, 103, 146, 147, 148

Cain, Helena (admiral) 102–106, 121, 124, 126, 128, 137, 157
Cally *see* Tyrol, Cally
Caprica (planet) 36, 37, 53, 97, 107, 124, 136, 143, 161, 172, 174, 176

211

Index

Caprica Six (character) 29, 43, 60, 62–65, **95–100**, 106, 108, 109, 154, 167, 178, 183
Cavil 1, 87, 88, 93–95, 106, 107, 109, 110, 120–121, 124, **134–139**, 143, 156, 158, 163, 186
Centurions 17, 19, 23, **80–88**, 93, 120, 137, 143, 165
Clarice *see* Willow, Clarice
Conoy, Leoben 29, 48, 50, 72–77, 91–94, 114, **151–156**, 160, 166, 184, 186
cyberpunk 13, 19–20, 186
Cyberspace *see* virtual space
Cyborgs 6, 11–13, 16, 44, 55, 64, 78, 79, 81–83, 85, 89, 134, 187, 189, 196*ch*4*n*1; *see also* Hera; hybrids

demons 2, 27, 41, 57, 58, 61, 63, 69, 95–99, 114, 180, 185
Devil 14, 27, 58, 59, 63, **134–139**, 185
Doral, Aaron 94, 137

Eight *see* Agathon, Sharon; Valerii, Sharon
Elosha 30, 36, 37, 69, 70
enlightenment 11, 14, 114, 123, 136, 167–170, 172, 185, 186, 188, 189, 197*ch*6*n*1
Eve (biblical) 96, 101, 108, 109, 135
Eve (character) 141, 143
Eve of destruction 79, 81, 82

The Face of the Enemy (webisodes) 19, 104, 133
Faustus 137–138
Final Five 74, 75, 85, 86, 87, 88, 89, 93, 94, 110, 111, 126, 134, 137, 139, 146, 155, 156, 158, 161, 163–164, 180
Fisk (colonel) 105, 106, 128
Foster, Tory 107, 110–111, 122, 156, 160, 163
Frankenstein 11, 13, 42

Gaeta, Felix 104, 124, 129, 130, 132–134, 136, 144, 157, 163, 186
Gemenon 80, 82, 119, 120
Gina *see* Invière, Gina
gnosticism 14, 84, 116, 178
Graystone, Amanda 119–120
Graystone, Daniel 18, 80–81, 83–84, 99, **111–115**, 117, 139, 140–141, 143–144, 186
Graystone, Zoe 18, 32, 65, 72, **79–85**, 90, 95, 100, 112, 114–115, 117–119, 139, 140, 146, 147, 149, 150; *see also* Messenger-Zoe; Zoe-A
Greece, Ancient 10, 39, 41, 58, 67, 73–74, 91, 92, 116, 188

Ha'la'tha (crime syndicate) 139, 141–143
Haraway, Donna 12, 44, 78, 79, 81, 189
heaven 27, 30, 31, 61, 102, 188; *see also* virtual space
Helo (character) *see* Agathon, Karl
Hera (character) 31, 35, **40–45**, 51, 54, 97, 127, 173
homosexuality 12, 103–104, 142, 143, 164
hybrids (BSG species) 67, **72–77**, 86, 92, 105, 154, 163–165; *see also* Cyborgs; Hera

Invière, Gina 92, 104, 173–175
Islam 27- 29, 41, 118, 148–151, 164, 197*ch*7*n*1

Jesus 9, 31, 34, 38, 39, 41–43, 45, 47–49, 61, 68, 109, 113, 117

Kendra *see* Shaw, Kendra
Kobol 17, 27, 69–70, 125, 126; Lords of 36, 69

Larson, Glenn A. 16, 27, 28
Leoben *see* Conoy, Leoben
Lilith 79, **95–100**, 106
Lucifer *see* Devil

messengers *see* angels
Messiah *see* savior
monotheism 18, 19, 28, 32, 57, 67, 69, 71, 72, 80, 82, 84, 101, 111–119, 147–151, 181, 182, 197*ch*7*n*1
Moore, Ronald D. 16, 18, 21, 22, 24, 27, 28, 103, 168, 196*intro.n*6
Mormonism 16, 27, 188

Natalie (character) 94
New Cap City 98–99
New Caprica 17, 19, 86, 108, 131, 132, 133, 146, 154, 157, 175, 177, 181

Olympic Carrier 169–170
opera house visions 43–44, 76
oracles 39, 56, 61, 67, 71–77, 154, 158, 196*ch*3*n*5

Index

paradise 30, 32, 35–38, 44, 45, 53, 54, 70, 87, 88, 92, 96, 98–101, 108, 109, 111, 137
Pegasus *see* Battlestar Pegasus
The Plan (film) 19, 134, 136, 137
polytheism 17, 28, 29, 57, 58, 66, 67, 70–72, 118, 181
posthumanism 3, 6, *10–16*, 19, 20, 26, 31–33, 40, 75, 78, 81, *90–95*, 114–117, 121, 135, 170, 178, 187, 188, 195*ch2n*3, 195*ch2n*4
postmodernism *12–16*, 20, 22, 25, 26, 32, 99, 129, 180, 183, 185–187, 189, 195*ch1n*2
Promised Land *see* paradise
prophets 6, 22, 24, 25, 30, 32, 36, 37, 39, 50, 56, 61, 67, 68, *71–75*, 77, 118, 119, 154
Pythia, scrolls of 36–39, 66–67, 69, 70

Quorum of Twelve 27, 37, 133, 167, 172, 174

Raiders (Cylon species) 85, 88, 137
Rand, Lacy 18, 81–84, 117–120, 140, 146–147, 149–150
Razor (film) 19, 76, 104–105
reproduction 31, 40–42, 44, 79–80, 85, 89, 98, 122, 152, 175
The Resistance (webisodes) 19, 146–148
resurrection 31, 45, 48–50, 52, 91, 113, 116, 154, 163; technological 63–64, 73–74, 87, 90–94, 112–114, 119, 158, 159, 163, 164, 179
Roslin, Laura 16, *35–41*, 43, 44, 49, 50, 52–54, 58, 66–70, 76, 103, 104, 106, 110, 118, 124–127, 130–132, 143, 146, 147, 152, 154, 157, 165, 170, 172–176, 183

Sagittaran 130, 131
salvation 4, *30- 32*, 34- 36, 39–41, 43, 45–46, 51, 54, 61, 63, 91, 94, 100, 106, 117, 134, 173, 181, 183
Satan *see* Devil
Savior 6, 9, 22, 24–26, 30, *34–55*, 61, 91, 110, 117–122, 174, 181, 185, 188, 196*ch2n*1
Shaw, Kendra 105–106, 121
Simon 94, 137
Six *see* Caprica Six; Invière, Gina; Messenger Six; Natalie

Soldiers of the One (STO) 18, 19, 81–82, 118–120, 146–147, 197*ch7n*1
soul 17, 18, 22, 29, 32, *91–92*, 114–116, 135, 152–154, 177, 197*ch5n*2
Star Trek (franchise) 6, 11, 16, 20, *21–26*, 28, 32, 36, 37, 197*ch5n*2
Star Wars 45
Starbuck *see* Thrace, Kara
Stargate SG-1 2, 9, 10, 32
suicide bombings *see* terrorism
Superman (franchise) 9, 10, 25, 34, 45, 47

Tamara-A 19, 98, 140, 141, 143; *see also* Adama, Tamara
Tauron 139, 141–143
Temple of Five 158, 161
Terminator (franchise) 45, 47, 64
terrorism 18, 64, 113, 118–119, 130–131, 134, 139–141, *145–151*, 157, 166, 172, 175, 176, 197*ch7n*1
Thorne (lieutenant) 128, 157
Thrace, Kara 29, 35, 37–39, *45–50*, 51–54, 59, 61, 65, 70, 72, 73, 76, 91, 93, 102, 104–106, 116, 118, 124, 126, 151–156, 158, 159, 161–163, 165, 166, 183
Three *see* Biers, D'Anna
Tigh, Ellen 86–87, 89–90, 100, 110, 135, 137, 146, 156, 158–159, 163
Tigh, Saul 37, 86, 87, 97, 126, 146, 147, 157, 163
torture 92–93, 103, 104, 146, 148, *151–154*, 176, 177–180
Tory *see* Foster, Tory
Tyrol, Cally 111, 160
Tyrol, Galen 103, 107, 111, 128, 136, 145–147, *156–161*, 162, 166, 184

v-world *see* virtual space
Valerii, Sharon 63, 64, 94, 102, *107–111*, 126, 130, 134, 137, 157, 159, 160; *see also* Agathon, Sharon
violence 19, 63, 66, 78, 81, 84, 99–100, 119, 122, 136, 142, *145–166*, 171, 175
virtual space 14, 18–19, 31, 62, 65, 80–85, 92, 98–99, *111–121*, 140–141, 143, 149, 170, 187; *see also* heaven

war 23, 38, 39, 64, 66, 88, 93, 102, 103, 129, 148; first Cylon war 16, 18, 19; war on terror 3, 17, 146, 151
Willow, Clarice 72, 81, 102, *112–122*, 136, 139, 147, 149, 150, 185–186

Index

Zarek, Tom 38, 70, 124, ***130–133***, 163, 172, 174–176
Zoe-A 18, 65, ***80–85***, 89, 95, 98–100, 106, 114, 116, 119–120, 122, 140–141, 143, 185, 187; *see also* Graystone, Zoe; Messenger-Zoe
Zoroastrism 56, 57, 113

www.ingramcontent.com/pod-product-compliance
Ingram Content Group UK Ltd.
Pitfield, Milton Keynes, MK11 3LW, UK
UKHW041955140426
5217IPUK00015B/806